Democracy in Britain

Democracy in Britain

A Reader

Edited by Jack Lively and Adam Lively

The British Council

BLACKWELL
Oxford UK & Cambridge USA

This collection copyright © The British Council, 1994

First published 1994

Blackwell Publishers
108 Cowley Road
Oxford OX4 1JF
UK

238 Main Street,
Cambridge, Massachusetts 02142
USA

British Library Cataloguing in Publication Data

A CIP catalogue record for this book is available from the British Library.

Library of Congress Cataloging-in-Publication Data

Democracy in Britain : a reader / edited by Jack Lively and Adam
  Lively.
    p.   cm.
  Includes bibliographical references and index.
  ISBN 0–631–18829–0 — ISBN 0–631–18831–2 (pbk.)
  1. Great Britain—Politics and government. 2. Democracy—Great
Britain. 3. Representative government and representation—Great
Britain. I. Lively, Jack. II. Lively, Adam.
JN125.D46 1994
320.441—dc20
                                                 93–44085
                                                            CIP

Typeset in 10½ on 12pt Bembo by Photoprint, Torquay, Devon

Printed in Great Britain by T J Press, Padstow, Cornwall

This book is printed on acid-free paper

To Jacob,
son and grandson

Contents

Editors' Note

Extract titles are followed by the date of first publication or of delivery in the case of speeches. Source lines at the end of extracts give the original titles of works from which the extracts are taken. Full details of editions used are given in the Bibliography of Sources. Biographical Notes on the authors of the extracts may be found on pp. 312–27.

Introduction

This book attempts to trace and illustrate the debate over time on representative democracy in Britain (or Great Britain and Northern Ireland, or the United Kingdom, or England – the name of the state is part of the debate).

It is concerned with a debate in the sense of presenting conflicting opinions and views. Disagreement and conflict have been constant in British constitutional development. The emergence of representative institutions and their democratization has not been a story of smooth, unbroken and agreed progress. There have been breaks and back-sliding. Every move which in retrospect has brought us closer to accountable, democratic government has been opposed. Those who, again in retrospect, we might identify as the forwarders of this progressive movement have often given their support for reasons and on grounds quite alien to modern democratic thought. Nor has the debate been dispassionate and rational. In the seventeenth century, a civil war was fought at least in part on the issues examined here; and, in the nineteenth and twentieth centuries, the threat and fear of violence have often been a part of the background to the debate. Moreover, the debate is not finished. There are still those who argue that there are severe deficiencies from a democratic standpoint in British politics and society, or alternatively that the democratic element has gone too far to be compatible with efficient or liberal government, or alternatively that recent developments, such as the movement into Europe, have created a serious threat to British democratic institutions.

The book is concerned with the debate on democracy rather than with the actual course of constitutional development. This does not imply that ideas have in any sense determined that development or have even provided the motives for those pressing for or opposing change. It may be that interests and ambitions or even inertia have more to do with how people act or fail to act politically than ideals or ideologically formulated objectives, and that many historical developments are the unintended consequences of human actions. Nevertheless, the debate has defined the options between which choices have had to be made, and even the most pragmatic or self-interested or intellectually incurious of us make our decisions within a mental frame which is shaped largely by society's intellectual dialectic. Keynes noted how far the behaviour of *soi-disant* hard-headed businessmen was dictated by the ideas of long-dead economists. We might note a parallel determination of the actions of pragmatic politicians by past political theories and controversy.

The question of the relationship between theory and practice, of ideology and political action, has of course been much debated by historians and social scientists. It has also attracted politicians and propagandists and has entered the political debate through the assertion that the British people are averse to any theoretical approach to social and political matters. This claim, particularly when coupled with a condemnation of any ideological mode of politics, has often come from within the conservative tradition. Burke, with his contrast of the theoretical politics of the French Revolutionaries and the quiet, unreflective traditionalism of the British, was one of the originators of this self-portrait (Introduction:1). But the assertion of the untheoretic bent of British attitudes has also been put forward by persons far distant from the Tory fold, as the extract from Richard Crossman shows (Introduction:2). Crossman follows Burke's characterization, although he was a committed socialist and was an academic political theorist when he wrote this. Of course, the fact that this picture has been so often and so widely canvassed is no guarantee of its accuracy. It appeared at the time of the French Revolution. Before then, the British political character had generally been depicted in terms of a revolutionary past. The British had a European reputation, whether admired or abhorred, as a politically volatile people given to regicide and rebellion. And, as this book will perhaps demonstrate, a society that has produced Hobbes and Locke and Adam Smith and Bentham and John Stuart Mill and Keynes – and, it must be added, Burke himself – cannot be said to be devoid of serious and influential social thought.

The debate on democracy has been centred on, but not confined to, constitutional issues. Other and wider social and intellectual concerns have been constantly brought into the arena. The attainment of political democracy, it has been claimed, would bring about changes in many other aspects of national life. The values implicit in a political democracy, particularly the value of equality, might be applicable to ideas and structures outside the political sphere. So the discussion has widened, and this book covers this wider debate by looking at the relationships between democracy on the one hand and liberty, communities, the economy and the general culture on the other.

Both the constitutional debates and these wider discussions have found expression in a number of different contexts. They have been pursued in formal works of social and political theory, in parliamentary confrontations, in the polemics of pamphlets, periodicals and newspapers, in party literature, in pressure group proposals, in fiction and in poetry. We shall here call on as wide a variety of this material as possible so as to illustrate not only the breadth and complexity of the arguments but also the passion, vigour and often the literary merits of their exponents.

1   Edmund Burke, In Defence of Prejudice (1790)

You see, Sir, that in this enlightened age I am bold enough to confess, that we are generally men of untaught feelings; that instead of casting away all our old prejudices, we cherish them to a very considerable degree, and, to take more shame to ourselves, we cherish them because they are prejudices; and the longer they have lasted and the more generally they have prevailed, the more we cherish them. We are afraid to put men to live and trade each on his own private stock of reason; because we suspect that the stock in each man is small, and that the individuals would do better to avail themselves of the general bank and capital of nations and of ages. Many of our men of speculation, instead of exploding general prejudices, employ their sagacity to discover the latent wisdom which prevails in them. If they find what they seek, and they seldom fail, they think it more wise to continue the prejudice, with the reason involved, than to cast away the coat of prejudice, and to leave nothing but the naked reason; because prejudice, with its reason, has a motive to give action to that reason, and an affection which will give it permanence. Prejudice is of ready application in the emergency; it previously engages the mind in a steady course of wisdom and virtue, and does not leave the man hesitating in the moment of decision, sceptical, puzzled, and unresolved. Prejudice renders a man's virtue his habit: and not a series of unconnected acts. Through just prejudice, his duty becomes a part of his nature.

Reflections on the Revolution in France

2 R. H. S. Crossman, English Distrust of Theory (1965)

Perhaps the most common generalisation about British states-manship is that it hates theory and prefers 'muddling through'. It is usually made by Englishmen in a tone which blends a mixture of condescension and self-depreciation, and is usually employed to excuse the vagaries of foreign policy or the existence of some glaring anomaly. We have become proud of our reputation as practical men of affairs, but we are also uneasily aware that 'the virtue of muddling through' is not really a virtue, and does not really explain the paradoxes of our political conduct.

Only a moment's serious consideration is necessary in order to see that theory and speculative thought are by no means foreign to the British mind. In natural science and economics, to mention only two departments, Great Britain has excelled, while in the realm of philosophy British thinkers have been as influential as those of any other country. In every nation the vast majority of the population are suspicious of the thinking minority, and the politicians and business men disregard the academics whenever they can. These are facts common to human nature at large, not peculiar to the British people.

The true peculiarity of Englishmen consists not in their disregard of theory but in the uses for which they employ it. Our thought, like our language, has a deep aversion to system-atisation. We have always been unwilling to base our actions upon a philosophy of life, indeed, we have no word to correspond to the German *Weltanschauung*. Theory, for us, is not the foundation upon which practice should be built, but an instrument to be employed in the achievement of given ends. The 'reasonable' man is the man who uses not *Vernunft* but *Verstand*, and it is again significant that the French *raison* and the German *Vernunft* have no equivalents in English. The Anglo-Saxon peoples have produced scientists, historians, and philoso-phers, but not one pre-eminent exponent of a systematic philosophy or theology. In short, our speculations are employed to destroy or to support a given belief, not to demonstrate the premises of belief itself.

In a very profound sense, then, British political thought is dialectical in character. It is always part of a controversy, and therefore it is only intelligible in the context of conflict which gave rise to it. Even our most academic theorists and our speculative thinkers have elaborated their theories to meet a given situation. We do not dislike theory as such, but we do suspect any theory which has no relation to immediate practical objectives.

Planning for Freedom

I
Does the British Constitution Exist?

The question seems an odd one. Weighty tomes have been written on the constitution, and constitutional law courses are taught in many universities. However, the question does have some meaning in the British context. Consider the fact that when constitutional issues arise, those who enter the discussion are as likely to be historians as lawyers. This is understandable since Britain has no formal written constitution and the 'constitution' is simply a description of those procedures and practices that have arisen over a long political history, which historians are perhaps more capable of expounding than lawyers. For some commentators, such appeals to an unwritten constitution are a virtual admission that no constitution actually exists. In this chapter the notion of an unwritten constitution and the arguments for and against it are examined, as are the different perceptions, past and present, of the character of the constitution as intimated by British history.

A. THE UNWRITTEN CONSTITUTION

Britain is one of the few advanced political societies – some would argue the only such society – not to have a written constitution. Of course, there is a large body of written law governing what would be generally regarded as constitutional matters, statutes regulating the duration of Parliaments, the right to vote, ministerial powers, court proceedings and so on. Such statutes are, however, ordinary laws capable of being abolished, amended or suspended by the ordinary processes of legislation. There is no formal constitutional document defining the structure of the political system and enjoying some entrenched position which would protect it against change through ordinary legal procedures.

Moreover, the constitution is supposed to exist not only in those statutes with constitutional implications but also in constitutional 'conventions' which have not been given written or statutory expression. This characterization of the British constitution as unwritten was given its classic expression by Dicey in the late nineteenth century in his heartfelt lament on the difficulties faced by the commentator on the British constitution as against the comparatively easy task of his American counterparts (I:1). In Britain, he points out, constitutional historians and theorists as well as lawyers must contribute to the discovery of the constitution. When he comes to define the substance of the unwritten constitution, he looks not just at the history of institutional development but also at the emergence of and changes in the 'conventions' of the constitution, the habits of behaviour and patterns of belief at large among the British public or at the least among the British political classes (I:2).

Long before Dicey wrote, Paine, in an attack upon Burke's defence of the ancient constitution, had poured scorn on the possibility of an unwritten constitution and asserted bluntly that Britain had no constitution (I:3). Coleridge directly countered Paine and, anticipating Dicey's notion of the conventions of the constitution, saw the constitution as being founded not in legal enactments but in an idea of the state historically rooted in the minds and the consciences of the people (I:4). This contention that the constitution is an aspect of the political culture rather than of law is still frequently made.

Proponents and critics of the unwritten constitution have had at least one idea in common, which is that some constitution is an essential basis for any kind of liberal democratic regime. Without some settled and recognized constitutional order, detailing the scope of legislation, the limits of executive action, the proper processes of government formation, the proper procedures for political and legislative decision-making, there could be no defence against arbitrary and tyrannical government, no protection of individual rights and liberties. The call for a written constitution has come from those who believe that the unwritten constitution has failed to provide such a secure and recognized order. Significantly, in recent years, this demand has often come from lawyers who see the subjection of politicians to the rule of constitutional law and the supervision of the courts as the only final safeguard of citizens' rights. Cited here are two eminent legal peers, Lord Hailsham, writing in the 1970s (I:5), and Lord Scarman, writing in the 1990s in support of the constitutional reform group, Charter 88 (I:6). The common theme of this legal scepticism is that modern British political practices have become incompatible with a truly liberal democratic regime. The powers of a sovereign Parliament have been over-extended; Parliament itself, through the development of party machinery and discipline, has become the creature of the executive; the arbitrary powers of government have grown; and the effectiveness of the electoral mechanism as a check on these developments has weakened.

1 A. V. Dicey, Written and Unwritten Constitutions (1885)

At the present day students of the constitution wish neither to criticise, nor to venerate, but to understand; and a professor whose duty it is to lecture on constitutional law, must feel that he is called upon to perform the part neither of a critic nor of an apologist, nor of an eulogist, but simply of an expounder; his duty is neither to attack nor to defend the constitution, but simply to explain its laws. He must also feel that, however attractive be the mysteries of the constitution, he has good reason to envy professors who belong to countries, such as France, Belgium, or the United States, endowed with constitutions of which the terms are to be found in printed documents, known to all citizens and accessible to every man who is able to read. Whatever may be the advantages of a so-called 'unwritten' constitution, its existence imposes special difficulties on teachers bound to expound its provisions. Any one will see that this is so who compares for a moment the position of writers, such as Kent or Story, who commented on the Constitution of America, with the situation of any person who undertakes to give instruction in the constitutional law of England . . .

The American lawyer has to ascertain the meaning of the Articles of the Constitution in the same way in which he tries to elicit the meaning of any other enactment. He must be guided by the rules of grammar, by his knowledge of the common law, by the light (occasionally) thrown on American legislation by American history, and by the conclusions to be deduced from a careful study of judicial decisions. The task, in short, which lay before the great American commentators was the explanation of a definite legal document in accordance with the received canons of legal interpretation. Their work, difficult as it might prove, was work of the kind to which lawyers are accustomed, and could be achieved by the use of ordinary legal methods. Story and Kent indeed were men of extraordinary capacity; so, however, were our own Blackstone, and at least one of Blackstone's editors. If, as is undoubtedly the case, the American jurists have produced commentaries on the constitution of the United States utterly unlike, and, one must in truth add, vastly superior to, any commentaries on the constitutional law of England, their success is partly due to the possession of advantages denied to the English commentator or lecturer. His position is entirely different from that of his American rivals. He may search the statute-book from beginning to end, but he will find no enactment which purports to contain the articles of the constitution; he will not possess any test by which to discriminate laws which are constitutional or fundamental from ordinary enactments; he will discover that the very term 'constitutional law', which is not (unless my memory deceives me) ever employed by Blackstone, is of comparatively modern origin; and in short, that before commenting on the law of the constitution he must make up his mind what is the nature and the extent of English constitutional law.

His natural, his inevitable resource is to recur to writers of authority on the law, the history, or the practice of the constitution.

The Law of the Constitution

2   A. V. Dicey, The Conventions of the Constitution (1885)

Constitutional law, as the term is used in England, appears to include all rules which directly or indirectly affect the distribution or the exercise of the sovereign power in the state. Hence it includes (among other things) all rules which define the members of the sovereign power, all rules which regulate the relation of such members to each other, or which determine the mode in which the sovereign power, or the members thereof, exercise their authority. Its rules prescribe the order of succession to the throne, regulate the prerogatives of the chief magistrate, determine the form of the legislature and its mode of election. These rules also deal with Ministers, with their responsibility, with their spheres of action, define the territory over which the sovereignty of the state extends and settle who are to be deemed subjects or citizens. Observe the use of the word 'rules', not 'laws'. This employment in terms is intentional. Its object is to call attention to the fact that the rules which make up constitutional law, as the term is used in England, include two sets of principles or maxims of a totally distinct character.

The one set of rules are in the strictest sense 'laws', since they are rules which (whether written or unwritten, whether enacted by statute or derived from the mass of custom, tradition, or judge-made maxims known as the Common Law) are enforced by the Courts; these rules constitute 'constitutional law' in the proper sense of that term, and may for the sake of distinction be called collectively 'the law of the constitution'.

The other set of rules consist of conventions, understandings, habits, or practices which, though they may regulate the conduct of the several members of the sovereign power, of the Ministry, or of other officials, are not in reality laws at all since they are not enforced by the Courts. This portion of constitutional law may, for the sake of distinction, be termed the 'conventions of the constitution', or constitutional morality.

The Law of the Constitution

3 Thomas Paine, There is no English Constitution (1791)

A Constitution is not a thing in name only, but in fact. It has not an ideal, but a real existence; and wherever it cannot be produced in a visible form, there is none. A Constitution is a thing antecedent to a Government, and a Government is only the creature of a Constitution. The Constitution of a country is not the act of its Government, but of the people constituting a Government. It is the body of elements, to which you can refer, and quote article by article; and which contains the principles on which the Government shall be established, the manner in which it shall be organised, the powers it shall have, the mode of elections, the duration of Parliaments, or by what other name such bodies may be called; the powers which the executive part of the Government shall have; and in fine, everything that relates to the complete organisation of a civil Government, and the principles on which it shall act, and by which it shall be bound. A Constitution, therefore, is to a Government what the laws made afterwards by that Government are to a Court of Judicature. The Court of Judicature does not make the laws, neither can it alter them; it only acts in conformity to the laws made: and the Government is in like manner governed by the Constitution.

Can, then, Mr Burke produce the English Constitution? If he cannot, we may fairly conclude that though it has been so much talked about, no such thing as a Constitution exists, or ever did exist, and consequently that the people have yet a Constitution to form.

Mr Burke will not, I presume, deny the position I have already advanced – namely, that Governments arise either *out* of the people or *over* the people. The English Government is one of those which arose out of a conquest, and not out of society, and consequently it arose over the people; and though it has been much modified from the opportunity of circumstances since the time of William the Conqueror, the country has never yet regenerated itself, and is therefore without a Constitution.

The Rights of Man

4   Samuel Taylor Coleridge, The Idea of the State (1830)

Ask any of our politicians what is meant by the constitution, and it is ten to one that he will give you a false explanation, *ex. gr.* that it is the body of our laws, or that it is the Bill of Rights; or perhaps, if he have read Tom Payne, he may tell you, that we have not yet got one; and yet not an hour may have elapsed, since you heard the same individual denouncing, and possibly with good reason, this or that code of laws, the excise and revenue laws, or those for including pheasants, or those for excluding Catholics, as altogether unconstitutional: and such and such acts of parliament as gross outrages on the constitution. . .

But a Constitution is an idea arising out of the idea of a state; and because our whole history from Alfred onward demonstrates the continued influence of such an idea, or ultimate aim, on the minds of our fore-fathers, in their characters and functions as public men; alike in what they resisted and in what they claimed; in the institutions and forms of polity which they established, and with regard to those, against which they more or less successfully contended; and because the result has been a progressive, though not always a direct, or equable advance in the gradual realization of the idea; and that it is actually, though even because it is an *idea* it cannot be *adequately*, represented in a correspondent scheme of means really existing; we speak, and have a right to speak, of the idea itself, as actually existing, i.e. as a *principle*, existing in the only way in which a principle can exist – in the minds and consciences of the persons, whose duties it prescribes, and whose rights it determines. In the same sense that the sciences of arithmetic and of geometry, that mind, that life itself, have reality; the constitution has real existence, and does not the less exist in reality, because it both is, and exists as, an IDEA.

On the Constitution of the Church and State

5   Lord Hailsham, A Model for a Written Constitution (1976)

I have reached the conclusion that our constitution is wearing out. Its central defects are gradually coming to outweigh its merits, and its central defects consist in the absolute powers we confer on our sovereign body, and the concentration of those powers in an executive government formed out of one party which may not fairly represent the popular will. I have come to think that, while there is much to be said for each of them, none of the reforms which I have examined is adequate by itself to redress the balance. I now owe it to you to give some indication of what might suffice and how it might be achieved.

I envisage nothing less than a written constitution for the United Kingdom, and by that I mean one which limits the powers of Parliament and provides a means of enforcing these limitations either by political or legal means. This is the essence of the matter, and every other detailed suggestion that I make must be considered as tentative, and in comparison unimportant.

I would myself visualise a Parliament divided into two Chambers, each elected. The one, the Commons, would, as now, determine the political colour of the executive Government and retain control of finance. Preferably, in my view, it would be elected as now by single member constituencies. The other, you might call it a senate, but I would prefer the old name, would, like the Senate of the United States, be elected to represent whole regions, and unlike that Senate, would be chosen by some system of proportional representation.

The powers of Parliament, so formed, would be limited both by law, and a system of checks and balances. Regions would have devolved assemblies, and the respective spheres of influence of these and of Parliament would be defined by law and policed by the ordinary Courts. There would be a Bill of Rights, equally entrenched, containing as a minimum the rights defined by the European convention to which we are already parties, and which can already be enforced against us by an international body. Thus, Scotland, Wales and Northern Ireland would all obtain self-government in certain fields within the framework of a federal constitution of which the regions of England would also be separate and equal parts. The interests of regions, minorities and individuals would be safeguarded by law, by the provision of a proportionately elected second Chamber, and by the separate regional assemblies. What we should have achieved is a recognisable version of the Westminster model modified so as to remove its disadvantages, as has already been done in Canada and Australia.

Elective Dictatorship (BBC Dimbleby Lectures)

6 Lord Scarman, The Need for a Written Constitution (1992)

My theme will be that government above and beyond the reach of the law is the menace to be defeated. Charter 88, as we all know, proposes the ultimate safeguard, a written constitution: I quote now what I believe to be a critical sentence: 'No democracy can be considered safe whose freedoms are not encoded in a basic constitution.' I hold that view strongly . . .

The constitution I ask you to envisage for Britain is a code having the force of a basic law and protected by an independent judiciary. 'Basic' means that the constitution cannot be amended or repealed (in part or in whole) like the ordinary statute law by a simple majority in Parliament: it can be amended only by a stringent and rigorous procedure not applicable to ordinary legislation. Such a constitution may properly be described as a fundamental or basic law binding on Parliament, the government and the people. There are only two ways of getting rid of it – the special procedure or revolution. Both, let us never forget are options always open, however unwanted.

I would see this basic constitution as embodying four essential safeguards for the people:

(1) the protection of the human rights and fundamental freedoms of everyone within the jurisdiction;
(2) the setting of legal limits upon the legislative and executive power of the Crown and Parliament;
(3) the protection of regional and local government by the adoption of the principle of subsidiarity;
(4) the establishment of an independent judiciary having the duty and power of protecting the constitution.

Why Britain Needs a Written Constitution
(Charter 88 Trust)

B. The Ancient Constitution

Clearly, the idea of the unwritten constitution has been closely associated in the British debate with the idea of traditionalism. The constitution is defined in terms not of formal rules but of traditional behaviour and values, traditional modes of practice and belief. Central to the idea of the constitution has been the assertion of its continuity and central to its definition has been the identification of 'the ancient constitution'.

The assertion of continuity has in the past often been associated with the assumption of progress. The constitution has not just been ageing; it has also been maturing, becoming a more and more complete expression of civilized political relations. This kind of triumphalist history, exemplified here by an extract from Lord Acton's inaugural lecture at Cambridge in 1895 (I:7), has been castigated more recently as a 'Whig' view of history which distorts the past by subjecting it to the values and perspectives of the present. Nevertheless, Sir David Lindsay Keir allows himself a congratulatory tone in isolating continuity and adaptability as the prime characteristics of the British system (I:8). How adaptable a constitution can be whilst maintaining any kind of continuity is a moot point and Ferdinand Mount has recently attacked what he terms the continuity myth, in part by criticizing Keir's claims and the language in which they were posed (I:9).

Yet, however true it might be that the Parliament of the thirteenth century has little in common with the Parliament of the twentieth, it is nevertheless the case that England has the longest continuous experience of representative institutions of any modern state. In 1965 the seven-hundredth anniversary of Parliament was proclaimed and celebrated. The precision of the dating has very little historical validity, but what can be said is that during the thirteenth and early fourteenth centuries Parliament emerged as an established part of political life and with a structure that has remained in many of its aspects intact until today. The meetings of the royal councils called by the King became more regular and formal; to the wealthy magnates and higher clergymen who were the earlier participants in the councils were added representatives of other social orders and economic interests, representatives from town and country, the boroughs and the shires; there emerged a formal institutional separation of the first two groups into the House of Lords and the second two into the House of Commons; and the term Parliament attached itself to these political assemblies.

Some features of the early history of Parliament have deeply affected its subsequent development. Parliament was, in the first place, the creation of the Crown, the regularization and formalization of councils called by the King to parley with the politically active and economically dominant sections of the community – parley in the two senses of consulting and of treating or negotiating. In no sense did it arise as an expression of the will of the people, claiming some sort of ultimate authority in the state as did representative bodies created from the eighteenth century on. These origins, many would say, have coloured the whole relationship between government and Parliament in England. Moreover, the Parliament that emerged was not wholly representative, including as it did persons who were summoned individually by the Crown or, once an hereditary peerage had developed, attended by individual right. Again this original settlement has persisted. One last point might serve to modify undue British pride in its parliamentary traditions. This is that the English experience was by no means unique. The period from the thirteenth century on saw the emergence of assemblies of estates, called variously Parliament or cortes or states-general or diet, in almost every European state from Scotland to Hungary, from the Iberian peninsula to Russia. In most states, these assemblies disappeared in the early modern period or were abolished in the French Revolutionary and Napoleonic periods. Britain was almost unique in retaining the medieval assembly through to the nineteenth and twentieth centuries. Nor was the thirteenth-century Parliament unique in a temporal sense. In pre-feudal Europe, there were a number of assemblies which might be regarded as precursors of the later Parliaments, and in particular in Anglo-Saxon England the witenage-mot, an assembly of notables, seems to have played an at times extensive political role.

The outlines of this ancient constitution are obscure even to modern historians. None the less, this has not prevented constant appeals to the ancient constitution as the final arbiter in constitutional disputes. In the seventeenth-century period of the Civil War and the so-called Glorious Revolution of 1689, both parliamentarian and royalist apologists looked to the past for justification even when, on both sides, their positions diverged from current practice. In his reaction to French Revolutionary doctrine and to British radicalism of his time, Burke both passionately asserted the primacy of the ancient constitution and sought to associate this traditionalist stance with a conservative repudiation of attempts to alter the prevailing political system (I:10).

Appeals to tradition are likely, however, to get confused or contradictory answers. Legalistic interpretations of written constitutions are no doubt capable of wide and politically significant divergences, but the historically based accounts of unwritten constitutions, particularly if these are thought to be embodied in conventions or traditional ideas, are capable of even greater discrepancies. In the British context, these discrepancies have been so great that traditionalism has on occasions been allied to radical objectives. From the seventeenth century on, democratic ambitions have often been posed as a return to a past golden age. This has been done by the use of what has come to be known as the 'Norman yoke' argument. The argument was that the representative system had pre-Norman Conquest origins and that the Anglo-Saxon system was much more democratic in character than the parliamentary regime that had evolved since the thirteenth century. This golden age of Anglo-Saxon democracy had been ended by the Norman invasion and the imposition by William the Conqueror of a feudal monarchy.

One of the most extensive recitals of this argument was given by Oldfield in his six-volume history of British representation published in 1816 (I:11). Oldfield demonstrates also the political intent behind the historical narrative by linking the Norman yoke history to the campaign for parliamentary reform in his own time. The association had long been made. In the seventeenth century, it was a recurrent part of radical rhetoric in the Civil War period (I:12). Although the ancient constitution has been called up in the radical as well as the conservative cause, there have been those, again at different points on the political spectrum, who have rejected this appeal and have turned to reason rather than historical inquiry as the path to constitutional truths. Lord Bolingbroke, who has been seen as one of the founders of the Tory tradition, based his search for the idea of a patriot kingship on a consideration of what ought to have been rather than of what has been (I:13). Bentham, writing from a democratic perspective, was even more scathing about an appeal to a barbarian past rather than to the true principles of government (I:14).

7 Lord Acton, The Progress of Liberty (1895)

What do people mean who proclaim that liberty is the palm, and the prize, and the crown, seeing that it is an idea of which there are two hundred definitions, and that this wealth of interpretation has caused more bloodshed than anything, except theology? Is it Democracy as in France, or Federalism as in America, or the national independence which bounds the Italian view, or the reign of the fittest, which is the ideal of Germans? I know not whether it will ever fall within my sphere of duty to trace the slow progress of that idea through the chequered scenes of our history, and to describe how subtle speculations touching the nature of conscience promoted a nobler and more spiritual conception of the liberty that protects it, until the guardian of rights developed into the guardian of duties which are the cause of rights, and that which had been prized as the material safeguard for treasures of earth became sacred as security for things that are divine. All that we require is a work-day key to history, and our present need can be supplied without pausing to satisfy philosophers. Without inquiring how far Sarasa or Butler, Kant or Vinet, is right as to the infallible voice of God in man, we may easily agree in this, that where absolutism reigned, by irresistible arms, concentrated possessions, auxiliary churches, and inhuman laws, it reigns no more; that commerce having risen against land, labour against wealth, the State against the forces dominant in society, the division of power against the State, the thought of individuals against the practice of ages, neither authorities nor minorities, nor majorities can command implicit obedience; and, where there has been long and arduous experience, a rampart of tried conviction and accumulated knowledge, where there is a fair level of general morality, education, courage and self-restraint, there, if there only, a society may be found that exhibits the condition of life towards which, by elimination of failures, the world has been moving through the allotted space. You will know it by outward signs: Representation, the extinction of slavery, the reign of opinion, and the like; better still by less apparent evidences: the security of the weaker groups and the liberty of conscience, which, effectually secured, secures the rest.

Lectures on Modern History

8   Sir David Lindsay Keir, Constitutional Continuity and Flexibility (1964)

Continuity has been the dominant characteristic in the development of English government. Its institutions, though unprotected by the fundamental or organic laws which safeguard the 'rigid' constitutions of most other states, have preserved the same general appearance throughout their history, and have been regulated in their working by principles which can be regarded as constant. Crown and Parliament, Council and great offices of state, courts with their judges and magistrates, have all retained, amid varying environments, many of the inherent attributes as well as much of the outward circumstance and dignity which were theirs in the medieval world of their origin. In no other European country is the constitution so largely a legacy from that remote but not unfamiliar age. Yet continuity has not meant changelessness. Ancient institutions have been ceaselessly adapted to meet purposes often very different from those for which they were originally intended, and have been combined in apparent harmony with newer organs of government devised to meet requirements which have manifested themselves only as society has developed the intricate patterns of its modern life. The very flexibility of the constitution has ensured that the process of modifying and adding to it has involved no sudden and capricious breach with the past. In the English constitution, to adapt a picturesque phrase, the centuries have 'given one another rendezvous'. Some of the institutions of former days have from time to time been swept away. But their disappearance has generally been preceded by atrophy, and their end has been painless. The destruction of living and working parts of the constitution has been rare. Even more subtle have been the changes, in their nature less easy to follow, in the unwritten customs and understandings – the 'conventions of the constitution' as they have been termed – which supplement the strict letter of constitutional law. These too have been profoundly altered from age to age. The assumptions made in the sixteenth century had in the eighteenth long since ceased to be accepted. In the nineteenth century, those of the eighteenth were dissolved away. Whatever has been their form, they have always been reinterpretations, under changed circumstances, of principles inherent in the constitution, and they have lain within the very logic of constitutional growth. Neither in its formal and legal, nor in its informal and practical aspect, has English government at any stage of its history violently and permanently repudiated its own tradition.

The Constitutional History of Modern Britain since 1485

9   Ferdinand Mount, An Objection (1992)

Let us pause briefly to note the crucial modifying phrases in this paean: 'the same general appearance'. . .'principles which can be regarded as constant'. . .'amid varying environments'. . .'the outward circumstance and dignity'. Already the ground is prepared for easy slithering between continuity in matters of form and continuity in matters of substance, between appearance and reality.

The British Constitution Now: Recovery or Decline?

10   Edmund Burke, The Ancient Constitution (1790)

You will observe, that from Magna Charta to the Declaration of Right, it has been the uniform policy of our constitution to claim and assert our liberties, as an *entailed inheritance* derived to us from our forefathers, and to be transmitted to our posterity; as an estate specially belonging to the people of this kingdom, without

any reference whatever to any other more general or prior right.
By this means our constitution preserves an unity in so great a
diversity of its parts. We have an inheritable crown; an inheritable
peerage; and a house of commons and a people inheriting
privileges, franchises, and liberties, from a long line of ancestors.

The policy appears to me to be the result of profound
reflection; or rather the happy effect of following nature, which
is wisdom without reflection, and above it. A spirit of innovation is generally the result of a selfish temper, and confined
views. People will not look forward to posterity, who never
look backward to their ancestors. Besides, the people of England well know, that the idea of inheritance furnishes a sure
principle of conservation, and a sure principle of transmission;
without at all excluding a principle of improvement. It leaves
acquisition free; but it secures what it acquires. Whatever
advantages are obtained by a state proceeding on these maxims,
are locked fast as in a sort of family settlement; grasped as in a
kind of mortmain for ever. By a constitutional policy working
after the pattern of nature, we receive, we hold, we transmit our
government and our privileges, in the same manner in which
we enjoy and transmit our property and our lives.

Reflections on the Revolution in France

11 T. H. B. Oldfield, Anglo-Saxon Democracy (1816)

In entering upon a work of such magnitude and importance as a
Representative History of Great Britain and Ireland, the Author
feels most sensibly the responsibility he has imposed upon
himself; and, to acquit himself in the faithful discharge of his
duty, he has had recourse to the best authorities he could obtain;
and the result proves that the Representative System is as
ancient as the establishment of civil society in the world.

The Dyots in Germany, the Tiers Etat in France, the Cortes
in Spain, the Legislative Assemblies in every nation in Europe,
were all composed of the Representatives of Cities and Districts;
and it cannot be imagined that the Parliament of England alone,
originated in an Oligarchy of Barons or feudal chiefs, when that
assembly is proved to have existed for so many centuries before
the feudal system was known.

Caesar acknowledges that the *Commune Concilium* of Britain chose Cassibelanus for their leader, and Pughe the celebrated Welch antiquarian has proved from the Tryads, or ancient records of the Britons that the *Kyfr-y-then* of the ancient British was the *Commune Concilium* mentioned by Caesar, afterwards called the *Wittena-Gemote* of the Saxons, and which assumed the name of *Parliament* in the reign of Edward the Confessor, who had received his education in France.

That this was a representative assembly, elected by the people, is proved by the Saxon View of Frankpledge. . .and that not only the Legislative Body, but every executive officer from the Tythingman to the Ealderman, or chief magistrate of a county, was elected by the respective Hundreds annually assembled in the County Court. . .

The assembling of a Parliament composed of four representatives from each county, in the 49th Henry III, was what Carew calls 'throwing off the yoke of the Conqueror, and the redemption of the people from slavery'.

It was the re-establishment of the ancient form of government which existed from the earliest times, but had been wrecked in the same tempest that had overturned the Saxon Throne, and it is as absurd to suppose that we had no representative Parliament antecedent to the forty-ninth of Henry III, as to assert that we had no King prior to the same period. . .

That the representation was *equal*, and the right of suffrage *general*, in the Housekeepers paying taxes, or, as it is now termed, scot and lot, is proved from the Statutes at large, and from the earliest history of every County, City, and Borough, in the kingdom. . .

The corruption that was infused into the Representative System at the restoration of the Stuart family, and which has since contaminated the whole frame, has been more destructive of public morals than any other cause that can be assigned; it is the root from which all other political crimes originate. He who receives a bribe, must commit perjury, and the person who gives it, is guilty of subornation; but the individual offence is as nothing compared with the evil which, by wars and consequent taxation, has been brought upon the country.

The only remedy for all these evils is a fair and equal representation of the people, a Parliament that upon every question will speak the sense of the nation, instead of being the tool of a minister. The great Earl of Chatham concurred in this

sentiment. The late Right Hon William Pitt declared it in the
House of Commons. It was the pillar on which the late Right
Hon Charles James Fox erected the standard of his popularity;
and which the late Duke of Richmond, the first Marquis of
Lansdowne, Sir George Savile, Sir Charles Turner, Doctor John
Jebb, James Martin Esq, Granville Sharp Esq and all the
departed patriots of the last generation united to promote.

We trust their descendants will not be less active in procuring
this great reform, on which our Constitution, our natural
rights, and our very existence, depends. It is not a favor we ask,
it is a birthright we demand, and to which we have as just a
claim as to the property we possess.

The Representative History of Great Britain and Ireland

12   The Norman Yoke (1649)

And so successively from that time the conquering enemy have
still laid these yokes upon Israel, to keep Jacob down. And the
last enslaving conquest which the enemy got over Israel, was
the Norman over England. And from that time kings, lords,
judges, justices, bailiffs, and the violent bitter people that are
freeholders, are and have been successively: the Norman bastard
William himself, his colonels, captains, inferior officers, and
common soldiers, who still are from that time to this day in
pursuit of that victory, imprisoning, robbing, and killing the
poor enslaved English Israelites.

And this appears clear. For when any trustee or state officer is
to be chosen, the freeholders or landlords must be the choosers,
who are the Norman common soldiers spread abroad in the land.
And who must be chosen but some very rich man who is the
successor of the Norman colonels or high officers? And to what
end have they been thus chosen but to establish that Norman
power the more forcibly over the enslaved English, and to beat
them down again whenas they gather heart to seek for liberty? For
what are all those binding and restraining laws that have been
made from one age to another since that conquest, and are still
upheld by fury over the people? I say, what are they but the
cords, bands, manacles, and yokes that the enslaved English, like
Newgate prisoners, wear upon their hands and legs as they walk
the streets; by which those Norman oppressors, and these their

successors from age to age, have enslaved the poor people by, killed their younger brother, and would not suffer Jacob to arise?

'The True Levellers' Standard Advanced'

13 Lord Bolingbroke, An Appeal to Reason not the Past (1738)

My intention is not to introduce what I have to say concerning the *duties of kings*, by any nice inquiry into the *original* of their institution. What is to be known of it will appear plainly enough, to such as are able and can spare time to trace it, in the broken traditions which are come down to us of a few nations. But those, who are not able to trace it there, may trace something better, and more worthy to be known, in their own thoughts: I mean what this institution *ought* to have been, whenever it began, according to the rule of *reason*, founded in the common *rights*, and *interests*, of *mankind*. On this head it is quite necessary to make some reflections, that will, like angular stones laid on a rock, support the little fabric, the model however of a great building, that I propose to raise.

So plain a matter could never have been rendered intricate and voluminous, had it not been for lawless ambition, extravagant vanity, and the detestable spirit of tyranny, abetted by the private interests of artful men, by adulation and superstition, two vices to which that staring timid creature man is excessively prone; if authority had not imposed on such as did not pretend to reason; and if such as did attempt to reason had not been caught in the common snares of sophism, and bewildered in the labyrinths of disputation. In this case, therefore, as in all those of great concernment, the shortest and the surest method of arriving at real knowledge is to *unlearn* the lessons we have been taught, to *remount* to *first principles*, and take no body's word about *them*; for it is about *them* that almost all the juggling and legerdemain, employed by men whose trade it is to deceive, are set to work.

The Idea of a Patriot King

14 Jeremy Bentham, Matchless Constitution? (1824)

Matchless constitution! There's your sheet-anchor! There's your true standard! Rally round the constitution, that is – rally round waste, rally round depredation, rally round oppression, rally round corruption, rally round election terrorism, rally round imposture – imposture on the hustings, imposture in the honorable House, imposture in every court of law.

Connected with all this boasting and toasting is a theory such as a Westminster or Eton boy of the sixth form, aye, or his grandmother, might be ashamed of. For among those who are the loudest in decrying theory, whenever any attempt is made at reasoning, some silly sentimental theory may almost always be found. The constitution, why must it not be looked into? Why is it that under pain of being *ipso facto* convicted of anarchism, we must never presume to look at it except with our eyes shut?

Because it was the work of our ancestors, of legislators, few of whom could so much as read, and those few having nothing before them that was worth reading. First theoretical presupposition: *wisdom of barbarian ancestors.*

And when from their ordinary occupation, the cutting of one another's throats, or those of Welshmen, or Scotchmen, or Irishmen, they could now and then steal a holiday, how did they employ it? In cutting Frenchmen's throats in order to get their money. This was active virtue; leaving Frenchmen's throats uncut was indolence, slumber, inglorious ease. Second theoretical presupposition: *virtue of barbarian ancestors.*

Thus fraught with habitual wisdom and habitual virtue, they sat down and devised; and setting before them the best ends, and pursuing those best ends by the best means, they framed in outline – at any rate – they planned and executed our matchless constitution – the constitution as it stands, and may it forever stand!

Planned and executed? On what occasion? On none. At what place? At none. By whom? By nobody. . .

The Handbook of Political Fallacies

C.   PRESENT PERSPECTIVES

The claimed possession of an unwritten constitution based on convention and tradition as well as on changeable statute law offers the British a wide scope for interpretation of the central features of their system. As in the past, so in the present, these perspectives can diverge widely. At least three can be identified, the first seeing the system as essentially a constitutional monarchy, the second emphasizing parliamentary sovereignty as the central principle and the third viewing the system as a flawed democracy or, at best, only a potential democracy.

The first perspective sees Crown rule as still the central constitutional principle, in the sense that ministers of the Crown, the Cabinet and in particular the Prime Minister, are the mainspring of the political system. Of course, this perspective accepts that government operates within an elaborate system of checks and balances; it must maintain the support of a majority in the House of Commons, it must answer to Parliament, it must face the electorate at least once every five years. Nevertheless, from this standpoint, government is the prime mover in the system. Cabinet decides the general lines of policy, it controls the legislative programme of Parliament, it can, given party discipline, normally be assured of a majority in the Commons. This point of view is naturally attractive to governments, of whatever political hue. Richard Crossman illustrated this well in his diary entry about Cabinet reactions to his proposals for the reform of procedure in the Commons, including the proposal to have some morning sittings of the House (I:15). Crossman's Cabinet colleagues received with little enthusiasm proposals which might have extended Commons' control over the executive. The view that government, acting as agent of the Crown, is the central organ of the state was put clearly by the prosecution in the trial of Clive Ponting, and was endorsed by the trial judge. Ponting was charged with a breach of the Official Secrets Act for sending to an MP documents available to him as a senior civil servant (I:16).

The second perspective sees Parliament, and in particular the House of Commons, as the centre of the British political world. Enoch Powell, one of the most controversial but also influential parliamentarians of his time, is a passionate advocate of this position (I:17). Clearly, Powell is pressing the notion of parliamentary legal sovereignty, which will be examined in the next chapter, but here and elsewhere he attaches an even wider significance to the authority and prestige of Parliament. He acknowledges present threats to this position of eminence, but whereas others – such as Crossman – have seen the threat to be the increasing dominance of the executive over the Commons, Powell points to the twin threats of loss of sovereignty and power to the European Community and the possible loss of sovereignty to devolved national governments in Scotland and Wales.

The last position, that the British system can best be characterized as an only partially achieved democracy, is of course one taken by those urging further constitutional reform. If England can lay claim to seven hundred years of representative institutions, it can claim only sixty years of democracy if universal adult suffrage is a minimal requirement of democracy. For those who subscribe to Charter 88, a stronger dose of popular sovereignty needs to be added to Crown and parliamentary sovereignty before the democratic credentials of the system can be fully established (I:18). Of course, there are also those who agree with the reformers' depiction of the system as a limited democracy but applaud the limitations and recommend the strength of a regime which allows only a limited role to 'the people'.

15 R. H. S. Crossman, A Labour Cabinet and Parliamentary Control (1966)

I put the case as well as I could knowing it was unpopular. I reminded them that I'd inherited this package from my predecessor and that the Party was deeply committed to it at the general election. The moment I'd finished George Brown said, 'Well, it's asking a terrible lot of us, Prime Minister. We're busy men. What you're asking is that busy Ministers should have morning sittings as well.' I explained that the aim was to get the back-benchers home early two nights a week. I couldn't guarantee that we should achieve this aim and I had put the topical debates in to spice things up in the mornings. Now, however, I realized that a topical debate was something which might take the time of a Foreign Office spokesman and that is the way in which George Brown considered it. He was followed by Minister after Minister round the table simply saying how busy they were, how they were harassed by all these Cabinet Committees, and how they simply couldn't be burdened with any more work by the House of Commons.

Barbara was the only person with any political sense. She said, 'I'm as bothered as anybody about the extra work but frankly, you know, if what's being said here was reported to the Parliamentary Party we would be blown to smithereens.' She was specifically referring to the remarks of the First Secretary. Michael Stewart had said to the Cabinet that these new Members on whose initiative morning sittings had been proposed really must be told that they'd got it all wrong – that a back-bench MP has a perfectly satisfactory full-time job to do and there's no reason to create work for him to keep him happy. Indeed, our back-benchers should be thankful that as a socialist government we want to keep the Executive strong, not to strengthen parliamentary control. Michael's remarks had been applauded by many people round the table. When I heard them I remembered that he'd hardly been a back-bencvher at any time in his twenty years in the House of Commons. He's always been either a junior Minister or a Shadow Minister on the front bench. I've had nineteen years as a back-bencher and I know what they are talking about so I was tickled when Jim Callaghan joined in and said, 'We've got to be careful of our Lord President now he has transferred his attention from boosting housing to boosting the House of Commons. Just as he knew nothing about housing before he went to the Ministry this fellow was never there when he was a back-bencher. Now he's boosting the Commons with all the strength and power he gave to his housing programme and we've got to resist him in the same way.'

Most of these Ministers were individually as well as collectively committed to parliamentary reform. Yet after two years they've become Whitehall figures who've lost contact with Parliament. And of course what they're saying is pure nonsense. Ministers aren't bothered by Parliament, indeed they're hardly ever there. A departmental Minister has many other major worries what with boxes, Ministerial committees, visits outside London. But the amount of time a Minister spends on the front bench or in his room in St Stephen's is very small. The Executive rides supreme in Britain and has minimum trouble from the legislature.

The Crossman Diaries: entry for Thursday, 17 November 1966

16   The Interests of the State – R. *v.* Ponting (1985)

Official Secrets

Whether duty to communicate information in the interests of the state – meaning of 'duty' and 'interests of the state'

The defendant was charged with an offence under section 2(1) of the Official Secrets Act 1911. On July 16, 1984 he sent to

Mr Tam Dalyell, duly elected Member of Parliament for Linlithgow, two Ministry of Defence documents relating to Parliamentary enquiries about the sinking of the Argentine vessel, the *General Belgrano*, during the Falklands conflict. The first of these documents was a draft reply written by the defendant, in his capacity as head of the relevant Ministry of Defence department, to questions asked by Mr Dalyell to the Secretary of State which was never in fact sent by the Minister. The second was a minute by another Ministry of Defence department indicating that certain answers should not be given to questions put by the Parliamentary Select Committee on Foreign Affairs concerning changes in the Rules of Engagement during the Falkland conflict. The first document was unclassified and the second was marked confidential.

It was conceded by the defence that the defendant had communicated this information to Mr Dalyell, that he had this information in his possession by virtue of his position as a civil servant, and that he had not been authorised to give this information to Mr Dalyell. The only live issue, therefore, was whether Mr Dalyell was a person to whom it was in the interest of the State the defendant's duty to communicate the information. . .

Held: That this section of the Official Secrets Act is primarily concerned with the preservation of information which has been obtained by the communicator by virtue of his position as a servant of Her Majesty and that whether or not the document touched on national security was irrelevant. The judge also held that on a proper construction of section 2, there was no requirement of *mens rea* for this section further than an intention to commit the *actus reus*. The prosecution did not have to show that the defendant did not reasonably and honestly believe that the communication was in the interest of the state. . .

The judge further held that the word duty in section 2(1) of the Official Secrets Act referred to an official duty imposed upon the communicator by virtue of his position as the duty arises out of the accused's office as a Crown servant. It must, therefore, indicate an official duty rather than a moral, contractual or civic duty. As to the meaning of the words 'in the interest of the state', the learned judge preferred the views that the interests of the state meant what was in the interests of the State according to its recognised organs of government and the policies as expounded by the particular Government of the day. It was not, he held, for the jury to decide what the Government's policy should have been nor was it for them to enter into a political debate. In this case it was not in dispute that the policy of the Government was not to give the information which Mr Ponting communicated.

Case and Comment

The defence had argued for a wider meaning of 'in the interest of the State', namely in the interest of the country or the realm or in the national interest. . .

The defence further argued that even if the learned judge directed the jury in accordance with the speeches of Lord Devlin and Lord Pearce, the policies of the government of the day had to be regarded as being subject to established constitutional conventions or rules one of which was that Ministers should always tell the truth to Parliament as far as was possible without harming national security.

The defendant was acquitted.

R. v. Ponting, in *Criminal Law Review*

17 Enoch Powell, Parliamentary Government (1978)

There can I believe be no dispute as to what for Britain has been the central institution which has embodied our national values, and whose history has been essential to our perception and acceptance of those values. That institution is Parliament. Our national experience has been unique and our national values are unique because there is no other nation of which the statement I have just made can be predicated. It cannot be said of the Congress of the United States any more than of the representative assemblies which the other Western nations have erected at various stages of their history. From the common root of the feudal court there grew and flourished in the special conditions of Britain alone, by a kind of ecological exception, the institution of Parliament. The British are a parliamentary nation: internally and externally they are conditioned and defined by that institution and that historical experience. If our values are in danger, and if our freedom and our independence are in danger, it is because Parliament is endangered, and endangered in the only way an institution can be – by inner loss of conviction. Whether such loss is temporary or permanent, an episode or an irreversible event, we from inside history can neither predict nor determine. We can only. . .perceive and warn. . .

Parliament is being ground – indeed, has voluntarily offered itself to be ground – between the upper and the nether millstones. The upper millstone is the European Economic Community, to which the Parliament of 1970 ceded overriding power to tax and make laws and policies for the British people – something for which there has not been the remotest precedent since the Middle Ages, and only dubiously then. Without as yet any sense, upon the part of Parliament or people, of the total and revolutionary effect of this abnegation, it is now anticipated that in no more than two years hence we shall have concurred in furnishing the superior taxing and legislating authority of the EEC with an elected parliament of its own, thus renouncing in the most explicit manner the political authority and independent existence of the British parliament and its constituency.

The nether millstone is the process – euphemistically called 'devolution' – of setting up within the United Kingdom directly elected bodies or anti-parliaments which purport to represent nations and which, being in principle endowed with the right to make or change the law, cannot logically be subordinated to Parliament itself or denied the power of taxation. Ironically, perhaps because the perspective is shorter, the consequences in this case have been perceived sooner and seem in Parliament itself to have aroused quicker antagonism. Those consequences are a conflict which could only be resolved by either dividing the United Kingdom into separate states or converting it into a federation.

A Nation or No Nation?

18   Charter 88 – A Flawed Democracy (1988)

We have been brought up in Britain to believe that we are free: that our Parliament is the mother of democracy; that our liberty is the envy of the world; that our system of justice is always fair; that the guardians of our safety, the police and security services, are subject to democratic, legal control; that our civil service is impartial; that our cities and communities maintain a proud identity; that our press is brave and honest. Today such beliefs are increasingly implausible. The gap between reality and the received ideas of Britain's 'unwritten constitution' has widened to a degree that many find hard to endure. Yet this year we are invited to celebrate the third centenary of the 'Glorious Revolution' of 1688, which established what was to become the United Kingdom's sovereign formula. In the name of freedom, our political, human and social rights are being curtailed while the powers of the executive have increased, are increasing and ought to be diminished.

A process is underway which endangers many of the freedoms we have had. Only in part deliberate, it began before 1979 and is now gathering momentum. Scotland is governed like a province from Whitehall. More generally, the government has eroded a number of important civil freedoms: for example, the universal rights to habeas corpus, to peaceful assembly, to freedom of movement, even to the birth-right itself. By taking these rights from some, the government puts them at risk for all.

A traditional British belief in the benign nature of the country's institutions encourages an unsystematic perception of these grave matters; each becomes an 'issue' considered in isolation from the rest. Being unwritten the constitution also encourages a piecemeal approach to politics; an approach that gives little protection against a determined, authoritarian state. For the events of 1688 only shifted the absolute power of the monarch into the hands of the parliamentary oligarchy.

The current administration is not an un-English interruption in the country's way of life. But while the government calls upon aspirations for liberty, it also exploits the dark side of a constitutional settlement which was always deficient in democracy.

The 1688 settlement had a positive side. In its time the Glorious Revolution was a historic victory over Royal tyranny. Britain was spared the rigours of dictatorship. A working compromise between many different interests was made possible at home, even if, from Ireland to India, quite different standards were imposed by Empire abroad. No criticism of contemporary developments in Britain should deny the significance of past democratic achievements, most dramatically illuminated in May 1940 when Britain defied the fascist domination of Europe.

But the eventual victory that liberated Western Europe preserved the paternalist attitudes and institutions of the United

Kingdom. These incorporated the popular desire for work and welfare into a post-war national consensus. Now this has broken down. So, too, have its conventions of compromise and tolerance: essential components of a free society. Instead, the inbuilt powers of the 1688 settlement have enabled the government to discipline British society to its ends: to impose its values on the civil service; to menace the independence of broadcasting; to threaten academic freedom in the universities and schools; to tolerate abuses committed in the name of national security. The break with the immediate past shows how vulnerable Britain has always been to elective dictatorship. The consequence is that today the British have fewer legal rights and less democracy than many other West Europeans.

The intensification of authoritarian rule in the United Kingdom has only recently begun. The time to reverse the process is now, but it cannot be reversed by an appeal to the past. Three hundred years of unwritten rule from above are enough. Britain needs a democratic programme that will end unfettered control by the executive of the day. It needs to reform a Parliament in which domination of the lower house can be decided by fewer than 40 per cent of the population; a Parliament in which a majority of the upper house is still determined by inheritance.

We have had less freedom than we believed. That which we have enjoyed has been too dependent on the benevolence of our rulers. Our freedoms have remained their possession, rationed out to us as subjects rather than being our own inalienable possession as citizens. To make real the freedoms we once took for granted means for the first time to take them for ourselves.

The time has come to demand political, civil and human rights in the United Kingdom. The first step is to establish them in constitutional form, so that they are no longer subject to the arbitrary diktat of Westminster and Whitehall.

Charter 88

II
Crown and Parliament, Government and People

Since the creation of Parliament in the thirteenth century – or its re-creation if the Norman yoke story is correct – the relationship between Crown and Parliament, in modern terms between government and the House of Commons, has been crucial within the British system. It has also been, and still is, a constant source of contention in British political argument. This chapter will follow the development of this theme by looking at its variants – the ideas of mixed government, checks and balances, separation of powers, parliamentary sovereignty, Cabinet government. Another recurrent theme is the relationship between government and people, the political public, and this will be examined through consideration of the status of the MP in face of his (and, more recently, her) constituents, the frequency of elections, the notion of the mandate and the use of referenda.

A. Mixed Government

By the end of the Middle Ages, Parliament had gone far towards establishing its position within the constitutional order. On taxation, both direct and indirect, there were by the end of the fourteenth century no obvious ways in which the King could impose taxes without parliamentary consent. Besides this, the House of Commons had come to assume a dominant position over the other estates in the imposition of taxes. On the question of general legislation, it had become an established principle that statute law required the consent of King, Lords and Commons. The implications of this were drawn by Sir John Fortescue writing in 1469 and contrasting the absolute monarchy of France with the constitutional monarchy of England through his distinction between *dominium regale* and *dominium politicum et regale* (II:1).

This identification of King-in-Parliament as the supreme sovereign power was not challenged in the Tudor period. Perhaps because Parliaments in this period were in any case so amenable to royal wishes, there was little incentive for monarchs to gainsay the theory of constitutional monarchy. Indeed, Sir Thomas Smith, one of Queen Elizabeth's Secretaries of State, could insist in the later sixteenth century that the English Parliament 'representeth and hath the power of the whole realm' (II:2).

Nevertheless the challenge was to come with the accession of the Stuarts. James I outlined in his speech to Parliament in 1610 the doctrine of the divine right of kings, which combined assertions of the sovereignty of the Crown, the divine ordination of royal authority and the hereditary title to the throne (II:3). It has been claimed that what James I expressed in theory, his son, Charles I, took as a pressing principle of action. In the years leading up to the Civil Wars of the 1640s, he pursued courses which, at least in the eyes of many parliamentarians, threatened to relegate Parliament to a subordinate constitutional position. His attempt to exact forced loans, not agreed to by Parliament, produced in June 1628 the parliamentary Petition of Right insisting on what were taken to be two central constitutional provisions, no taxation without parliamentary consent and the rule of law over the executive power (II:4). Charles accepted the Petition but after eleven years of rule without Parliament was faced with a much more radical parliamentary challenge. In the Nineteen Propositions of 1642, Parliament claimed for itself a large part of the Crown's prerogative powers – the right to nominate ministers and judges, the right to change the Church, the control of the militia. In the royal reply to this virtual declaration of civil war, Charles put a view of the constitution as a mixed government and a system of checks and balances which was to dominate constitutional attitudes until the nineteenth century (II:5). The Reply, although it asserts the equality of the King with the Lords and the Commons in the making of law and the vesting of government in the King, was a far cry from the notion of divine kingship presented by James I. Some royalists believed it had moved too far from the old constitution arguing that the Crown had never been regarded as an estate of the realm (see Chapter III), but was itself the sovereign power over the estates.

This interwoven account and defence of the constitution – in terms of mixed monarchy, checks and balances and the separation of powers – was to become almost universally acknowledged. Throughout the eighteenth century, it was a commonplace that the

balance between the estates of Parliament, the restraints on government and the separation of executive and legislature made the
constitution an ideal blend of monarchy, aristocracy and democracy
and thereby achieved a delicate reconciliation of authority and liberty.
The terms of this admirable balance were recited in the authoritative
Commentaries on the Laws of England of Sir William Blackstone (II:6).
The three different forms of government each had its peculiar virtues
and vices; democracy encouraged public spirit but was frequently
foolish or head-strong: aristocracy empowered wisdom and experience but was subject to corruption: monarchy gave strength to
government but was liable to degenerate into tyranny. The British
constitution, by its mixture of the three forms, constructed a political
frame in which the three virtues were nurtured and the three vices
constrained.

Yet it was obvious that political practice contradicted many of the
precepts of the balance of powers theory. The settlement after the
Glorious Revolution left to the King at least in theory certain
independent powers, notably that of choosing his own ministers. At
the same time, the supremacy of Parliament, and in particular the
House of Commons, came to be asserted in many areas of government as well as in legislation.

In theoretical terms, the contradictions were revealed in the
contrast between the theory of checks and balances and the principle
of parliamentary sovereignty, outlined also by Blackstone (II:7). On
this principle, Parliament has an exclusive and unlimited legislative
power. It can, said Blackstone, 'do everything that is not naturally
impossible' or, in the words of the French observer de Lolme, 'do
everything but make a woman a man, and a man a woman'. Of
course, parliamentary sovereignty could be reconciled with checks
and balances by stressing the divided nature of Parliament itself.
Formally, it is still the case that legislative proposals must be placed
before both Houses and receive royal assent before they are enacted.
In practice, the House of Commons has for long been the main
legislative arena. Even in the eighteenth century it was often
recognized that the 'balanced' constitution was achieved not by King-
in-Parliament but by the ability of the Crown and individual peers to
exercise influence in the Commons either through the dispensation of
Crown patronage or, in the case of peers, through their ability, as
great land-owners, virtually to nominate members of the Commons.

The practical reflection of this theoretic tension was the need for
some mechanism by which to co-ordinate government and the
Commons. In a situation in which general policy and administration

was the business of the Crown acting through the King's ministers, but in which Parliament had a monopoly over law-making and provided most governmental revenue, no stable administration could be sustained if the King's ministers could not control the Commons. In the course of the nineteenth century, the means of control were to be found in organized political parties. In the eighteenth, they were found in a combination of the use of Crown patronage, the use of ministerial connections and reliance on the 'independent' members whose distaste for faction, or organized opposition to the Crown, made them on most occasions supporters of the King's ministers (see Chapter V).

1   Sir John Fortescue, Royal and Political Dominion (c. 1473)

Ther bith ij kyndes off kyngdomes, of the wich that on is a lordship callid in laten *dominium regale*, and that other is callid *dominium politicum et regale*. And thai diuersen in that the first kynge mey rule his peple bi suche lawes as he makyth hym self. And therfore he mey sett vppon thaim tayles and other imposicions, such as he wol hym self, with owt thair assent. The secounde kynge may not rule his peple bi other lawes than such as thai assenten unto. And therfore he mey sett vpon thaim non imposicions with owt thair own assent.

[There are two kinds of kingdom, one of which is a lordship called in Latin *dominium regale* and the other is called *dominium politicum et regale*. And they differ in that the first king may rule his people by such laws as he himself makes. And therefore he may set upon them tallages and other impositions, such as he himself wills, without their consent. The second king may not rule his people by laws other than those to which they consent. And therefore he may set upon them no impositions without their own consent.]

On The Governance of England

2   Sir Thomas Smith, Supremacy of Parliament (1589)

The most high and absolute power of the realme of Englande, consisteth in the Parliament. For as in warre where the king himselfe in person, the nobilitie, the rest of the gentilitie, and the yeomanrie are, is the force and power of Englande: so in peace and consultation where the Prince is to give life, and the last and highest commaundement, the Baronie for the nobilitie and higher, the knightes, esquiers, gentlemen and commons for the lower part of the common wealth, the bishoppes for the clergie bee present to advertise, consult and shew what is good and necessarie for the common wealth, and to consult together, and upon mature deliberation everie bill or lawe being thrise reade and disputed uppon in either house, the other two partes first each a part, and after the Prince himselfe in presence of both the parties doeth consent unto and alloweth. That is the Princes and whole realmes deede: whereupon justlie no man can complaine, but must accommodate himselfe to finde it good and obey it.

That which is doone by this consent is called firme, stable and *sanctum*, and is taken for lawe. The Parliament abrogateth olde lawes, maketh newe, giveth orders for thinges past, and for thinges hereafter to be followed, changeth rightes, and possessions of private men, legittimateth bastards, establisheth formes of religion, altereth weightes and measures, giveth formes of succession to the crowne, defineth of doubtfull rightes, whereof is no lawe alreadie made, appointeth subsidies, tailes, taxes, and impositions, giveth most free pardons and absolutions, restoreth in bloud and name as the highest court, condemneth or absolveth them whom the Prince will put to that triall: And to be short, all that ever the people of Rome might do either in *Centuriatis comitijs* or *tributis*, the same may be doone by the parliament of Englande, which representeth and hath the power of the whole realme both the head and the bodie. For everie Englishman is entended to bee there present, either in person or by procuration and attornies, of what preheminence, state, dignitie, or qualitie soever he be, from the Prince (be he King or Queene) to the lowest person of Englande. And the consent of the Parliament is taken to be everie mans consent.

De Republica Anglorum

3 James VI and I, Divine Right of Kings (1610)

The state of monarchy is the supremest thing upon earth; for kings are not only God's lieutenants upon earth, and sit upon

God's throne, but even by God himself they are called gods. There be three principal similitudes that illustrates the state of monarchy: one taken out of the word of God; and the two other out of the grounds of policy and philosophy. In the Scriptures kings are called gods and so their power after a certain relation compared to the divine power. Kings are also compared to fathers of families for a king is truly *Parens Patriae*, the politic father of his people. And lastly, kings are compared to the head of this microcosm of the body of man.

Kings are justly called gods for that they exercise a manner or resemblance of divine power upon earth. For if you will consider the attributes to God, you shall see how they agree in the person of a king. God hath power to create or destroy, make or unmake at his pleasure, to give life or send death, to judge all and to be judged nor accountable to none, to raise low things and to make high things low at his pleasure, and to God are both soul and body due. And the like power have kings: they make and unmake their subjects; they have power of raising and casting down; of life and of death; judges over all their subjects, and in all causes, and yet accountable to none but God only. They have power to exalt low things, and abase high things, and make of their subjects like men at the chess – a pawn to take a bishop or a knight – and to cry up or down any of their subjects as they do their money. And to the king is due both the affections of the soul and the service of the body of his subjects. . .

A father may dispose of his inheritance to his children at his pleasure, yea, even disinherit the eldest upon just occasions and prefer the youngest, according to his liking; make them beggars or rich at his pleasure; restrain, or banish out of his presence as he finds them give cause of offence; or restore then in favour again with the penitent sinners. So may the king deal with his subjects.

And lastly, as for the head of the natural body, the head hath the power of directing all the members of the body to that use which the judgement in the head thinks most convenient. It may apply sharp cures or cut off corrupt members, let blood in what proportion it thinks fit and as the body may spare, but yet is all this power ordained by God *ad aedificationem, non ad destructionem*. . .

In the first original of kings, whereof some had their beginning by conquest and some by election of the people, their wills at that time served for law. Yet how soon kingdoms began to be settled in civility and policy, then did kings set down their minds by laws which are properly made by the king only, but at the rogation of the people, the king's grant being obtained thereunto. And so the king became to be *Lex Loquens* after a sort, binding himself by a double oath to the observation of the fundamental laws of the kingdom: tacitly, as by being a king and so bound to protect as well the people, as the laws of his kingdom; and expressly, by his oath at his coronation. So, as every just king in a settled kingdom is bound to observe that paction made to his people by his laws, in framing his government agreeable thereunto, according to that paction which God made with Noah after the deluge, 'Hereafter seed time and harvest, cold and heat, summer and winter, and day and night shall not cease, so long as the earth remains' (Genesis 8:22). And therefore a king governing in a settled kingdom leaves to be a king and degenerates into a tyrant, as soon as he leaves off to rule according to his laws. . . As for my part, I thank God I have ever given good proof that I never had intention to the contrary, and I am sure to go to my grave with that reputation and comfort, that never king was in all his time more careful to have his laws duly observed, and himself to govern thereafter, than I. . .

James's speech to the Parliament, 21 March 1610

4 Assertion of Parliamentary Rights (1628)

To the King's Most Excellent Majesty.

Humbly show unto our Sovereign Lord the King, the Lords Spiritual and Temporal, and Commons in Parliament assembled, that. . .your subjects have inherited this freedom, that they should not be compelled to contribute to any tax, tallage, aid, or other like charge, not set by common consent in Parliament.

Yet nevertheless, of late divers commissions directed to sundry Commissioners in several counties with instructions have issued, by means whereof your people have been in divers places assembled, and required to lend certain sums of money unto your Majesty, and many of them upon their refusal so to do, have had an oath administered unto them, not warrantable by the laws or statutes of this realm, and have been constrained to become bound to make appearance and give attendance before your Privy Council, and in other places, and others of them have been therefore imprisoned, confined, and sundry other ways molested and disquieted: and divers other charges have been laid and levied upon your people in several counties, by Lords Lieutenants, Deputy Lieutenants, Commissioners for Musters, Justices of Peace and others, by command or direction from your Majesty or your Privy Council, against the laws and free customs of this realm.

And where also by the statute called, 'The Great Charter of the Liberties of England', it is declared and enacted, that no freeman may be taken or imprisoned or be disseised of his freeholds or liberties, or his free customs, or be outlawed or exiled; or in any manner destroyed, but by the lawful judgement of his peers, or by the law of the land. . .

Nevertheless, against the tenor of the said statutes, and others the good laws and statutes of your realm, to that end provided, divers of your subjects have of late been imprisoned without any cause showed, and when for their deliverance they were brought before your Justices, by your Majesty's writs of Habeas Corpus, there to undergo and receive as the Court should order, and their keepers commanded to certify the causes of their detainer; no cause was certified, but that they were detained by your Majesty's special command, signified by the Lords of your Privy Council, and yet were returned back to several prisons, without being charged with anything to which they might make answer according to the law. . .

And whereas also by authority of Parliament, in the 25th year of the reign of King Edward the Third, it is declared and enacted, that no man should be forejudged of life or limb against the form of the Great Charter, and the law of the land. . .nevertheless of late divers commissions under your Majesty's Great Seal have issued forth, by which certain persons have been assigned and appointed Commissioners with power and authority to proceed within the land, according to the justice of martial law against such soldiers and mariners, or other dissolute persons joining with them. . .

They do therefore humbly pray your Most Excellent Majesty, that no man hereafter be compelled to make or yield any gift, loan, benevolence, tax, or such like charge, without common consent by Act of Parliament; and that none be called to make answer, or take such oath, or to give attendance, or be confined, or otherwise molested or disquieted concerning the same . . .; and that the foresaid commissions for proceeding by martial law, may be revoked and annulled; and that hereafter no commissions of like nature may issue forth to any person or persons whatsoever, to be executed as aforesaid, lest by colour of them any of your Majesty's subjects be destroyed or put to death, contrary to the laws and franchise of the land.

All which they most humbly pray of your Most Excellent Majesty, as their rights and liberties according to the laws and statutes of this realm.

The Petition of Right, June 1628

5   Charles I, Royalist Assertion of Mixed Government (1642)

There being three kinds of government among men, absolute monarchy, aristocracy and democracy, and all these having their particular conveniences and inconveniences, the experience and wisdom of your ancestors hath so moulded this out of a mixture of these as to give to this kingdom (as far as human prudence can provide) the conveniences of all three, without the inconveniences of any one, as long as the balance hangs even between the three estates, and they run jointly on in their proper channel (begetting verdure and fertility in the meadows on both sides) and the overflowing of either on either side raise no deluge or inundation. The ill of absolute monarchy is tyranny, the ill of aristocracy is faction and division, the ills of democracy are tumults, violence and licentiousness. The good of monarchy is the uniting a nation under one head to resist invasion from abroad and insurrection at home; the good of aristocracy is the conjunction of counsel in the ablest persons of a state for the public benefit; the good of democracy is liberty, and the courage and industry which liberty begets.

In this kingdom the laws are jointly made by a king, by a house of peers, and by a House of Commons chosen by the people, all having free votes and particular privileges. The government, according to these laws is [en]trusted to the King; power of treaties of war and peace, of making peers, of choosing officers and councillors for state, judges for law, commanders for forts and castles, giving commissions for raising men, to make war abroad, or to prevent or provide against invasions or insurrections at home, benefit of confiscations, power of pardoning, and some more of the like kind are placed in the King. And this kind of regulated monarchy, having this power to preserve that authority without which it would be disabled to preserve the laws in their force and the subjects in their liberties and properties, is intended to draw to him such a respect and relation from the great ones, as may hinder the ills of division and faction, and such a fear and reverence from the people as may hinder tumults, violence and licentiousness.

Again, that the prince may not make use of this high and perpetual power to the hurt of those for whose good he hath it, and make use of followers, to the detriment of his people, the House of Commons (an excellent convener of liberty, but never intended for any share in government, or the choosing of them that govern) is solely entrusted with the first propositions concerning the levy of money (which is the sinews as well of peace as of war), and the impeaching of those who for their own ends, though countenanced by any surreptitiously gotten command of the King, have violated the law, which he is bound (when he knows it) to protect; and to the prosecution of which they are bound to advise him, at least not to serve him to the contrary. And the Lords, being trusted with a judicatory power, are an excellent screen and bank between the prince and people, to assist each against any encroachments of the other, and by just judgements to preserve that law which ought to be the rule of every one of the three. . .

Since therefore the power, legally placed in both houses, is more than sufficient to prevent and restrain the power of tyranny, and without the power which is now asked from us we shall not be able to discharge that trust which is the end of monarchy, since this would be a total subversion of the fundamental laws, and that excellent constitution of this kingdom which hath made this nation so many years both famous and happy to a great degree of envy, since to the power of punishing (which is already in your hands according to law) if the power of preferring be added, we shall have nothing left for us but to look on, since the encroaching of one of these estates upon the power of the other is unhappy in the effects, both to them and all the rest.

Reply to the Nineteen Propositions, 18 June 1642

6   Sir William Blackstone, The Balanced Constitution (1765)

The political writers of antiquity will not allow more than three regular forms of government; the first, when the sovereign power is lodged in an aggregate assembly consisting of all the members of a community, which is called a democracy; the second, when it is lodged in a council, composed of select members, and then it is stiled an aristocracy; the last, when it is entrusted in the hands of a single person, and then it takes the name of a monarchy. All other species of government, they say, are either corruptions of, or reducible to, these three.

By the sovereign power, as was before observed, is meant the making of laws; for wherever that power resides, all others must conform to, and be directed by it, whatever appearance the outward form and administration of the government may put on. For it is at any time in the option of the legislature to alter that form and administration by a new edict or rule, and to put the execution of the laws into whatever hands it pleases: and all the other powers of the state must obey the legislative power in the execution of their several functions, or else the constitution is at an end.

In a democracy, where the right of making laws resides in the people at large, public virtue, or goodness of intention, is more likely to be found, than either of the other qualities of government. Popular assemblies are frequently foolish in their contrivance, and weak in their execution; but generally mean to do the thing that is right and just, and have always a degree of patriotism or public spirit. In aristocracies there is more wisdom to be found, than in the other frames of government; being composed, or intended to be composed, of the most experienced citizens; but there is less honesty than in a republic, and less strength than in a monarchy. A monarchy is indeed the most powerful of any, all the sinews of government being knit together, and united in the hand of the prince; but then there is imminent danger of his employing that strength to improvident or oppressive purposes.

Thus these three species of government have, all of them, their several perfections and imperfections. Democracies are usually the best calculated to direct the end of a law; aristocracies to invent the means by which that end shall be obtained; and

monarchies to carry those means into execution. And the
antients, as was observed, had in general no idea of any other
permanent form of government but these three. . .

But happily for us of this island, the British constitution has
long remained, and I trust will long continue, a standing
exception to the truth of this observation. For, as with us the
executive power of the laws is lodged in a single person, they
have all the advantages of strength and dispatch, that are to be
found in the most absolute monarchy; and, as the legislature of
the kingdom is entrusted to three distinct powers, entirely
independent of each other; first, the king; secondly, the lords
spiritual and temporal, which is an aristocratical assembly of
persons selected for their piety, their birth, their wisdom, their
valour, or their property; and, thirdly, the house of commons,
freely chosen by the people from among themselves, which
makes it a kind of democracy; as this aggregate body, actuated
by different springs, and attentive to different interests, com-
poses the British parliament, and has the supreme disposal of
every thing; there can no inconvenience be attempted by either
of the three branches, but will be withstood by one of the other
two; each branch being armed with a negative power, sufficient
to repel any innovation which it shall think inexpedient or
dangerous.

Commentaries on the Laws of England

7 Sir William Blackstone, Parliamentary Sovereignty (1765)

The power and jurisdiction of parliament, says Sir Edward
Coke, is so transcendent and absolute, that it cannot be
confined, either for causes or persons, within any bounds. . . It
hath sovereign and uncontrolable authority in making, confirming, enlarging, restraining, abrogating, repealing, reviving, and
expounding of laws, concerning matters of all possible denominations, ecclesiastical, or temporal, civil, military, maritime, or
criminal: this being the place where that absolute despotic
power, which must in all governments reside somewhere, is
entrusted by the constitution of these kingdoms. All mischiefs
and grievances, operations and remedies, that transcend the
ordinary course of the laws, are within the reach of this
extraordinary tribunal. It can regulate or new model the

succession to the crown; as was done in the reign of Henry VIII and William III. It can alter the established religion of the land; as was done in a variety of instances, in the reigns of king Henry VIII and his three children. It can change and create afresh even the constitution of the kingdom and of parliaments themselves; as was done by the act of union, and the several statutes for triennial and septennial elections. It can, in short, do every thing that is not naturally impossible; and therefore some have not scrupled to call its power, by a figure rather too bold, the omnipotence of parliament. True it is, that what they do, no authority upon earth can undo.

Commentaries on the Laws of England

B.   CABINET GOVERNMENT AND 'ELECTIVE DICTATORSHIP'

The forms of what has been called the 'classical' constitution of the eighteenth century have survived, but, many would argue, much of its substance has disappeared. On this view, the system of checks and balances which bounded governmental powers has been seriously corroded and needs to be reinforced or replaced by the constitutional constraints of a written constitution, the legal constraints of a bill of rights or the democratic constraints of closer popular control over both government and parliamentarians. Similarly, it has been argued that the idea of a mixed government has no great relevance to a modern system in which royal and aristocratic political influence has been severely curtailed.

That curtailment has come about in part as a consequence of the parliamentary reforms of the late eighteenth and nineteenth centuries. On the one side, the enactment of so-called 'economical' reform, the exclusion of Crown placemen and pensioners from the Commons, cut down the Crown's ability to secure parliamentary support through patronage. On the other side, the extension of the franchise, the redistribution of seats and the imposition of a secret ballot undermined the power of both the crown and the landowning aristocracy to sway electoral decisions.

The influence of the peerage persisted throughout the nineteenth century, measured at any rate in terms of aristocratic intervention in high politics. Nevertheless, the formal powers of the House of Lords have been diminished and the House has been relegated to a subsidiary legislative role (a process which will be traced in Chapter

III). The decline in the personal influence of the King or Queen has been no less marked. By the time that Queen Victoria came to the throne, it had become clear that the Queen could not, by means of royal patronage, provide parliamentary support for ministers of her choice and that for the most part she would have to choose ministers (and particularly a Prime Minister) capable of commanding a majority in the House of Commons on grounds other than that they were the Queen's choice.

This decline in the position of the Crown was pictured in its most extreme, perhaps exaggerated, form by Walter Bagehot, who, writing shortly before the second Reform Act of 1867, claimed to have uncovered the hidden truths behind constitutional rhetoric (II:8). The particular rhetoric he was concerned to counter was the theory of checks and balances which, in his eyes, heavily obscured the reality of constitutional relations. That reality could best be discerned by using the distinction between the dignified and the efficient parts of the constitution, the Crown being a dignified part whilst the central efficient institution was a Cabinet in which legislative and executive power was fused. Not that kings and lords were useless; they could help to generate loyalty to the regime amongst the masses, who were more likely to be moved by the emotional and theatrical, by that which had a hallowed whiff of the ancient and appealed to large if incoherent ideas, than by cool consideration of practical utility. The Cabinet, as the Queen's ministers, retained the trappings of dignity, but its real power derived from the fact that it had become a 'committee of the legislative body selected to be the executive body'. Bagehot's stress on the crucial role of the Cabinet was such that it can be overlooked that he was equally asserting the dominance of the Commons, which had, on his analysis, added the selection of the executive to its legislative and taxation powers.

Bagehot has often been hailed as the clear-eyed revealer of abiding truths about the hidden constitution. But there have also been claims either that his theoretical arguments were flawed or that developments since he wrote have made his conclusions now inappropriate. His discussion of mixed government is flawed by his confusion of monarchy with hereditary royalty. The theorists of the classical constitution did not make this mistake, but saw that monarchy, as the rule of the one, could take forms other than that of hereditary monarchy. As an illustration of this, we can look to Lord Bolingbroke who expressed two preferences: for a limited monarchy and for an hereditary monarchy (II:9). Implicit in this is that limited monarchies could be non-hereditary and that hereditary monarchs could be unlimited. Bagehot drew a parallel between the British Prime Minister and the American President, claiming of both that they were elective first magistrates and implying that the republican parallel demonstrated the decline in the monarchical element in the British system. In fact, the framers of the American constitution operated within the assumptions of mixed government and discussion of the role, status and powers of the President revolved around the questions of how far and in what ways a monarchic element (the rule of one) should be incorporated into the constitution. In this context, Bagehot's parallel between Prime Minister and President could as well have implied that the Prime Minister was the true, albeit an indirectly elected, monarch and not the Queen.

To such criticism of Bagehot's analysis have been added arguments that, whatever its accuracy at the time it was written, it has now become a wholly misleading portrait. The claim is broadly that the emergence in the late nineteenth century of highly disciplined, mass, extra-parliamentary parties has altered the relationship between government and the Commons. The individual MP has lost his or her independence and a government commanding a majority party in the House is faced with a Commons which is normally subservient. Fears of the loss of back-bencher independence have long been voiced. Lord Robert Cecil, giving evidence to a Commons select committee inquiring in 1914 into complaints by MPs about their loss of power to initiate or amend legislation, expressed them clearly (II:10). When Richard Crossman came to edit a new edition of Bagehot, he too in his introduction pointed to what he saw as the fundamental transformation of the constitution since Bagehot's day and the decline in the position of the Commons as a consequence of the government's control of both the majority party machine and the state bureaucracy. Crossman went even further in consigning not only the Commons but also the Cabinet to the category of dignified parts of the constitution. In the post-Second World War epoch, he argued, Cabinet government had itself been displaced by prime-ministerial government (II:11). Interestingly, Crossman had a subsequent opportunity as a Cabinet minister to test this academic judgement. Although in his diaries he wavered on the question, he did in the end endorse from his experience the demise of Cabinet government and the rise of prime-ministerial government (II:12). This account of constitutional change, put in the more emotive terms of movement towards 'elective dictatorship', was reiterated from a different political start-point by Lord Hailsham (I:13).

Such warnings of the decline of Commons and Cabinet as

determiners of or even checks on governmental actions may be exaggerated. The degree to which a government is controllable by the Commons and a Prime Minister by the Cabinet is governed by many factors – the size of the Commons majority, the electoral popularity of the government, the relative political standing of the Prime Minister and his senior colleagues, the presence or absence of fundamental splits on policy within the governing party. Despite this, in most circumstances the only real check that can be mounted is from the back-benchers of the governing party and there are severe constraints on rebellion if that will damage the political standing of individual MPs or bring about the downfall of their own government.

For many, these developments run counter to Bagehot's conclusion that the democratic (or parliamentary) element in the constitution had been strengthened. They can be seen rather as the strengthening of the monarchic element, through the subordination of Parliament to the Queen's ministers and particularly the Prime Minister who directly control a powerful Crown bureaucracy and who are ordinarily unencumbered by any extensive restraints imposed by the representatives of the people.

8 Walter Bagehot, Dignified and Efficient Parts of the Constitution (1867)

It is insisted that the peculiar excellence of the British Constitution lies in a balanced union of three powers. It is said that the monarchical element, the aristocratic element, and the democratic element, have each a share in the supreme sovereignty, and that the assent of all three is necessary to the action of that sovereignty. Kings, lords, and commons, by this theory, are alleged to be not only the outward form, but the inner moving essence, the vitality of the Constitution. A great theory, called the theory of 'Checks and Balances', pervades an immense part of political literature, and much of it is collected from or supported by English experience. Monarchy, it is said, has some faults, some bad tendencies, aristocracy others, democracy, again, others; but England has shown that a Government can be constructed in which these evil tendencies exactly check, balance, and destroy one another – in which a good whole is constructed not simply in spite of, but by means of, the counteracting defects of the constituent parts. . .

No one can approach to an understanding of the English institutions, or of others, which, being the growth of many centuries, exercise a wide sway over mixed populations, unless he divide them into two classes. In such constitutions there are two parts (not indeed separable with microscopic accuracy, for the genius of great affairs abhors nicety of division): first, those which excise and preserve the reverence of the population – the *dignified* parts, if I may so call them; and next, the *efficient* parts – those by which it, in fact, works and rules. There are two great objects which every constitution must attain to be successful, which every old and celebrated one must have wonderfully achieved: every constitution must first *gain* authority, and then *use* authority; it must first win the loyalty and confidence of mankind, and then employ that homage in the work of government.

There are indeed practical men who reject the dignified parts of Government. They say, we want only to attain results, to do business: a constitution is a collection of political means for political ends, and if you admit that any part of a constitution does no business, or that a simpler machine would do equally well what it does, you admit that this part of the constitution, however dignified or awful it may be, is nevertheless in truth useless. And other reasoners, who distrust this bare philosophy, have propounded subtle arguments to prove that these dignified parts of old Governments are cardinal components of the essential apparatus, great pivots of substantial utility; and so they manufactured fallacies which the plainer school have well exposed. But both schools are in error. The dignified parts of Government are those which bring it force – which attract its motive power. The efficient parts only employ that power. The comely parts of a Government *have* need, for they are those upon which its vital strength depends. They may not do anything definite that a simpler polity would not do better; but they are the preliminaries, the needful prerequisites of *all* work. They raise the army, though they do not win the battle.

Doubtless, if all subjects of the same Government only thought of what was useful to them, and if they all thought the same thing useful, and all thought that same thing could be attained in the same way, the efficient members of a constitution would suffice, and no impressive adjuncts would be needed. But the world in which we live is organised far otherwise. . .

The brief description of the characteristic merit of the English

Constitution is, that its dignified parts are very complicated and somewhat imposing, very old and rather venerable; while its efficient part, at least when in great and critical action, is decidedly simple and rather modern. We have made, or rather stumbled on, a constitution which – though full of every species of incidental defect, though of the worst *workmanship* in all out-of-the-way matters of any constitution in the world – yet has two capital merits: it contains a simple efficient part which, on occasion, and when wanted, *can* work more simply and easily, and better, than any instrument of government that has yet been tried; and it contains likewise historical, complex, august, theatrical parts, which it has inherited from a long past – which *take* the multitude – which guide by an insensible but an omnipotent influence the associations of its subjects. Its essence is strong with the strength of modern simplicity; its exterior is august with the Gothic grandeur of a more imposing age. Its simple essence may, *mutatis mutandis*, be transplanted to many very various countries, but its august outside – what most men think it is – is narrowly confined to nations with an analogous history and similar political materials.

The efficient secret of the English Constitution may be described as the close union, the nearly complete fusion, of the executive and legislative powers. No doubt by the traditional theory, as it exists in all the books, the goodness of our constitution consists in the entire separation of the legislative and executive authorities, but in truth its merit consists in their singular approximation. The connecting link is *the Cabinet*. By that new word we mean a committee of the legislative body selected to be the executive body. The legislature has many committees, but this is its greatest. It chooses for this, its main committee, the men in whom it has most confidence. It does not, it is true, choose them directly; but it is nearly omnipotent in choosing them indirectly. . . As a rule, the nominal Prime Minister is chosen by the legislature, and the real Prime Minister for most purposes – the leader of the House of Commons – almost without exception is so. There is nearly always some one man plainly selected by the voice of the predominant party in the predominant house of the legislature to head that party, and consequently to rule the nation. We have in England an elective first magistrate as truly as the Americans have an elective first magistrate. The Queen is only at the head of the dignified part of the Constitution. The Prime Minister is at the head of the efficient part. The Crown is, according to the saying, the 'fountain of honour'; but the Treasury is the spring of business. Nevertheless, our first magistrate differs from the American. He is not elected directly by the people; he is elected by the representatives of the people. He is an example of 'double election'. The legislature chosen, in name, to make laws, in fact finds its principal business in making and in keeping an executive.

The leading Minister so selected has to choose his associates, but he only chooses among a charmed circle. The position of most men in Parliament forbids their being invited to the Cabinet; the position of a few men ensures their being invited. Between the compulsory list whom he must take, and the impossible list whom he cannot take, a Prime Minister's independent choice in the formation of a Cabinet is not very large; it extends rather to the division of the Cabinet offices than to the choice of Cabinet Ministers. Parliament and the nation have pretty well settled who shall have the first places; but they have not discriminated with the same accuracy which man shall have which place. The highest patronage of a Prime Minister is, of course, a considerable power, though it is exercised under close and imperative restrictions – though it is far less than it seems to be when stated in theory, or looked at from a distance.

The Cabinet, in a word, is a board of control chosen by the legislature, out of persons whom it trusts and knows, to rule the nation. The particular mode in which the English Ministers are selected; the fiction that they are, in any political sense, the Queen's servants; the rule which limits the choice of the Cabinet to the members of the legislature – are accidents unessential to its definition – historical incidents separable from its nature. . .

But a cabinet, though it is a committee of the legislative assembly, is a committee with a power which no assembly would – unless for historical accidents, and after happy experience – have been persuaded to entrust to any committee. It is a committee which can dissolve the assembly which appointed it; it is a committee with a suspensive veto – a committee with a power of appeal. Though appointed by one Parliament, it can appeal if it chooses to the next. Theoretically, indeed, the power to dissolve Parliament is entrusted to the sovereign only, and there are vestiges of doubt whether in *all* cases a sovereign is bound to dissolve Parliament when the Cabinet asks him to do so. But neglecting such small and dubious exceptions, the

Cabinet which was chosen by one House of Commons has an appeal to the next House of Commons. The chief committee of the legislature has the power of dissolving the predominant part of that legislature – that which at a crisis is the supreme legislature. The English system, therefore, is not an absorption of the executive power by the legislative power; it is a fusion of the two. Either the Cabinet legislates and acts, or else it can dissolve. It is a creature, but it has the power of destroying its creators. It is an executive which can annihilate the legislature, as well as an executive which is the nominee of the legislature. It *was* made, but it *can* unmake; it was derivative in its origin, but it is destructive in its action.

The English Constitution

9   Lord Bolingbroke, Types of Monarchy (1738)

To conclude this head therefore; as I think a *limited monarchy* the best of governments, so I think an *hereditary monarchy* the best of monarchies. I said a *limited monarchy*; for an *unlimited monarchy*, wherein arbitrary will, which is in truth no rule, is however the sole rule, or stands instead of all rule of government, must be allowed so great an absurdity, both in reason informed and uninformed by experience, that it seems a government fitter for savages than for civilised people. . .

Among many reasons which determine me to prefer *monarchy* to every other form of government, this is a principal one. When monarchy is the essential form, it may be more easily and more usefully *tempered* with *aristocracy* or *democracy*, or both, than either of them, when they are the essential forms, can be *tempered* with *monarchy*. It seems to me, that the introduction of a real permanent monarchical power, or any thing more than the pageantry of it, into either of these, must destroy them and extinguish them, as a greater light extinguishes a less. Whereas it may easily be shewn, and the true form of our government will demonstrate, without seeking any other example, that very considerable *aristocratical* and *democratical powers* may be grafted on a *monarchical stock*, without diminishing the lustre, or restraining the power and authority of the prince, enough to alter in any degree the essential form.

The Idea of a Patriot King

10   Loss of Back–Benchers' Independence (1914)

Lord Robert Cecil examined by the Select Committee on Public Business of 1914:

919. But you know there was no mandate from the people for the Land Bill? – **No, I do not think mandates matter much**.

920. I am glad to hear you say that. – **I do not say they ought not to matter**.

921. My point is this, and is it not true, that in former days the House of Commons might have been regarded in some small degree as a deliberative assembly because pressure from without was less strong? – There were no printed reports? – **I think that was one of the reasons certainly**.

922. There was no proper education of public opinion? – **I will not put it that way**.

923. I would. People then were more Members of Parliament and less delegates? – **Certainly, but may I say that I think the real change is not that Members have become more delegates of their constituents, but that they have become more delegates of the Party organisations, which is quite a different thing**.

924. And then the Party organisation (I think you will agree with me in this) is much more represented by the Cabinet than by Members of the House of Commons? – **I should say that if you really looked into the real principle of our constitution now, it is purely plebiscitical, that you have really a plebiscite by which a particular man is selected as Prime Minister, he then selects his Ministry himself, and it is pretty much what he likes subject to what affects the rule that he has to consider – namely, that he must not do anything that is very unpopular**.

925. And this particular man is selected by indications by the people, so that the choice is irresistible? – **I think, generally speaking, that would be true, not always**. . .

927. I want to put this to you. You think there is no real discussion in the House of Commons, and I agree with you, but I want to bring out from you that the real reason why there is no real discussion of an important nature in the House of Commons is that the people have given a mandate to the Prime Minister, and the Prime Minister then carries it out with the aid of Parliament? – **I**

should agree with you, generally speaking, that the procedure questions are only a part of the evil under which the House of Commons is suffering, and that is my view (and, of course, that is one of the reasons I am such a strong advocate of the Referendum). You want to restore a greater and more intimate connection between Members of the House of Commons and the electors who choose them.

935. . . . Is this not the main object of debating now in the House of Commons, not to affect the issue, but to affect public opinion outside? – I think that is true of a good deal of the debate, but I do not think it is true of the debates in Committee. I think the debates on the Second Reading are almost all addressed to the public outside; the debates in Committee I do not think are addressed to the public outside, and they do not have any opportunity of knowing what they are, generally speaking, because they are not reported.

Lord Robert Cecil examined by the Select Committee
on Public Business

11 R. H. S. Crossman, Cabinet Government and Prime Ministerial Government (1964)

It seems to me, therefore, that *The English Constitution* can still be read as the classical account of the classical period of parliamentary government. The secret which Bagehot claimed to have discovered does indeed provide the correct explanation of the relationship between the Commons and the Cabinet as it emerged between 1832 and 1867. . .

It was not until well after Bagehot's death that this system was fundamentally transformed by the transfer of effective power from the floor of the Commons to the great party machines and the bureaucracy in Whitehall. Yet this was the very period when *The English Constitution* was finally accepted, not only as the *locus classicus* for the *mores* of Whitehall and Westminster, but as the definitive and authoritative account of how, in a democracy, power is divided between the electorate, the Commons and the Cabinet. . .

When Bagehot, for example, described the Commons as the place where 'ministries are made and unmade' and Congress as the place where 'the debates are prologues without a play' the contrast was valid because the House of Commons in the 1860s still enjoyed effective sovereignty. But the contrast has become less and less true, as the suffrage was extended in this country and the modern party system developed. The right to appoint the Prime Minister – which Bagehot and Mill agreed to be the most important constitutional power belonging to the Commons, was gradually removed from it and shared between the parties and the Monarch. And once it had lost its status as an 'electoral college' the House of Commons began to lose its collective will and finally became merely the forum of debate between well-disciplined political armies. Britain had left the epoch of classical parliamentary government, and entered a new epoch of bureaucratic democracy – with its new division between the dignified and efficient elements in the constitution. . .

The growth of Party was of course directly related to the extension of the suffrage that began in the year *The English Constitution* was published. Once votes became too numerous to buy, organised corruption was gradually replaced by party organisation; and the voter was wooed not with offers of ready cash but with promises of state benefits to come. The party which, up to now, had been a weak organisation, functioning informally in the lobbies and political clubs, became a central-ised, extra-parliamentary machine, constantly seeking to impose its discipline and its doctrine on the Member of Parliament as well as on the party worker. By the turn of the century, when the party caucuses were firmly entrenched, the efficient secret of the Constitution was no longer the fusion of the executive and the legislature, in that supreme committee of the House of Commons called the Cabinet, but the secret links that connected the Cabinet with the party on the one side and with the civil service on the other. . .

The post-war epoch has seen the final transformation of Cabinet Government into Prime Ministerial Government. Under this system the 'hyphen which joins, the buckle which fastens, the legislative part of the state to the executive part' becomes one single man. Even in Bagehot's time it was probably a misnomer to describe the Premier as chairman, and *primus inter pares*. His right to select his own Cabinet and dismiss them at will; his power to decide the Cabinet's agenda and announce the decisions reached without taking a vote; his control, through the Chief Whip, over patronage – all this had already before 1867 given him near-Presidential powers. Since then his powers have been steadily increased, first by the centralisation of the party machine under his personal rule, and secondly by the growth of a centralised bureaucracy, so vast that it could no longer be managed by a Cabinet behaving like the board of directors of an old-fashioned company.

Under Prime Ministerial government, secondary decisions are normally taken either by the department concerned or in Cabinet committee, and the Cabinet becomes the place where busy executives seek formal sanction for their actions from colleagues usually too busy – even if they do disagree – to do more than protest. Each of these executives, moreover, owes his allegiance not to the Cabinet collectively but to the Prime Minister who gave him his job, and who may well have dictated the policy he must adopt. In so far as ministers feel themselves to be agents of the Premier, the British Cabinet has now come to resemble the American Cabinet. . .

But there is one important difference. The old doctrine of collective Cabinet responsibility is scrupulously maintained and enforced, even though many of the decisions for which members must assume responsibility have been taken above their heads and without their knowledge. And this collective responsibility now extends downwards from the Cabinet through the ministers outside the Cabinet, to the parliamentary under-secretaries and even to the private parliamentary secretaries.

Under this doctrine, today, about a third of the Government's parliamentary strength is automatically required not merely to accept but actively to support policy decisions which, if they are of great importance, will nearly always have been taken by one man after consultation with a handful of advisers he has picked for the occasion.

Introduction to Walter Bagehot, *The English Constitution*

12   R. H. S. Crossman, The Demise of Cabinet Government (1965)

Broadly speaking, the analysis I made in the Introduction to Bagehot is being confirmed. Certainly it is true that the Cabinet is now part of the 'dignified' element in the constitution, in the sense that the real decisions are rarely taken there, unless the Prime Minister deliberately chooses to give the appearance of letting Cabinet decide a matter. I was also right to recognise the importance of Cabinet Committees. I am a permanent member of two, the Home Affairs Committee and the Economic Development Committee. In addition, I attend the Immigration Committee and the Broadcasting Committee as well as the Legislation Committee. But I am not a member of the Social Services Committee. Nor, of course, am I a member of the two really important Committees, on Defence and Foreign Affairs. From these I am totally excluded. So I am very much a home-front Cabinet Minister.

The really big thing I completely failed to notice when I wrote that Introduction was that, in addition to the Cabinet Committees which only Ministers normally attend, there is a full network of official committees; and the work of the Ministers is therefore strictly and completely paralleled at the official level. This means that very often the whole job is pre-cooked in the official committee to a point from which it is extremely difficult to reach any other conclusion than that already determined by the officials in advance; and if agreement is reached at the lower level of a Cabinet Committee, only formal approval is needed from the full Cabinet. This is the way in which Whitehall ensure that the Cabinet system is relatively harmless.

The Crossman Diaries: entry for Easter Sunday, 18 April 1965

13   Lord Hailsham, Elective Dictatorship (1976)

But how far are the Commons themselves really masters of their own House? Until fairly recently influence was fairly evenly balanced between Government and Opposition, and between front and back benches. Today the centre of gravity has moved decisively towards the Government side of the house, and on that side to the members of the Government itself. The opposition is gradually being reduced to insignificance, and the Government majority, where power resides, is itself becoming a tool in the hands of the Cabinet. Back-benchers, where they show promise, are soon absorbed into the administration, and thus lose their powers of independent action. When Trollope wrote the Palliser novels a hundred years ago, parties were fluid, and Government time less extensive. Even in 1906, a back-bench speech like F. E. Smith's maiden could make a considerable impact. But, in present conditions, the whole absolute powers of Parliament, except in a few matters like divorce or abortion, are wielded by the Cabinet alone and sometimes by a relatively small group within the Cabinet. To begin with, the actual members of the Government, with their Parliamentary private secretaries, are one of the largest and most disciplined single groups in the House. They number, I suppose, not much short of a hundred and thirty out of the three hundred-odd members of the government party, and not one, so long as he retains his position, can exercise an independent judgement. But, far more important than numbers, is the disproportionate influence of Ministers in debate as the result of their possession of the Civil Service brief. The increasing complexity of public affairs makes meticulous research and specialisation almost indispensable for speaking in Parliament. The decreasing leisure and increasing economic pressures upon Private Members, few of whom live upon their Parliamentary salaries, make it more and more difficult to bring a Minister to book. Even when he is wrong, he can usually make it look sufficiently as if he were right to get his own supporters into the lobby when the division bell rings. I have been often enough both on the giving and the receiving end myself, and I must say frankly that, more often than not, right or wrong, it is the Minister who wins the argument. So the sovereignty of Parliament has increasingly become, in practice, the sovereignty of the Commons, and the sovereignty of the Commons has increasingly become the sovereignty of the government, which, in addition to its influence in Parliament, controls the party whips, the party machine and the civil service. This means that what has always been an elective dictatorship in theory, but one in which the component parts operated in practice to control one another, has become a machine in which one of those parts has come to exercise a predominant influence over the rest. . .

At the centre of the web sits the Prime Minister. There he sits with his hand on the lever of dissolution, which he is free to operate at any moment of his choice. In selecting that moment he is able, with the Chancellor of the Exchequer, to manipulate the economy, so as to make it possible for things to appear for a time better than they really are.

Elective Dictatorship (BBC Dimbleby Lectures)

C.   GOVERNMENT, PARLIAMENT AND THE PEOPLE

Questions of the relationship between Parliament and the people or government and the people have tended to be treated in British political argument as secondary to the problem of the relationship between Crown or government and Parliament. The widening of the franchise was the crucial constitutional issue in the century following the first Reform Act but this was seldom envisaged as a move towards popular sovereignty. And those institutions or practices that might enhance popular control over either government or Parliament or both have taken only shallow roots in British political soil.

A general and repeated view of parliamentarians has been that Parliament is a deliberative body in which the merits of different cases and the needs of different interests could be heard and assessed. From this standpoint, Bentham's derisive description of Parliament as a talking-shop was an acceptable truth since parliamentary decisions were supposedly the outcomes of reasoned debate and were not in any way the expression of some monolithic popular will. Parallel to this idea of the deliberative character of Parliament has been the portrayal of the MP as a representative rather than as a delegate. Burke, in a much quoted passage, urged that the MP was elected to exercise his own independent judgement on matters of the national interest (II:14). Democratic radicals pressed an alternative model of the MP as ideally a simple delegate or deputy of his constituents, solely their mouthpiece. As has been seen, by 1914 the fear was being expressed that the MP was becoming a mere delegate, but of the party not of local constituents (see II:10). Nevertheless, the Burkean view has remained the generally accepted depiction of the proper functions of the MP.

Another method of enhancing popular control of government and the Commons pressed by nineteenth-century radicals was the holding of frequent elections. Rousseau remarked that the English were free only once in seven years (this was at that time the period within which an election was required in Britain). The nineteenth-century radical wanted freedom more often; indeed the Chartists demanded annual Parliaments. This is the one of the six Chartist demands that has never come near to being satisfied; and now even the most dedicated of democrats is unlikely to push for an arrangement that would achieve only a dangerous combination of political exhaustion and administrative chaos. Nevertheless, the rationale behind the radical demands still stands. An election, and the prospect of political death, wonderfully concentrates the mind of a government on the wants and needs of the electorate, and this stimulus, it could be argued, is insufficiently provided by the present British requirement of an election at least once every five years. Recently, more attention has been paid to the fact that within the five-year limit there is no fixed date for elections and the timing is decided on by the incumbent Prime Minister. Naturally, that timing is usually determined by party considerations and so, it has been claimed, the incumbent party has a built-in electoral advantage.

The mandate has been put forward as another device by which firmer democratic control might be established. What this involves has never been entirely clear or agreed. The issue is the relationship between a government's policies and the commitments made in its election manifesto. At one level, the principle of the mandate has been taken to imply that a government is authorized to carry out whatever it has proposed in its election programme; at another level, that indeed it is obliged to carry out what it has proposed; and at a further level, that it has no authority to initiate major policies not mentioned in its election programme. Whether or not the mandate, in any of these forms, has become an accepted constitutional convention is doubtful. In 1888, Bryce could write as though it was a recent, but none the less established, addition to constitutional practice (II:15); but in the debates on the 1911 Parliament Act Morley forthrightly put a view, since then widely canvassed in democratic theorizing, that general elections are not popular decisions on issues but simply decisions on who is to form the government (II:16). Appeals to mandate are certainly now part of the rhetoric of both government and opposition, but governments often, and perhaps rightly, ignore the doctrine when political expediency or change of circumstances demand it. In any case, it has been argued, the moral force of such appeals to an electoral mandate is weak. It is unlikely that the voter for a particular party is by his vote endorsing all the policy proposals in that party's electoral package. Even if this were the case, in British circumstances parties can, and usually do, win parliamentary majorities on something much less than an absolute majority of the votes cast, and election victory cannot therefore be interpreted as majority approval of the winning party's proclaimed policies.

The referendum, a popular vote on particular issues, avoids many of these difficulties of inferring a mandate from a general election result and the referendum has found an established place in many constitutional systems. In Britain, this method of extending democratic control has been used only sparingly and generally grudgingly. In recent years, referenda have been held on constitutional issues – membership of the European Community and the proposed devolution of power to Scottish and Welsh assemblies. These uses of referenda have been more to do with settling intra-party conflicts than with boosting the power of the people. Generally there is considerable scepticism, particularly at the top of the political hierarchy, about the validity of such populist practices; this scepticism is illustrated by a senior civil servant's assessment in 1983 of the desirability and possibility of a more extended resort to referenda in Britain (II:17).

14   Edmund Burke, The MP as Representative (1774)

Certainly, gentlemen, it ought to be the happiness and glory of a representative to live in the strictest union, the closest correspondence, and the most unreserved communication with his constituents. Their wishes ought to have great weight with him; their opinion high respect; their business unremitted attention. It is his duty to sacrifice his repose, his pleasures, his satisfactions, to theirs; and above all, ever, and in all cases, to prefer their interest to his own. But, his unbiassed opinion, his mature judgement, his enlightened conscience, he ought not to sacrifice to you, to any man, or to any set of men living. These he does not derive from your pleasure; no, nor from the law and the constitution. They are a trust from Providence, for the abuse of which he is deeply answerable. Your representative owes you, not his industry only, but his judgment; and he betrays, instead of serving you, if he sacrifices it to your opinion. . .

To deliver an opinion, is the right of all men; that of constituents is a weighty and respectable opinion, which a representative ought always to rejoice to hear; and which he ought always most seriously to consider. But *authoritative* instructions; *mandates* issued, which the member is bound blindly and implicitly to obey, to vote, and to argue for, though contrary to the clearest conviction of his judgment and conscience, – these are things utterly unknown to the laws of this land, and which arise from a fundamental mistake of the whole order and tenour of our constitution.

Speech to the Electors of Bristol

15   James Bryce, Elections as Mandates (1888)

It is now beginning to be maintained as a constitutional doctrine, that when any large measure of change is carried through the House of Commons, the House of Lords has a right to reject it for the purpose of compelling a dissolution of Parliament, that is, an appeal to the voters. And there are some signs that the view is making way, that even putting the House of Lords out of sight, the House of Commons is not morally, though of course it is legally, entitled to pass a bill seriously changing the Constitution, which was not submitted to the electors at the preceding general election. A general election, although in form a choice of particular persons as members, has now practically become an expression of popular opinion on the two or three leading measures then propounded and discussed by the party leaders, as well as a vote of confidence or no confidence in the Ministry of the day. It is in substance a vote upon those measures; although, of course, a vote only on their general principles, and not, like the Swiss Referendum, upon the statute which the legislature has passed. Even therefore in a country which clings to and founds itself upon the absolute supremacy of its representative chamber, the notion of a direct appeal to the people has made progress.

The American Commonwealth

16   John Morley, Elections as Choices of Government (1911)

My argument was that when a General Election returned a Parliament, it entrusted power to Ministers to pass whatever Bills they thought fit.

Let us take the great case of the most active and most fertile

Administration in recent history, Mr Gladstone's first Government, which sat from 1868 to 1874. He got his majority and the electors had in the forefront of their electoral vision the Irish Church. But before that Ministry came to an end six years later the fact of that being the central question did not hinder the radical reform of land in Ireland, the complete reform of the Army, the establishment of a system of national elementary education, the introduction of the ballot, the abolition of tests at Oxford and Cambridge, and the opening of the Civil Service to competition. These things were not in the minds of the electors. How could they be? Probably they were not even in the minds of Ministers at the election, but the electors did what I believe most electors would do. They returned a First Minister in whom they had confidence and to whom they were determined to give a chance of showing his power and force and constructive ability, and they left it in his hands and in the hands of his colleagues. That is my view of the right theory of the result of a general election.

Parliamentary Debates, House of Lords 5th Series,
vol. viii, 23 May 1911

17   Douglas Wass, Referenda – A Critical View (1983)

The difficulties of determining the popular will apply also to the holding of referenda on issues of public interest, one of the techniques considered from time to time as a means of popular participation, but applied nationwide in this country only once – on the issues of our continued membership of the European Community. The advocates of referenda view them either as a means of checking or promoting constitutional change or of establishing public support for a policy which may be opposed by sectional and influential interests. Although they are widely used in the United States, where at the local and state level the electorate is frequently invited to decide some public issue, and in a more limited way in Europe too, they have not found favour here. The Burkean doctrine of the right of the elected representative to decide issues on behalf of his constituency is deeply entrenched. And our politicians are reluctant to surrender this right. In any case, it is a rare political issue that can be presented to a mass audience in a simple 'either/or' form. Some questions, like the one in 1975 on our continued membership of the European Community, may lend themselves to such treatment. But others, like the issue of capital punishment, do not. To establish a clear view from the electorate of its position on this matter, it would be necessary to define with some care the crimes for which capital punishment was being considered, what – if any – degree of judicial discretion would be allowed, and so on.

In a parliamentary debate, all these aspects can be deployed at length and Parliament can then reach a precise decision which can be turned into law. A public debate lacks this precision and a public decision can at best be only a general one. Nor can there be much confidence, as things stand, in the public's decision being an informed one. If it is to reach an enlightened view for or against capital punishment, the public should have available a great deal of factual and analytical material. They should, for instance, have statistics of the incidence of the crime, evidence about those who commit it, facts about recidivism, evidence about deterrence, facts too about the circumstances in which capital punishment is administered. But if capital punishment is a difficult issue on which to poll public opinion, how much more complex is a matter like, for instance, the level of National Insurance Benefits. The question 'Do you think that the retirement pension for a married couple should be set at £55 or £60, or £70 a week?' would produce one set of answers. But if the question also spelt out the consequences of each level of benefit – if we were told, for instance, what the insurance contributions for people in work would have to be in each case – the answer would almost certainly be different. Without a good deal of education and enlightenment public opinion, polled in this way, could well be a poor guide to policy – poor not in the sense that it would not correspond to elite opinion, but poor in that it would be ill-informed and in the long run unacceptable, even to those expressing it. The perverse way in which voting takes place on the various fiscal propositions put to the electorate by the State of California is a sufficient illustration of this point. The binding referendum therefore cannot take the place of a parliamentary decision on complicated public issues.

Government and the Governed (BBC Reith Lectures)

III
Representation of Groups

The developing relationship between Crown and Parliament, government and representative assembly has been one major theme in British constitutional debate. Another has been the structure of representation, the ways in which social groups and individuals have been represented in Parliament. In this chapter, we shall look at the devices through which, it has been thought, the complex (and increasingly complex) social and economic life of the community can be reflected in the political realm and can influence political decision-making. More specifically, we shall look at those principles of representation which informed the original composition of Parliament – the representation of estates, the representation of communities, the representation of property and the representation of interests – and which have continued to shape views on what a representative system should ideally achieve. By the twentieth century, this has amounted to a statement and defence of a social and economic pluralism which both reinforces and justifies the constitutional pluralism depicted in Chapter II.

A.   THE ORIGINAL PRINCIPLES OF REPRESENTATION

As has been said, the emergence of Parliament from a feudal court came about through the summoning of representatives of the boroughs and shires to add to the lay and ecclesiastical magnates. What principles of representation were embodied in such a medieval assembly? In the first place it represented the estates of the realm, as was clearly shown in the name given to many continental assemblies, the estates-general. The notion of estates rests on the idea that the community is divided into clearly articulated social orders, bound together in a natural or even divinely ordained hierarchy, which are given separate but privileged positions within the political order. Shakespeare was one who pressed the necessity of such an ordered social and political structure, relating it to the governance by 'degree, priority and place' of all the created universe and picturing the horrors that follow from the dissolution of degree (III:1). The three estates represented in the English Parliament were the clergy, the barons and the commons – those who prayed, those who fought and those who worked. The higher clergy (the bishops and abbots) and the barons were summoned individually and came to be banded together, as the lords spiritual and the lords temporal, in the House of Lords. Initially the barons were in the main just the largest of the tenants-in-chief of the Crown and there was some doubt about whether the barony was an attribute of the person or of the tenure, but, by the end of the Middle Ages, there had evolved a fairly definite hereditary peerage whose members had an inherited title and right of attendance in the House of Lords. The third estate, after the lords spiritual and temporal, was the commons, the representatives of the county freeholders and the burgesses. Early moves to add representatives of the lower clergy came to nothing. In this sense the 'third' estate was not one estate but a number of estates grouped together in the Commons.

In particular, the Commons did not represent 'commoners' as opposed to the hereditary peers of the Lords. For the term Commons had the connotations of the French *communes*, and was a House of communities rather than a House of commoners. This points to a second broad principle of representation, the representation of communities. Representatives were called from the shires, the cities and the boroughs and these were not arbitrary collections of individuals divided by lines on an electoral map but organic communities with their own social life and unified political organization. The methods of election or appointment of representatives varied; in the counties, they were made by the county courts, probably assemblies of shire freeholders, whilst in the boroughs electoral qualifications varied from the fairly democratic to the highly oligarchic. The role of the representative was nearer to that of a modern national ambassador than that of a delegate within a democratic structure. He was someone sent to treat with the Crown (and other ambassadors) and was authorized to act in the name of his community.

A third principle of representation implicit in the early structure of Parliament was the representation of property. As we have seen, one of the most important functions of early Parliaments was agreement to taxation, and the linkage between taxation and representation demanded a parallel linkage between representation and property. Barons, bishops and abbots were for the most part owners or controllers of large estates. The shire freeholder franchise, narrowed in 1430 to a forty-shilling freeholder franchise, implied a property-owning electorate. In all but the most democratic boroughs, the franchise was limited by some property qualification.

Closely allied to the principle of the representation of property was the principle of the representation of interests. The division of labour in society, pictured by Shakespeare in his analogy of the beehive, implied the division of society into groups with differing productive functions and concerns (III:2). Before the invention of the notion of the market in the eighteenth century, the co-ordination of these different efforts and interests was taken to be the task mainly of 'a king and officers of sorts' which Shakespeare assumed even a hive to have. The basic social division of labour is between town and country, agriculture on the one side and commerce and manufacture on the other, and this division was encompassed in the House of Commons in the separate representation of shires and boroughs. This objective of expressing the views and interests within a representative assembly of the various productive groups was to remain a central operative principle of the British system.

These principles of representation were not theoretically stated or consciously pursued. They were no more than implicit in the practice and structure of Parliament and the electoral system as they evolved. What, in their operation, these principles implied was that the representative assembly should set before the Crown the wishes and grievances of the various orders, communities and economic group-ings within the realm and that its members should be empowered both to treat with government and authoritatively to commit those they represented to both legislation and the payment of taxes. The structure of the electoral system was geared towards producing an assembly capable of performing these functions. What the assembly spoke for were groups within a variegated social order. What it did not speak for was either a unified will of the people or the separate wills of the individuals constituting society. The system sought to represent a social pluralism and to present to a governing Crown the information and counsel which it needed to govern.

1   William Shakespeare, Degree, Priority, and Place (c.1602)

The heavens themselves, the planets, and this centre,
Observe degree, priority, and place,

Insisture, course, proportion, season, form,
Office, and custom, in all line of order:
And therefore is the glorious planet Sol
In noble eminence enthron'd and spher'd
Amidst the other; whose medicinable eye
Corrects the ill aspects of planets evil,
And posts, like the commandment of a king,
Sans check, to good and bad: but when the planets,
In evil mixture, to disorder wander,
What plagues and what portents! what mutiny!
What raging of the sea! shaking of earth!
Commotion in the winds! frights, changes, horrors,
Divert and crack, rend and deracinate
The unity and married calm of states
Quite from their fixture!   O, when degree is shak'd,
Which is the ladder to all high designs,
The enterprise is sick!   How could communities,
Degrees in schools, and brotherhoods in cities,
Peaceful commerce from dividable shores,
The primogenitive and due of birth,
Prerogative of age, crowns, sceptres, laurels,
But by degree, stand in authentic place?
Take but degree away, untune that string,
And, hark, what discord follows! each thing meets
In mere oppugnancy: the bounded waters
Should lift their bosoms higher than the shores,
And make a sop of all this solid globe:
Strength should be lord of imbecility,
And the rude son should strike his father dead:
Force should be right; or, rather, right and wrong, –
Between whose endless jar justice resides, –
Should lose their names, and so should justice too.
Then everything includes itself in power,
Power into will, will into appetite;
And appetite, an universal wolf,
So doubly seconded with will and power,
Must make perforce an universal prey,
And last eat up himself.

Troilus and Cressida

2   William Shakespeare, The Division of Labour (1599)

Therefore doth heaven divide
The state of man in divers functions,
Setting endeavour in continual motion;
To which is fixed, as an aim or butt,
Obedience: for so work the honey bees;
Creatures that, by a rule in nature, teach
The act of order to a peopled kingdom.
They have a king, and officers of sorts:
Where some, like magistrates, correct at home;
Others, like merchants, venture trade abroad;
Others, like soldiers, armed in their stings,
Make boot upon the summer's velvet buds;
Which pillage they with merry march bring home
To the tent-royal of their emperor:
Who, busied in his majesty, surveys
The singing masons building roofs of gold;
The civil citizens kneading up the honey;
The poor mechanic porters crowding in
Their heavy burdens at his narrow gate;
The sad-ey'd justice, with his surly hum,
Delivering o'er to executors pale
The lazy yawning drone. I this infer, –
That many things, having full reference
To one concent, may work contrariously:
As many arrows, loosed several ways,
Fly to one mark;
As many several ways meet in one town;
As many fresh streams meet in one salt sea;
As many lines close in the dial's centre:
So may a thousand actions, once afoot,
End in one purpose, and be all well borne
Without defeat.

Henry V

B.   ESTATES AND COMMUNITIES

Much of this original parliamentary structure seems to have survived
to the present day. Parliament is, for instance, still divided into a

House of Lords and a House of Commons. However, this structural continuity might be misleading. Does the persistence of a House of Lords mean that the representation of estates still operates and that peers and bishops are given an active political role in recognition of their leading positions within an hierarchical social order?

Disraeli, writing in his novel *Coningsby* of the 1832 Reform Act, suggested that the representation of estates could have formed the basis of the reformation of the electorate, but he also acknowledged that the Act itself, although it allowed for only a limited extension of the franchise, was a virtual concession to the alternative democratic principle of universal suffrage (III:3). In fact, a democratic electorate was a long time coming. Equally the habit of social deference, and together with it a leading role for the aristocracy in British politics, survived at least until the end of the nineteenth century. Burke, in a typical blend of historical description and ideological justification, argued for a natural aristocracy in Britain, an aristocracy which, if wider than the hereditary peerage, nevertheless included it (III:4). In 1871, the Liberal Prime Minister, Gladstone, in countering proposals for Lords reform, endorsed Burke's views and, like Burke, reinforced his argument by contrasting French and English attitudes (III:5). In Burke's own day and since, there have been constant criticisms of both the honours system and the parliamentary status of the peerage. Paine, defending the abolition by the French Revolutionaries of titles, foresaw the sweeping away of such, in his eyes, ridiculous distinctions by the rise of reason (III:6). Southey too predicted a decline in the prestige of the peerage and a weakening of its political role because of the indiscriminate creation of new peers and the sale of titles (III:7). Given the fact that the honours system has not only survived but been extended, despite continued objections that titles are given for political services and continued allegations that they are given in return for contributions to party funds, it might seem that Paine and Southey were wildly astray in their predictions.

Nevertheless, whatever may be the truth about the social prestige of the titled, the political influence of the hereditary peerage has declined and the powers of the House of Lords have over time been curtailed. Demands for Lords reform have been constant. Aside from complete abolition, these have taken the form of demands for the reduction of the powers and demands for changes in the composition of the House. Both of these demands have had some success during this century. The Parliament Acts of 1911 and 1949 have eliminated any role for the Lords in money bills and reduced its power in ordinary legislation to that of delay. The Preamble to the 1911 Act

promised to substitute in the future a democratic second Chamber for
the hereditary Lords (III:8), but this promise has not as yet been
redeemed. One change in composition that was made in 1958 was a
long-advocated proposal for the introduction of life peers (non-
hereditary members of the Lords). In recent decades, there has also
been a substantial reduction in the creation of new hereditary
peerages. A problem here is a potential conflict between the two
reform demands, since revision of the composition of the Lords in a
democratic direction might increase its prestige and so allow for the
expansion of its ability to oppose the Commons. Given this dilemma,
some critics of the Lords would prefer outright abolition. Others,
such as Lord Hailsham writing in the late 1970s, saw this possible
expansion of power as the best reason for a democratic second
chamber since it would provide a counter to the danger of elective
dictatorship (III:9).

The arguments of those like Lord Hailsham who wish to retain a
second Chamber, even of those who favour a second Chamber in its
present form, are usually now far removed from the principle of the
representation of estates, and from Burke's and Gladstone's assertions
about the Englishman's love of a lord. Present defences of a second
Chamber fit more readily into the context of another, no less
significant, constitutional principle – the need for checks and
balances.

Another of the original principles, that of the representation of
geographical communities, has equally survived only in an attenuated
form. There has been a decline in local institutional structures, local
self-government and local feelings. At times, it seems that sport
provides the last bastions of local community – is Warwickshire more
than a cricket team, Liverpool more than a football team? All sorts of
factors have contributed to this decline – industrialization, the growth
of cities, the expansion of population, geographical mobility and so
on. There have, however, been political and constitutional contributions. Politically, the development of highly organized and disciplined parliamentary parties have moved the primary concerns of MPs
away from local views and interests and towards party commitments. Of course MPs may oppose party policy if there are strong
local feelings against it, particularly if those feelings are strong in the
local party. Nevertheless they see themselves as, on the whole,
Conservative or Labour MPs rather than as MPs for this constituency
or that. Constitutionally, the emergence at the end of the nineteenth
century of the single-member constituency as the basic unit of the
electoral system and the triumph of the idea of political equality as its

organizing principle have meant that there is only a tenuous connection between what remains of local communities and constituency boundaries. The need to keep constituency populations roughly comparable means that political geography can pay only slight regard to social geography. Of course, the MP in the single-member constituency is likely to maintain close contacts with his or her constituents: most MPs wish to be good constituency MPs both out of a sense of duty and because most perceive it as a requirement of political survival. They will then seek to protect or further local economic interests and to attend to the grievances of individual constituents, but this representation of interests and persons hardly adds up to the representation of a community.

3 Benjamin Disraeli, The Estates of the Realm (1844)

In the protracted discussions to which this celebrated measure gave rise, nothing is more remarkable than the perplexities into which the speakers of both sides are thrown, when they touch upon the nature of the representative principle. On one hand it was maintained, that, under the old system, the people were virtually represented; while, on the other, it was triumphantly urged, that if the principle be conceded, the people should not be virtually, but actually, represented. But who are the people? And where are you to draw a line? And why should there be any? It was urged that a contribution to the taxes was the constitutional qualification for the suffrage. But we have established a system of taxation in this country of so remarkable a nature, that the beggar who chews his quid as he sweeps a crossing, is contributing to the imposts! Is he to have a vote? He is one of the people, and he yields his quota to the public burthens.

Amid these conflicting statements, and these confounding conclusions, it is singular that no member of either House should have recurred to the original character of these popular assemblies, which have always prevailed among the northern nations. We still retain in the antique phraseology of our statutes the term which might have beneficially guided a modern Reformer in his reconstructive labours.

When the crowned Northman consulted on the welfare of his kingdom, he assembled the ESTATES of his realm. Now an estate is a class of the nation invested with political rights. There appeared the estate of the clergy, of the barons, of other classes. In the Scandinavian kingdoms to this day, the estate of the peasants sends its representatives to the Diet. In England, under the Normans, the Church and the Baronage were convoked, together with the estate of the Community, a term which then probably described the inferior holders of land, whose tenure was not immediate of the Crown. This Third Estate was so numerous, that convenience suggested its appearance by representation; while the others, more limited, appeared, and still appear, personally. The Third Estate was reconstructed as circumstances developed themselves. It was a Reform of Parliament when the towns were summoned.

In treating the House of the Third Estate as the House of the People, and not as the House of a privileged class, the Ministry and Parliament of 1831 virtually conceded the principle of Universal Suffrage. In this point of view the ten-pound franchise was an arbitrary, irrational, and impolitic qualification. It had, indeed, the merit of simplicity, and so had the constitutions of Abbé Siéyès. But its immediate and inevitable result was Chartism.

But if the Ministry and Parliament of 1831 had announced that the time had arrived when the Third Estate should be enlarged and reconstructed, they would have occupied an intelligible position; and if, instead of simplicity of elements in its reconstruction, they had sought, on the contrary, various and varying materials which would have neutralised the painful predominance of any particular interest in the new scheme, and prevented those banded jealousies which have been its consequences, the nation would have found itself in a secure condition. Another class not less numerous than the existing one, and invested with privileges not less important, would have been added to the public estates of the realm; and the bewildering phrase 'the People' would have remained, what it really is, a term of natural philosophy, and not of political science.

Coningsby

4 Edmund Burke, A Natural Aristocracy (1791)

To enable men to act with the weight and character of a people, and to answer the ends for which they are incorporated into that capacity, we must suppose them (by means immediate or consequential) to be in that state of habitual social discipline, in which the wiser, the more expert, and the more opulent conduct, and by conducting enlighten and protect, the weaker, the less knowing, and the less provided with the goods of fortune. When the multitude are not under this discipline, they can scarcely be said to be in civil society. . .

A true natural aristocracy is not a separate interest in the state, or separable from it. It is an essential integrant part of any large body rightly constituted. It is formed out of a class of legitimate presumptions, which, taken as generalities, must be admitted for actual truths. To be bred in a place of estimation; to see nothing low and sordid from one's infancy; to be taught to respect one's self; to be habituated to the censorial inspection of the publick eye; to look early to publick opinion; to stand upon such elevated ground as to be enabled to take a large view of the wide-spread and infinitely diversified combinations of men and affairs in a large society; to have leisure to read, to reflect, to converse; to be enabled to draw the court and attention of the wise and learned wherever they are to be found; – to be habituated in armies to command and to obey; to be taught to despise danger in the pursuit of honour and duty; to be formed to the greatest degree of vigilance, foresight, and circumspection, in a state of things in which no fault is committed with impunity, and the slightest mistakes draw on the most ruinous consequences – to be led to a guarded and regulated conduct, from a sense that you are considered as an instructor of your fellow-citizens in their highest concerns, and that you act as a reconciler between God and man – to be employed as an administrator of law and justice, and to be thereby amongst the first benefactors to mankind – to be a professor of high science, or of liberal and ingenuous art – to be amongst rich traders, who from their success are presumed to have sharp and vigorous understandings, and to possess the virtues of diligence, order, constancy, and regularity, and to have cultivated an habitual regard to commutative justice – these are the circumstances of men, that form what I should call a *natural* aristocracy, without which there is no nation.

Appeal from the New to the Old Whigs

5   W. E. Gladstone, The English Love a Lord (1871)

Before you determine to expel the hereditary principle from the House of Lords, I first ask you, the people of Greenwich, as representing the people of England, what you will substitute for the hereditary principle? (*A Voice* – 'five years' election.') That is a fruitful hint, but yet I have another point to suggest, and it is this: I have a shrewd suspicion in my mind that a very large proportion of the people of England have a sneaking kindness for this hereditary principle.

I do not mean, gentlemen, by these words that a large proportion of the people of England either desire, or intend, or would permit that which I hope that they never will desire, or intend, or permit – namely, that the House of Lords should exercise a paramount control over the legislation of the country. That is quite another matter. But this I do say – that the people of England are not, like the people of France, lovers of naked political equality. England is a great lover of liberty; but of equality she never has been so much enamoured. Gentlemen, in judging of this question, I must say that possibly the obser-vation of the manner in which, for such long periods, and under so many varieties of form, the love of equality in France has proved insufficient to save our generous and distinguished neighbours from the loss of liberty – the observation of these facts may tend to confirm the people of the three kingdoms in the feelings that I think they entertain; but I want to put this to you as a practical question. The only mode of judging whether an Englishman – and I use the word 'Englishman' for the people of the three kingdoms – is not unfriendly to social inequalities is by watching the working of our institutions in detail. My observation has not been of a very brief term – I wish it had been, for then I should have been younger than I am now – and it is this: that whenever there is anything to be done, or to be given, and there are two candidates for it who are exactly alike – alike in opinions, alike in characters, alike in possessions, – and one is a commoner and the other a lord, the Englishman is very apt indeed to prefer the lord.

Gladstone's Speeches

6 Thomas Paine, Titles are but Nicknames (1791)

Titles are but nicknames, and every nickname is a title. The thing is perfectly harmless in itself, but it marks a sort of foppery in the human character, which degrades it. It reduces man into the diminutive of man in things which are great, and the counterfeit of woman in things which are little. It talks about its fine *blue ribbon* like a girl, and shows its new *garter* like a child. A certain writer of some antiquity, says: '*When I was a child, I thought as a child; but when I became a man, I put away childish things.*'. . .

Is it, then, any wonder that titles should fall in France? Is it not a greater wonder they should be kept up anywhere? What are they? What is their worth, and 'what is their amount'?

When we think or speak of a *Judge* or a *General*, we associate with it the ideas of office and character; we think of gravity in the one and bravery in the other; but when we use a word *merely as a title*, no ideas associate with it. Through all the vocabulary of Adam there is not such an animal as a Duke or a Count; neither can we connect any certain idea with the words. Whether they mean strength or weakness, wisdom or folly, a child or a man, or the rider or the horse, is all equivocal. What respect then can be paid to that which describes nothing, and which means nothing? Imagination has given figure and character to centaurs, satyrs, and down to all the fairy tribe; but titles baffle even the powers of fancy, and are a chimerical nondescript.

But this is not all. If a whole country is disposed to hold them in contempt, all their value is gone, and none will own them. It is common opinion only that makes them anything or nothing, or worse than nothing. There is no occasion to take titles away, for they take themselves away when society concurs to ridicule them. This species of imaginary consequence has visibly declined in every part of Europe, and it hastens to its exit as the world of reason continues to rise.

The Rights of Man

7   Robert Southey, The Creation and Sale of Titles (1807)

Merchants and bankers and contractors make their way by wealth even into the ranks of nobility. James I. . .invented the title of baronet, and offered fifty of these titles for sale at a thousand pounds each, – in those days a weighty sum. This title has never indeed since been publicly put up to sale, yet it is still to be purchased. . .

The indiscriminate admission to nobility is a practice which produces the same mischievous effect upon public opinion. They must be short-sighted politicians who do not see that, if they would have nobility respected, they should reserve it as the reward of great and signal services; that it is monstrous to give the same honours and privileges to a man because he has the command of three or four boroughs, as to Nelson for the battle of the Nile. This however is not all the evil; the political system of the country is altered by it, and the power of the old nobles gradually transferred to a set of new men, to an aristocracy of wealth. The Lords in England form the second power in the state, and no law can be enacted till it has received their approbation. About a century ago the party in opposition to the crown was known to be the strongest in the house of lords, and the queen, knowing that her measures would else be out-voted, created twelve new peers, who turned the scale. This open and undisguised exertion of the prerogative, to the actual subversion of the constitution as it then stood, provoked nothing more than a sarcasm. When the first of these new peers gave his vote upon the question, one of the old nobles addressed himself to the rest, and said, 'I suppose, gentleman, you all vote by your foreman,' alluding to their number, which was the same as that of a common jury. This practice of granting peerages has been more frequent during the present reign than at any former period, not less than three-fifths of the house of lords having been created, and the number is every year increased. But to the old aristocracy of the country every new creation is a diminution of their power and weight in the political scale.

Letters from England

8   The Parliament Act 1911

Whereas it is expedient that provision should be made for regulating the relations between the two Houses of Parliament:

And whereas it is intended to substitute for the House of Lords as it at present exists a Second Chamber constituted on a popular instead of hereditary basis, but such substitution cannot be immediately brought into operation:

And whereas provision will require hereafter to be made by Parliament in a measure affecting such substitution for limiting and defining the powers of the new Second Chamber, but it is expedient to make such provision as in this Act appears for restricting the existing powers of the House of Lords:. . .

Be it therefore enacted. . .

1 & 2 Geo. V, c.13

9   Lord Hailsham, A Democratic Second Chamber (1978)

Various attempts have been made since the makeshift legislation of 1911 (not improved by the equally makeshift amendments of 1949) to introduce compromise proposals designed to make the composition of the House of Lords more acceptable to the electorate. All have foundered for two reasons, each conclusive in its own sphere. The first is that it is simply not theoretically possible to make either a nominated membership or a hereditary membership compatible with the principles of democracy. The second is that the House of Commons is not prepared to share effective power with any chamber which is partly nominated and partly hereditary, or partly ex-officio, partly nominated, and partly hereditary, however the proportions or methods of selection may be juggled about. This is not in any way to criticize the existing House of Lords, least of all its hereditary element, which in my experience contributes a desirable element of common sense, and occasionally, an acceptable element of independence, into an assembly of persons whose members are sometimes lacking at least in the first. It is simply to say that the alternative to radical reform is to maintain the status quo more or less as it is, and, if I am right in describing the status quo as intolerable, there is no genuine alternative to radical reform.

Fortunately, the matter is no longer capable of argument. Sooner or later the Labour Party is going to abolish the status quo. The more radical and foolish wish to go in for a single chamber government with the House of Lords no longer in existence at all and no replacement having been made, the House of Commons would then be left without its chaperon. The wiser, but far more dangerous, proposal would be to leave the anomalous assembly as it is, but further emasculate its powers. An even sillier proposal by the Labour peers is to render it a positive replica of the House of Commons by making membership of it dependent on approval by a select committee of MPs. These would be worse than outright abolition since it would retain a façade of a two-chamber legislature, while concealing the reality of elective dictatorship by one. Outright abolition would at least force Conservatives and Liberals to devise a replacement when the reality of elective dictatorship became obvious. But, in either case, the present House of Lords is doomed, and there is therefore no longer any point in arguing whether or not it should be retained.

The only question is, with what to replace it and when. To my mind there is no alternative to an elected chamber. It must not be elected on the same constituencies, or by the same voting method as the Commons, as a mere mirror image of the Commons would be valueless. Some method of proportional representation is desirable, since the function of a second chamber is to legislate, and to restrain legislation not acceptable to majority opinion. It is no part of its function to act as a Court of Appeal from the verdict of the people, and therefore, legislation should pass through when it is proposed, or amended in a form acceptable to the majority.

The Dilemma of Democracy

C.   Property and Interests

The question of the representation of property was to become central to the nineteenth-century debate on parliamentary and electoral reform. For two centuries before that, though, the more general question of the relationship between property systems and political orders had been a major concern of British political thinking. Two themes dominated this discussion – the argument that the primary end of government is the protection of individual property rights and the argument that there is a close relationship between the distribution of property in any society and its governmental structure.

The classic statement of the first theme was made by Locke (III:10). His founding of political authority on individual consent will be explored in the next chapter. Here we can notice his firm assertion that the only reason the individual could have to renounce his natural liberty was to secure his property. He gives a wide meaning to property, including under it life and liberty as well as estates, but it is clear that the security of property in a modern understanding of the term ('estates') is a primary end of government. This Lockean message was accepted as axiomatic in eighteenth-century British thought and was highly influential in the America of the Revolution and of the Founding Fathers.

In modern social thought, the second theme, that the pattern of political relations in any society is closely connected with its property relations, has been seen as a particularly Marxist preoccupation. It was, however, a theme that had for long been heard in Britain. This is illustrated by extracts from two of its most eminent exponents: James Harrington, writing in the mid-seventeenth century, and Adam Smith, writing in the mid-eighteenth. Harrington puts, in his aphoristic style, the argument that the distribution of property, whether in the family or in the nation, determines the style of government (III:11). Smith, in tracing the origins of government to the move from a hunter–gatherer society to a nomadic shepherd society in which large-scale ownership arose, repeats the Lockean view that government is a means to the security of property and the Harrington view that the particular form and distribution of property determines the structure of political authority (III:12).

Ideas such as these became important in the constitutional debate when the reform movement revived after the Napoleonic wars. In the late eighteenth century, reform demands were commonly justified in terms of a restoration of a constitutional balance of power. Now, changes in the regime were pressed as a way of closing what was claimed to be a growing gap between that regime and the property structure. The Industrial Revolution had created new sources of wealth, new wealthy classes, new and prosperous cities, and these new riches must be given political expression. The specific means towards this general objective were the redistribution of Commons seats in favour of the new industrial towns and the alteration of the property qualifications for voters. Macaulay, in one of his influential speeches in the Commons debates leading up to the 1832 Reform Act, put eloquently this case that economic and social change had created an unavoidable need to reconstruct the ancient constitution (III:13).

The three great Reform Acts of the nineteenth century – of 1832, 1867 and 1884 – all extended the electorate through the lowering of property qualifications. The principle of a property qualification for the right to vote was itself maintained until 1918. The principle had long been defended by the 'stake in the country' argument, that only the possession of some property, more particularly real estate, could guarantee the attachment to the general good, the moderation of views, the soundness of character and intellect that justified entry into the political public. Similar arguments were used to justify property qualifications for MPs, which existed from 1710 to 1858. The payment of MPs, which the People's Charter of 1838 associated with abolition of Members' property qualifications, was claimed on the ground that its absence amounted to a property qualification.

Of all the original principles of representation, it is the representation of interests that has most obviously survived into the modern world both as a central feature of representative democracies and as a justification of such regimes. The idea that a representative system should express the interests and views of all parts of a pluralist society and that a prime function of government in such a system is to seek the mutual accommodation of these different and often conflicting interests is a commonplace of modern defences of representative democracy, although it has come under periodic attack. Such defences have been heard since the early nineteenth century. The primary economic division incorporated into the initial organization of the Commons, between town and country, was still at the centre of many political conflicts, at least when translated into the political economists' terminology as the conflict between land on the one side and capital and labour on the other. The Industrial Revolution had however greatly complicated the social and economic consequences of the division of labour. The emergence of a range of new manufacturing industries and new areas of trade created new needs and demands for parliamentary representation. George Eliot pictures the transformation of an eighteenth-century market town connected with national trade, and traces the political consequences of both this transformation and the granting of a parliamentary seat to Treby

Magna in the 1832 Reform Act (III:14). The generally accepted theory of representation in the debate leading up to the Reform Act was that the House of Commons should incorporate representatives of all the varied social interests. This is the common refrain of Charles Jenkinson, the future Tory Prime Minister Lord Liverpool (III:15), and Lord John Russell, an architect of the first Reform Act and future Whig Prime Minister (III:16). Whig and Tory were agreed on the objectives of representation, but they were disagreed about the means towards these objectives. On the reformist side was pressed the need for granting seats in Parliament to the new industrial towns; on the anti-reform side, it was argued by speakers like Sir Robert Inglis that the unreformed House of Commons admirably achieved such a representation through virtual representation (III:17). This notion, given its classic expression by Burke (III:18), was that a person could represent a group if he was a typical member of the group, sharing its interests or views or characteristics, even if he was not elected by it. So someone like Inglis could argue that the cotton industry of Manchester was better represented by a cotton manufacturer who had bought a rotten borough than a man elected by a wide electorate in Manchester.

There were then, as there are now, critics of this pluralist vision of the ideal representative system, and the critics were of different political hues. The conservative Burke, despite his defence of virtual representation, was absolutely opposed to the idea that the House of Commons should be a 'congress of ambassadors from different and hostile interests' (III:19) and the radical James Mill believed such an assembly would be a cockpit for 'sinister interests' (III:20). Both believed the proper task of the assembly was to identify and express a single national interest.

Subsequent demands for further parliamentary reform were fuelled at least in part by representation of interests arguments. These played their parts in demands for both redistribution of seats and extensions of the franchise. The movements for working-class representation and for votes for women both used the argument that the interests of those excluded from the vote would never be properly considered or protected by government. An 1836 pamphlet written by Lovett, a Chartist leader, and issued by the London Working Men's Association, hammered home the message that, without some political power, the working class would never have adequate means of self-protection (III:21). Universal male suffrage was not to be achieved until 1885, and this still left women excluded from the franchise. When a suffragette movement emerged in the early twentieth century, it used a similar plea that the condition of women could not be improved without their possessing the vote (III:22).

As Lovett's pamphlet showed, what was needed, it was believed, was not only a working-class franchise but also working-class MPs. This was a virtual representation argument – that it was only working men who could adequately plead the cause of labour. The Labour Party itself originated in the Labour Representation Committee whose prime purpose was to increase the number of working-class MPs. And still in the 1950s, Aneurin Bevan could insist on the need for representatives to be of the same kind as those they represent (III:23). Attempts to increase the number of women and of members of minority ethnic groups in the Commons rest on the same virtual representation assumptions.

The tradition of the representation of interests is reflected in modern interpretations of Western democracies in pluralist terms. In general, the pluralist perspective sees these systems as ones in which all the varied interests in society have some access to the political arena and thus some leverage in policy formulation. This influence is achieved partly by the ability of minority groups to use their electoral power as a means of shaping party policies, but more importantly it follows from the activities of pressure groups seeking to forward the objectives of their members through influencing government decisions. In this pressure process, Parliament itself may be by-passed. Organized groups may try to secure individual MPs to speak for them, but groups may achieve much more by acting directly on the administration without using the intermediary of back-bench MPs. On this pluralist analysis, one of the main functions of government is seen as the accommodation of the demands of different groups. Margaret Thatcher, speaking shortly after she had come to power in 1979, rejected this pluralist defence of the activities of pressure groups and the politics of accommodation, consensual politics (III:24). For her, this kind of politics was a recipe for governments evading their clear duty to act for the national interest as they understand it.

10   John Locke, Government as Defender of Property Rights (1690)

If Man in the State of Nature be so free, as has been said; If he be absolute Lord of his own Person and Possessions, equal to the greatest, and subject to no Body, why will he part with his

Freedom? Why will he give up this Empire, and subject himself to the Dominion and Controul of any other Power? To which 'tis obvious to Answer, that though in the state of Nature he hath such a right, yet the Enjoyment of it is very uncertain, and constantly exposed to the Invasion of others. For all being Kings as much as he, every Man his Equal, and the greater part no strict Observers of Equity and Justice, the enjoyment of the property he has in this state is very unsafe, very unsecure. This makes him willing to quit a Condition, which however free, is full of fears and continual dangers: And 'tis not without reason, that he seeks out, and is willing to joyn in Society with others who are already united, or have a mind to unite for the mutual *Preservation* of their Lives, Liberties and Estates, which I call by the general Name, *Property*.

The great and chief end therefore, of Mens uniting into Commonwealths, and putting themselves under Government, is the Preservation of their Property.

The Second Treatise on Government

11   James Harrington, Property and Political Power (1661)

Distribution of shares in land as to the three grand interests, the king, the nobility, and the people, must be equal or inequal.

Equal distribution of land, as if one man or a few men have one half of the territory and the people have the other half, causes privation of government and a state of civil war, for the lord or lords on the one side being able to assert their pretension or right to rule, and the people on the other their pretension or right to liberty; that nation can never come under any form of government till that question be decided; and property being not by any law to be violated or moved, any such question cannot be decided but by the sword only.

Unequal distribution of shares in land as to the three grand interests, or the whole land in any one of these, is that which causes one of these three to be the predominant interest.

All government is interest, and the predominant interest gives the matter or foundation of the government.

If one man has the whole or two parts in three of the whole land or territory, the interest of one man is the pre–dominant interest and causes absolute monarchy.

If a few men have the whole or two parts in three of the whole land or territory, the interest of the few or of the nobility is the predominant interest and, were there any such thing in nature, would cause a pure aristocracy.

It being so that pure aristocracy or the nobility, having the whole or two parts in three of the whole land or territory without a moderator or prince to balance them, is a state of war in which everyone as he grows eminent or potent aspires to monarchy; and that not any nobility can have peace or can reign without having such a moderator or prince as on the one side they may balance or hold in from being absolute, and on the other side may balance or hold them and their factions from flying out into arms, it follows that if a few men have the whole or two parts in three of the whole land or territory, the interest of the nobility being the predominant interest must of necessity produce regulated monarchy,

If the many or the people have the whole or two parts in three of the whole land or territory, the interest of the many or of the people is the predominant interest and causes democracy.

A people neither under absolute or under regulated monarchy, not yet under democracy, are under a privation of government.

A System of Politics

12 Adam Smith, Economic Structures and Political Authority (1766)

Property and civil government very much depend on one another. The preservation of property and the inequality of possession first formed it, and the state of property must always vary with the form of government. . .

The forms of government however various may not improperly be reduced to these three, Monarchical, Aristocratical, and Democratical. These may be blended in a great number of ways, and we usually denominate the government from that one which prevails. . .

To acquire proper notions of government it is necessary to consider the first form of it, and observe how the other forms arose out of it.

In a nation of hunters there is properly no government at all. The society consists of a few independent families, who live in the same village and speak the same language, and have agreed among themselves to keep together for their mutual safety. But they have no authority one over another. The whole society interests itself in any offence. If possible they make it up between the parties, if not they banish from their society, kill, or deliver up to the resentment of the injured, him who has committed the crime. But this is no regular government. For tho' there may be some among them who are much respected, and have great influence in their determinations, yet he never can do anything without the consent of the whole.

Thus among hunters there is no regular government; they live according to the laws of nature.

The appropriation of herds and flocks, which introduced an inequality of fortune, was that which first gave rise to regular government. Till there be property there can be no government, the very end of which is to secure wealth, and to defend the rich from the poor. In this age of shepherds if one man possessed 500 oxen, and another had none at all, unless there were some government to secure them to him, he would not be allowed to possess them. This inequality of fortune, making a distinction between the rich and the poor, gave the former much influence over the latter, for they who had no flocks or herds must have depended on those who had them, because they could not now gain a subsistence from hunting as the rich had made the game, now become tame, their own property. They therefore who had appropriated a number of flocks and herds, necessarily came to have great influence over the rest; and accordingly we find in the Old Testament that Abraham, Lot, and the other patriarchs were like little petty princes.

Lectures on Jurisprudence

13   Lord Macaulay, Economic Change and Constitutional Reform (1831)

[Our ancestors] framed a representative system, which, though not without defects and irregularities, was well adapted to the state of England in their time. But a great revolution took place. The character of the old corporations changed. New forms of property came into existence. New portions of society rose into importance. There were in our rural districts rich cultivators, who were not freeholders. There were in our capital rich traders, who were not livery-men. Towns shrank into villages. Villages swelled into cities larger than the London of the Plantagenets. Unhappily while the natural growth of society went on, the artificial polity continued unchanged. The ancient form of the representation remained; and precisely because the form remained, the spirit departed. Then came that pressure almost to bursting, the new wine in the old bottles, the new society under the old institutions. It is now time for us to pay a decent, a rational, a manly reverence to our ancestors, not by superstitiously adhering to what they, in other circumstances, did, but by doing what they, in our circumstances, would have done. All history is full of revolutions, produced by causes similar to those which are now operating in England. A portion of the community which had been of no account expands and becomes strong. It demands a place in the system, suited, not to its former weakness, but to its present power. If this is granted, all is well. If this is refused, then comes the struggle between the young energy of one class and the ancient privileges of another. Such was the struggle between the Plebeians and the Patricians of Rome. Such was the struggle of the Italian allies for admission to the full rights of Roman citizens. Such was the struggle of our North American colonies against the mother country. Such was the struggle which the Third Estate of France maintained against the aristocracy of birth. Such was the struggle which the Roman Catholics of Ireland maintained against the aristocracy of creed. Such is the struggle which the free people of colour in Jamaica are now maintaining against the aristocracy of skin. Such, finally, is the struggle which the middle classes in England are maintaining against an aristocracy of mere locality, against an aristocracy the principle of which is to invest a hundred drunken potwallopers in one place, or the owner of a ruined hovel in another, with the powers which are withheld from cities renowned to the furthest ends of the earth, for the marvels of their wealth and of their industry.

Miscellaneous Writings and Speeches

14   George Eliot, Industrial Growth and Parliamentary Reform (1866)

Treby Magna, on which the Reform Bill had thrust the new honour of being a polling-place, had been, at the beginning of the century, quite a typical old market-town, lying in pleasant sleepiness among green pastures, with a rush-fringed river meandering through them. Its principal street had various handsome and tall-windowed brick houses with walled gardens behind them; and at the end, where it widened into the market-place, there was the cheerful rough-stuccoed front of that excellent inn, the Marquis of Granby, where the farmers put up their gigs, not only on fair and market days, but on exceptional Sundays when they came to church. And the church was one of those fine old English structures worth travelling to see, standing in a broad churchyard with a line of solemn yew-trees beside it, and lifting a majestic tower and spire far above the red-and-purple roofs of the town. It was not large enough to hold all the parishioners of a parish which stretched over distant villages and hamlets; but then they were never so unreasonable as to wish to be all in at once, and had never complained that the space of a large side-chapel was taken up by the tombs of the Debarrys, and shut in by a handsome iron screen. For when the black Benedictines ceased to pray and chant in this church, when the Blessed Virgin and St Gregory were expelled, the Debarrys, as lords of the manor, naturally came next to Providence and took the place of the saints. Long before that time indeed, there had been a Sir Maximus Debarry who had been at the fortifying of the old castle, which now stood in ruins in the midst of the green pastures, and with its sheltering wall towards the north made an excellent strawyard for the pigs of Wace & Co., brewers of the celebrated Treby beer. Wace & Co. did not stand alone in the town as prosperous traders on a large scale, to say nothing of those who had retired from business; and in no country town of the same small size as Treby was there a larger proportion of families who had handsome sets of china without handles, hereditary punchbowls, and large silver ladles with a Queen Anne's guinea in the centre. . .

Such was the old-fashioned, grazing, brewing, wool-packing, cheese-loading life of Treby Magna, until there befell new conditions, complicating its relating with the rest of the world, and gradually awakening in it that higher consciousness which is known to bring higher pains. First came the canal; next, the working of the coal-mines at Sproxton, two miles off the town; and, thirdly, the discovery of a saline spring, which suggested to a too constructive brain the possibility of turning Treby Magna into a fashionable watering-place. . .

In this way it happened that Treby Magna gradually passed from being simply a respectable market-town – the heart of a great rural district, where the trade was only such as had close relations with the local landed interest – and took on the more complex life brought by mines and manufactures, which belong more directly to the greater circulating system of the nation than to the local system to which they have been superadded. . .

Thus Treby Magna, which had lived quietly through the great earthquakes of the French Revolution and the Napoleonic wars, which had remained unmoved by the *Rights of Man*, and saw little in Mr Cobbett's *Weekly Register* except that he held eccentric views about potatoes, began at last to know the higher pains of a dim political consciousness; and the development had been greatly helped by the recent agitation about the Reform Bill. Tory, Whig, and Radical did not perhaps become clearer in their definition of each other; but the names seemed to acquire so strong a stamp of honour or infamy, that definitions would only have weakened the impression. As to the short and easy method of judging opinions by the personal character of those who held them, it was liable to be much frustrated in Treby. It so happened in that particular town that the Reformers were not all of them large-hearted patriots or ardent lovers of justice; indeed, one of them, in the very midst of the agitation, was detected in using unequal scales – a fact to which many Tories pointed with disgust as showing plainly enough, without further argument, that the cry for a change in the representative system was hollow trickery. Again, the Tories were far from being all oppressors, disposed to grind down the working classes into serfdom; and it was undeniable that the inspector at the tape manufactory, who spoke with much eloquence on the extension of the suffrage, was a more tyrannical personage than open-handed Mr Wace, whose chief political tenet was, that it was all nonsense giving men votes when they had no stake in the country. On the other hand, there were some Tories who gave themselves a great deal of leisure to abuse hypocrites, Radicals, Dissenters, and atheism generally, but whose inflamed faces, theistic swearing, and frankness in expressing a wish to borrow, certainly did not mark them out strongly as holding opinions likely to save society.

Felix Holt

15   Lord Liverpool, Representation of Interests: A Tory View (1793)

If all persons have not a natural right to vote for members of parliament, no particular class of persons can have that right; the line could never be drawn. The question, then, is placed upon its proper ground; it was a question of wisdom, a question of expediency, but not a question of right. Considering it in this point of view, we ought to examine this question on the same principle on which all questions of the sort must be examined, viz. by inquiring what was the end that was to be produced; and then considering what were the means likely to produce that end. . .[We] ought to begin by considering who ought to be the elected, and then constitute such persons electors as would be likely to produce the best elected. Three questions, then, arise out of this principle: 1. What is the House of Commons? 2. How ought it to be composed to answer its object? 3. What is the way of so composing it?

Supposing, then, that there can be no doubt on the first of these questions; that we must be all agreed that the House of Commons is meant to be a legislative body, representing all descriptions of men in this country, without troubling the House any farther on that proposition, he would proceed to the second, and consider how it ought to be formed. In the first place, he supposed every person would agree, that the landed interest ought to have the preponderant weight. The landed interest was, in fact, the stamina of the country. In the second place, in a commercial country like this, the manufacturing and commercial interest ought to have a considerable weight, secondary to the landed interest, but secondary to the landed interest only. But was this all that was necessary? There were other descriptions of people, which, to distinguish from those already mentioned, he should style professional people and whom he considered as absolutely necessary to the composition of a House of Commons.

Parliamentary History, vol. XXX, *Hansard* 1817

16   Lord John Russell, Representation of Interests: A Whig View (1821)

The grand principle of all is, that the representative body should be the image of the represented; not that it should represent property only, or multitude only, or farmers, or merchants, or manufacturers only; not that it should govern with the pride of an insulated aristocracy, or be carried to and fro by the breath of transient popularity; but that it should unite somewhat of all these things, and blend these various colours into one agreeable picture. . .

The general scheme of the representation is evidently calculated to give the right of voting to persons of all classes. Landed property is represented in counties; commercial, in cities; and the boroughs contain various modes of suffrage, and are subject to various influences; in one place of a great landowner, in another of a club, in another of the multitude. These, too, are all so blended together – the towns have so much influence in the neighbouring city or town, that one kind of members does not feel much jealousy of another kind. It is always a great misfortune when they are pitted against each other.

But although no class is excluded from our constituent body, there were parts of the country which before the Reform Act were very inadequately represented. The county of Lancaster, and the county of York, comprising Manchester, Bolton, Leeds, Sheffield, Halifax, and Huddersfield, and containing 2,500,000 of inhabitants, were represented by four persons. This was evidently a practical grievance, and as such it was felt.

An Essay on the History of the English Government and Constitution

17   Sir Robert Inglis, In Defence of the Unreformed House of Commons (1831)

Such, generally speaking, as the House of Commons is now, such it has been for a long succession of years: it is the most complete representation of the interests of the people, which was ever assembled in any age or country. It is the only constituent body that ever existed, which comprehends within itself, those who can urge the wants and defend the claims of the landed, the commercial, the professional classes of the country; those who are bound to uphold the prerogatives of the Crown, the privileges of the nobility, the interests of the lower classes, the rights and liberties of the whole people. It is the very absence of symmetry in our elective franchises which admits of the introduction to this House of classes so various. The *concordia discors* opens the door to the admission here of all talents, and of all classes, and of all interests. How far, under any other than the present circumstances, the rights of the distant dependencies, of the East Indies, of the West Indies, of the Colonies, of the great Corporations, of the commercial interests generally. . .could find their just support in this House, I know not.

3 Hansard II

18   Edmund Burke, Virtual Representation (1792)

Virtual representation is that in which there is a communion of interests, and a sympathy in feelings and desires between those who act in the name of any description of people, and the people in whose name they act, though the trustees are not actually chosen by them. This is virtual representation. Such a representation I think to be, in many cases, even better than the actual. It possesses most of its advantages, and is free from any of its inconveniences; it corrects the irregularities in the literal representation, when the shifting current of human affairs, or the acting of public interests in different ways, carry it obliquely from its first line of direction. The people may err in their choice; but common interest and common sentiment are rarely mistaken.

A Letter to Sir Hercules Langrishe, MP

19   Edmund Burke, Parliament as Representative of National Interest (1774)

Parliament is not a *congress* of ambassadors from different and hostile interests; which interests each must maintain, as an agent and advocate, against other agents and advocates; but parliament is a *deliberative* assembly of *one* interest, that of the whole; where, not local purposes, not local prejudices, ought to guide, but the general good, resulting from the general reason of the whole. You choose a member indeed; but when you have chosen him, he is not member of Bristol, but he is a member of *parliament*.

Speech at the Conclusion of the Poll

20   James Mill, Sinister Interests (1820)

According to the ideas of Lord Liverpool, the landholders ought to be represented; the merchants and manufacturers ought to be represented; the officers of the army and navy ought to be represented; and the practitioners of the law ought to be represented. Other patrons of the scheme have added, that literary men ought to be represented. And these, we believe, are almost all the fraternities, which have been named for this purpose, by any of the advocates of representation by clubs. To insure the choice of Representatives of the landholders, landholders must be the choosers; to insure the choice of Representatives of the merchants and manufacturers, merchants and manufacturers must be the choosers; and so with respect to the other fraternities, whether few or many. Thus it must be at least in *substance*; whatever the form, under which the visible acts may be performed. According to the scheme in question, these several fraternities are represented *directly*, the rest of the community is *not* represented directly; but it will be said by the patrons of the scheme, that it is represented *virtually*, which, in this case, answers the same purpose.

From what has already been ascertained, it will appear certain, that each of these fraternities has its sinister interest, and will be led to seek the benefit of misrule, if it is able to obtain it. This is frankly and distinctly avowed by Lord Liverpool. And by those by whom it is not avowed, it seems impossible to suppose that it should be disputed.

Essay on Government

21   William Lovett, Working-class Representation
   (*c.*1836)

'Is the *Landholder*, whose interests lead him to keep up his rents
by unjust and exclusive laws, a fit representative for working
men?

'Are the whole host of *Money-makers*, *Speculators*, and *Usurers*,
who live on the corruptions of the system, fit representatives for
the sons of labour?

'Are the immense numbers of *Lords*, *Earls*, *Marquises*, *Knights*,
Baronets, *Honourables*, and *Right Honourables*, who have seats in
that house, fit to represent our interests? Many of whom have
the certainty before them of being the *hereditary legislators* of the
other house, or are the craving expectants of place or emolu-
ment; persons who cringe in the gilded circle of a court, flutter
among the gaieties of the ballroom, to court the passing smile of
Royalty, or whine at the Ministers of the day; and when the
interests of the people are at stake in the Commons are often
found the revelling debauchees of fashion, or the duelling
wranglers of a gambling-house?

'Are the multitude of *Military* and *Naval Officers* in the present
House of Commons, whose interest it is to support that system
which secures them their pay and promotion, and whose only
utility, at any time, is to direct one portion of our brethren to
keep the other in subjection, fit to represent our grievances?'

'Have we fit representatives in the multitude of *Barristers*,
Attorneys, and *Solicitors*, most of them seeking places, and all of
them having interests depending on the dissensions and corruptions of the people? – persons whose prosperity depends on the
obscurity and intricacy of the laws, and who seek to perpetuate
the interests of "*their order*" by rendering them so abstruse and
voluminous that none but *law conjurers* like themselves shall
understand them – persons whose *legal* knowledge (that is, of
fraud and deception) often procures them seats in the Government, and the highest offices corruption can confer?

'Is the *Manufacturer* and *Capitalist*, whose exclusive monopoly
of the combined powers of wood, iron, and steam enables them
to cause the destitution of thousands, and who have an interest
in forcing labour down to the *minimum* reward, fit to represent
the interests of working men?

'Is the *Master*, whose interests it is to purchase labour at the cheapest rate, a fit representative for the *Workman*, whose interest it is to get the most he can for his labour?

'Yet such is the only description of persons composing that house, and such the interests represented, to whom we, session after session, address *our humble petitions*, and whom we in our ignorant simplicity imagine will generously sacrifice their hopes and interests by beginning the great work of political and social reformation.

'Working men, inquire if this be not true, and then if you feel with us, stand apart from all projects, and refuse to be the tools of any party, who will not, as *a first and essential measure*, give to the working classes *equal political and social rights*, so that they may send their own representatives from the ranks of those who live by labour into that house, to deliberate and determine along with *all other interests*, that the interests of the labouring classes – of those who are the foundation of the social edifice – shall not be daily sacrificed to glut the extravagance of the pampered few. If you feel with us, then you will proclaim it in the workshop, preach it in your societies, publish it from town to village, from county to county, and from nation to nation, that there is no hope for the sons of toil, till those who feel with them, who sympathize with them, and whose interests are identified with theirs, have *an equal right to determine what laws shall be enacted or plans adopted for justly governing this country*.'

Life and Struggles

22   Christabel Pankhurst, Representation of Women (1905)

It has been decided to oppose Mr Winston Churchill at the General Election, on the ground that he is a member of the Liberal Government which refuses to give Women the Vote.

The Government is anxious to have freedom for the Chinese in South Africa, but will not give political freedom to British Women.

'The Passive Resisters' are to have satisfaction, but women are not to have the votes which they have been demanding for some half a century.

The working women of the country who are earning starvation wages stand in urgent need of the vote. These helpless workers must have political power. It is all very well to promise cheap bread, but good wages are quite as important as cheap food and unless working women get votes, their wages and conditions of labour cannot be improved. The vote is the worker's best friend. Evidently, the Liberal Government cares nothing about the sufferings of underpaid working women, or else votes for women would have a foremost place on the Government programme.

Suffragette Manifesto, in Unshackled.
The Story of How We Won the Vote

23   Aneurin Bevan, Working–class MPs (1952)

A representative person is one who will act in a given situation in much the same way as those he represents would act in that same situation. In short, he must be of their kind. They may not know the facts as he knows them. Indeed, they cannot expect to do so. In our complicated society there must be division of labour, but that division will operate in an atmosphere of confidence only if those working it are of like mind. Thus a political party which begins to pick its personnel from unrepresentative types is in for trouble. Confidence declines.

Election is only one part of representation. It becomes full representation only if the elected person speaks with the authentic accents of those who elected him. That does not mean he need be provincial, nor that he speaks in the local vernacular. It does mean he should share their values; that is, be in touch with their realities.

In Place of Fear

24   Margaret Thatcher, A Critique of Consensus (lecture delivered in 1979)

In the old days, political writers used to argue about something called 'the protection of minorities'. How could minority groups in a democracy be protected against the majority? Surely the 51 per cent might claim legitimacy for persecution of the 49 per cent? But democracy is about more than majorities. It is about the right of every individual to freedom and justice: a right founded upon the Old and New Testaments, which remind us of the dignity of each individual, his right to choose and his duty to serve. These rights are God-given, not State-given. They are rights which have been evolved and upheld across the centuries by our rule of law: a rule of law which safeguards individuals and minorities; a rule of law which is the cement of a free society.

But what I think we are now seeing is the reverse problem, and we haven't properly faced up to it yet – the problem of the protection of the majority. There has come into existence a fashionable view, convenient to many special interest groups, that there is no need to accept the verdict of the majority: that the minority should be quite free to bully, even coerce, to get the verdict reversed.

Marxists, of course, always had an excuse when they were outvoted: their opponents must have 'false consciousness': their views didn't really count. But the Marxists, as usual, only provide a bogus intellectual top-dressing for groups who seek only their own self-interest.

Plenty of groups operate more simply. They don't care whether they have persuaded their fellow-citizens or not, or whether constitutionally elected Governments undertake properly approved policies. These minorities will coerce the system to meet their own objectives, if we let them get away with it.

Many of the new 'campaigning' pressure groups, run by professionals who move from campaign to campaign – some in the trade unions; some even in parts of the system of Government itself – have seen how our democracy has evolved rules to temper the power of the majority and provide safeguards and rights for the minority. They have spotted that, if minorities bend the rules or simply ignore them, they may succeed in manipulating the whole system. The minority indeed may, in the end, effectively coerce the majority. You may recall that Burke had a phrase for it, as always: 'All that is needed for evil men to triumph is for good men to do nothing.'

Now I hope I won't be thought too provocative if I complain again about the sloppy use of the word 'consensus' in such cases. If there is a national debate and a constitutional vote about some matter, and if a recalcitrant minority says 'the vote be damned, we are going to do our level best to stop the majority having its way', then it's no good saying, 'we must seek consensus, we must negotiate'. Such a group will never consent, whatever the majority thinks, until it gets what it wants. That is when we have to stand up and be counted, that is when we have to do what we believe to be right.

The Revival of Britain

IV
Agreeing to be Governed

In the last chapter we traced the evolution of the originally medieval idea of the representation of groups, of communities and interests. In this chapter we turn to the history of the idea of the representation of individuals. The first section places its origins in seventeenth-century theories of a 'social contract' and, in particular, in the belief in political equality and consent that was inherent in those theories. The second section traces the evolution of this idea of government being legitimized by an original contract into the more radical idea of a universal right to democratic representation. We also illustrate two other important ways in which extensions of the franchise were argued for in the nineteenth century – the utilitarian argument, that democracy most efficiently promotes material contentment; and the argument that the vote is a recognition of the moral worth of each individual. This latter perspective on democracy was especially important both as an argument for reform and as a source of anxiety about extensions of the franchise. If the vote was a badge of moral worthiness, should it be given to those thought morally unworthy?

A.   THE SOCIAL CONTRACT

Until the seventeenth century, the legitimacy of governments was derived either from theology or tradition. Rulers derived their authority to rule from God's will or from the fact of succession to a title. The great change that occurred during the course of the seventeenth century was that people began to look to different sources of legitimacy, to rationality and (what was often seen as the same thing) to 'natural law'. The two most prominent figures who contributed, in very different ways, to this important shift were

Thomas Hobbes (IV:1) and John Locke (IV:2). Both saw government as being founded on 'contract', and explained it in terms of a pre-political 'state of nature' to escape from which men entered into the contract. What they escaped into was political society – the world of rulers, authority and obedience. The state of nature was for both Hobbes and Locke a state of natural equality among men (men only – the 'natural' subjection of women was unquestioned). But neither philosopher drew the conclusion that this natural equality implied the necessity or desirability of democratic structures of government.

Despite these similarities, Hobbes and Locke were in important respects diametrically opposed as political thinkers. Hobbes's political theory was condemned by both sides during the Civil War and he was widely reviled during his lifetime as an atheist. It was only in the nineteenth century that interest in his writing was revived, especially by the utilitarians. Since then, many commentators have been struck by the modernity of his thought, particularly regarding his rationalist view of power and his theory of indivisible sovereignty. Locke, on the other hand, was widely hailed as having provided the philosophical justification for the Revolution of 1688 (though some historians have argued that much of the important work on the *Two Treatises of Government* was done before the Revolution – see Peter Laslett's Introduction to the edition quoted here), and founded a Whig tradition that was to dominate British political thought throughout the eighteenth and well into the nineteenth century. He was an important influence both on the American Founding Fathers and, as we shall see, on the radicalism that blossomed at the time of the French Revolution.

According to Hobbes, before men lived under governments they lived in a 'state of nature', which was a state of natural equality. But this equality was not a source of harmony. It was a cause of perpetual warfare of each upon each, as each man attempted to gain the upper hand over every other. The life of man, in Hobbes's famous phrase, was 'solitary, poor, nasty, brutish and short'. This nightmarish, atomistic world of fear and uncertainty is men's natural condition, the world that men may lapse into without strong government. (It is, of course, significant that Hobbes was writing during the Civil War. *Leviathan*, the book in which his ideas achieve their fullest and most forceful expression, was published in 1651.) To escape this world, and to protect themselves from each other, men have entered into a contract with each other to place themselves under a supreme and absolute authority, a sovereign, who will prevent them all from pursuing their individual, selfish interests. The immediate motivation for agreeing to be governed is thus a rational calculation concerning fear and security. We can see now why Hobbes was attacked by both sides during the Civil War. From the point of view of parliamentarians, he was defending monarchical absolutism, while from the point of view of royalists he was destroying the traditional religious props of monarchical authority and justifying usurpation. (For in Hobbes's brutally realistic theory, men owe allegiance simply to the strongest ruler, the one who can provide the best protection against the potential violence of their fellow men.)

It might be wondered what place Hobbes's justification of absolute rule has in an anthology concerned with democracy. The first point to remember in this regard is that Hobbes's starting point is equality. It is the fact of men's equality that leads them, paradoxically, to place themselves under a supreme authority. Second, although the supreme authority under which men place themselves is not elected, and admits of no right of disobedience (otherwise it would not be sovereign, and thus could not provide the necessary protection), its legitimacy does derive from a kind of consent in the form of that original contract by which men escaped the State of Nature. And third, at the end of the extract quoted here, it will be seen that Hobbes refers to the sovereign power as 'some Man, or Assembly of men'. It is not who holds supreme power that is important so much as the existence of that supreme power. Hobbes's theory could as easily be used to defend parliamentary sovereignty as the sovereignty of a king.

The differences between Hobbes's theory of political authority and that of Locke begin with the contrasting pictures they paint of life in the pre-political, anarchic State of Nature. Unlike Hobbes's picture of perpetual warfare, the actions of men in Locke's State of Nature are circumscribed by a Law of Nature that forbids them from harming each other's 'Life, Health, Liberty, or Possessions'. This Law of Nature is revealed to men through their reason, but derives its authority from the fact that men are not free to dispose of themselves or each other as they wish since, as His creation, they are subject to God. The Natural Law is God's Law. In the State of Nature, each man has the right to enforce the Law of Nature, punishing those who transgress it. It is this 'executive power' of the Law of Nature that leads to 'inconveniences' in the State of Nature, for it leads to men being judges in cases that affect their own interests. It is this partiality that leads men to leave the State of Nature and come together (this is Locke's 'contract') in 'civil society', surrendering their executive power of the Law of Nature to the community. The community, the 'civil society', entrusts this collective executive power to government. The legitimacy of government thus derives from the consent of the governed. But this consent need not be explicit; 'tacit consent' can be given simply by being physically within the territories of a government. If government breaks the trust upon which it is based, then power reverts to the people. There is, then, a right of rebellion against arbitrary and tyrannical rulers.

For all his later influence, Locke's theories were largely a synthesis of earlier writers, and his theory contains a number of ambiguities and potential contradictions – for example, between his empiricism and the remnants of religious dogma in his philosophy, and between proto-socialist and proto-capitalist elements in his theory of property. It is scarcely surprising, therefore, that while some later writers have utterly rejected his idea of government being based on an original contract, others have used it to draw widely differing conclusions. It is with reactions to Locke's theory – and especially with the radical and conservative directions in which it could be pointed – that the rest of this section is concerned.

John Dryden's *Absalom and Achitophel* was written as a poetic attack on the Earl of Shaftesbury, Locke's patron (IV:3). Dryden pours scorn on the Lockean idea that the people retain a right to rebel against their rulers. Another conservative, David Hume (IV:4), directs his scepticism towards the proposition that people obey governments because their ancestors once consented to some original contract. Political obedience, Hume argues, is often established by force, and always maintained by habit. The contrast between the conservative and radical conclusions that could be drawn from the theory of the original contract can be seen most dramatically in the debate between Edmund Burke and Tom Paine in the 1790s. In his *Reflections on the Revolution in France* (IV:5), Burke argues, like Dryden, that the original contract obligates all those who come after, and that the dead, the living and the unborn are bound together 'in the great primaeval contract of eternal society'. Burke's *Reflections* was an attack not just on the French Revolution, but also on those who would seek to give to Whig political thought a radical twist. Foremost among these was Tom Paine, whose *Rights of Man* (IV:6) was written as a reply to Burke's *Reflections*. In the passage quoted here, Paine replies to Burke's argument that the wording of parliamentary statutes passed a hundred years before bound the people in obedience to the sovereign perpetually. As against this conservative idea that consent was irrevocably given once, Paine argues the need for continuous consent and popular sovereignty.

1   Thomas Hobbes, Hobbes's Social Contract (1651)

NATURE hath made men so equall, in the faculties of body, and mind; as that though there bee found one man sometimes manifestly stronger in body, or of quicker mind than another; yet when all is reckoned together, the difference between man, and man, is not so considerable, as that one man can thereupon claim to himselfe any benefit, to which another may not pretend, as well as he. For as to the strength of body, the weakest has strength enough to kill the strongest, either by secret machination, or by confederacy with others, that are in the same danger with himselfe.

And as to the faculties of the mind, (setting aside the arts grounded upon words, and especially that skill of proceeding upon generall, and infallible rules, called Science; which very few have, and but in few things; as being not a native faculty, born with us; nor attained, (as Prudence,) while we look after somewhat els,) I find yet a greater equality amongst men, than that of strength. For Prudence, is but Experience; which equall time, equally bestowes on all men, in those things they equally apply themselves unto. . .

From this equality of ability, ariseth equality of hope in the attaining of our Ends. And therefore if any two men desire the same thing, which neverthelesse they cannot both enjoy, they become enemies; and in the way to their End, (which is principally their owne conservation, and sometimes their delectation only,) endeavour to destroy, or subdue one another. . .

In the nature of man, we find three principall causes of quarrell. First, Competition: Secondly, Diffidence; Thirdly, Glory.

The first, maketh men invade for Gain; the second, for Safety; and the third, for Reputation. The first use Violence, to make themselves Masters of other mens persons, wives, children, and cattell; the second, to defend them; the third, for trifles, as a word, a smile, a different opinion, and any other signe of undervalue, either direct in their Persons, or by reflexion in their Kindred, their Friends, their Nation, their Profession, or their Name.

Hereby it is manifest, that during the time men live without a common Power to keep them all in awe, they are in that condition which is called Warre; and such a warre, as is of every man, against every man. For WARRE, consisteth not in Battell onely, or the act of fighting; but in a tract of time, wherein the Will to contend by Battell is sufficiently known: and therefore the notion of *Time*, is to be considered in the nature of Warre; as it is in the nature of Weather. For as the nature of Foule weather, lyeth not in a showre or two of rain; but in an inclination thereto of many dayes together; So the nature of War, consisteth not in actuall fighting; but in the known disposition thereto, during all the time there is no assurance to the contrary. All other time is PEACE.

Whatsoever therefore is consequent to a time of Warre, where every man is Enemy to every man; the same is consequent to the time, wherein men live without other security, than what their own strength, and their own invention shall furnish them withall. In such condition, there is no place for Industry; because the fruit thereof is uncertain; and consequently no Culture of the Earth, no Navigation, nor use of the commodities that may be imported by Sea; no commodious Building; no Instruments of moving, and removing such things as require much force; no Knowledge of the face of the Earth; no account of Time; no Arts; no Letters; no Society; and which is worst of all, continuall feare, and danger of violent death; And the life of man, solitary, poore, nasty, brutish, and short. . .

The finall Cause, End, or Designe of men, (who naturally love Liberty, and Dominion over others,) in the introduction of that restraint upon themselves, (in which wee see them live in Common-wealths,) is the foresight of their own preservation, and of a more contented life thereby; that is to say, of getting themselves out from that miserable condition of Warre, which is necessarily consequent (as hath been shewn) to the naturall Passions of men, when there is no visible Power to keep them in awe, and tye them by feare of punishment to the performance of their Covenants, and observation of those Lawes of Nature. . .

For the Lawes of Nature (as *Justice, Equity, Modesty, Mercy*, and (in summe) *doing to others, as wee would be done to*,) of themselves, without the terrour of some Power, to cause them to be observed, are contrary to our naturall Passions, that carry us to Partiality, Pride, Revenge, and the like. And Covenants, without the Sword, are but Words, and of no strength to secure a man at all. Therefore notwithstanding the Lawes of Nature (which every one hath then kept, when he has the them, when he can do it safely,) if there be no Power not great enough for our security; every man will lawfully rely on his own strength and art, for caution against all other men. . .

The only way to erect such a Common Power, as may be able to defend them from the invasion of Forraigners, and the injuries of one another, and thereby to secure them in such sort, as that by their owne industrie, and by the fruites of the Earth, they may nourish themselves and live contentedly; is to conferre all their power and strength upon one Man, or upon one Assembly of men, that may reduce all their Wills, by plurality of voices, unto one Will: which is as much as to say, to appoint one Man, or Assembly of men, to beare their Person; and every one to owne, and acknowledge himselfe to be Author of whatsoever he that so beareth their Person, shall Act, or cause to be Acted, in those things which concerne the Common Peace and Safetie; and therein to submit their Wills, every one to his Will, and their Judgements, to his Judgment. . .

And he that carryeth this Person, is called SOVERAIGNE, and said to have *Soveraigne Power*; and every one besides, his SUBJECT.

Leviathan

2 John Locke, Locke's Social Contract (1690)

To understand Political Power right, and derive it from its Original, we must consider what State all Men are naturally in, and that is, a State of perfect Freedom to order their Actions, and dispose of their Possessions, and Persons as they think fit, within the bounds of the Law of Nature, without asking leave, or depending upon the Will of any other Man.

A State also of Equality, wherein all the Power and Jurisdiction is reciprocal, no one having more than another: there being nothing more evident, than that Creatures of the same species and rank promiscuously born to all the same advantages of Nature, and the use of the same faculties, should also be equal one amongst another without Subordination or Subjection, unless the Lord and Master of them all, should by any manifest Declaration of his will set one above another, and confer on him by an evident and clear appointment an undoubted Right to Dominion and Sovereignty. . .

But though this be a *State of Liberty*, yet it is not a *State of Licence*, though Man in that State have an uncontroleable Liberty, to dispose of his Person or Possessions, yet he has not Liberty to destroy himself, or so much as any Creature in his Possession, but where some nobler use, than its bare Preservation calls for it. *The State of Nature* has a Law of Nature to govern it, which obliges every one: And Reason, which is that Law, teaches all Mankind, who will but consult it, that being all equal and independent, no one ought to harm another in his Life, Health, Liberty or Possessions. For Men being all the Workmanship of one Omnipotent, and infinitely wise Maker; All the Servants of one Sovereign Master, sent into the World by his order and about his business, they are his Property, whose Workmanship they are, made to last during his, not one another's Pleasure. . .

And that all Men may be restrained from invading others Rights, and from doing hurt to one another, and the Law of Nature be observed, which willeth the Peace and Preservation of all Mankind, the Execution of the Law of Nature is in that State, put into every man's hands, whereby every one has a right to punish the transgressors of that Law to such a Degree, as may hinder its Violation. For the Law of Nature would, as all other Laws that concern Men in this World, be in vain, if there were no body that in the State of Nature, had a Power to Execute that Law, and thereby preserve the innocent and restrain offenders, and if any one in the State of Nature may punish another, for any evil he has done, every one may do so. For in that *State of perfect Equality*, where naturally there is no superiority or jurisdiction of one, over another, what any may do in Prosecution of that Law, every one must needs have a Right to do. . .

To this strange Doctrine, *viz.* That *in the State of Nature, every one has the Executive Power* of the Law of Nature, I doubt not but it will be objected, That it is unreasonable for Men to be Judges in their own Cases, that Self-love will make Men partial to themselves and their Friends. And on the other side, that Ill Nature, Passion and Revenge will carry them too far in punishing others. And hence nothing but Confusion and Disorder will follow, and that therefore God hath certainly appointed Government to restrain the partiality and violence of Men. I easily grant, that *Civil Government* is the proper Remedy for the Inconveniences of the State of Nature, which must certainly be Great, where Men may be Judges in their own Case, since 'tis easily to be imagined, that he who was so unjust as to do his Brother an Injury, will scarce be so just as to condemn himself for it: But I shall desire those who make this Objection, to remember that *Absolute Monarchs* are but Men, and if Government is to be the Remedy of those Evils, which necessarily follow from Mens being Judges in their own Cases, and the State of Nature is therefore not to be endured, I desire to know what kind of Government that is, and how much better it is than the State of Nature, where one Man commanding a multitude, has the Liberty to be Judge in his own Case, and may do to all his Subjects whatever he pleases, without the least liberty to any one to question or controle those who Execute his Pleasure? And in whatsoever he doth, whether led by Reason, Mistake or Passion, must be submitted to? Much better it is in the State of Nature wherein Men are not bound to submit to the unjust will of another: And if he that judges, judges amiss in his own, or any other Case, he, not is answerable for it to the rest of Mankind. . .

Man being born, as has been proved, with a Title to perfect Freedom, and an uncontrouled enjoyment of all the Rights and Priviledges of the Law of Nature, equally with any other Man, or Number of men in the World, hath by Nature a Power not only to preserve his Property, that is, his Life, Liberty and Estate, against the Injuries and Attempts of other Men; but to judge of, and punish the breaches of that Law in others, as he is perswaded the Offence deserves, even with Death it self, in Crimes where the heinousness of the Fact, in his Opinion, requires it. But because no *Political Society* can be, nor subsist without having in it self the Power to preserve the Property, and in order thereunto punish the Offences of all those of that Society; there, and there only is *Political Society*, where every one of the Members hath quitted this natural Power, resign'd it up into the hands of the Community in all cases that exclude him not from appealing for Protection to the Law established by it. And thus all private judgement of every particular Member being excluded, the Community comes to be Umpire, by settled standing Rules, indifferent, and the same to all Parties; and by Men having Authority from the Community, for the execution of those Rules, decides all the differences that may happen between any Members of that Society, concerning any matter of right; and punishes those Offences, which any

Member hath committed against the Society, with such Penalties as the Law has established: Whereby it is easie to discern who are, and who are not, in *Political Society* together. Those who are united into one Body, and have a common establish'd Law and Judicature to appeal to, with Authority to decide Controversies between them, and punish Offenders, *are in Civil Society* one with another: but those who have no such common Appeal, I mean on Earth, are still in the state of Nature, each being, where there is no other, Judge for himself, and Executioner; which is, as I have before shew'd it, the perfect *state of Nature*. . .

Where-ever therefore any number of Men are so united into one Society, as to quit every one his Executive Power of the Law of Nature, and to resign it to the publick, there and there only is a *Political, or Civil Society*. And this is done where-ever any number of Men, in the state of Nature, enter into Society to make one People, one Body Politick under one Supreme Government, or else when any one joyns himself to, and incorporates with any Government already made. For hereby he authorizes the Society, or which is all one, the Legislative thereof to make Laws for him as the publick good of the Society shall require; to the Execution whereof, his own assistance (as to his own Decrees) is due. And this *puts Men* out of a State of Nature *into* that of a *Commonwealth*, by setting up a Judge on Earth, with Authority to determine all the Controversies, and redress the Injuries, that may happen to any Member of the Commonwealth; which Judge is the Legislative, or Magistrates appointed by it. And where-ever there are any number of Men, however associated, that have no such decisive power to appeal to, there they are still *in the state of Nature*. . .

Every Man being, as has been shewed, *naturally free*, and nothing being able to put him into subjection to any Earthly Power, but only his own Consent; it is to be considered, what shall be understood to be *a sufficient Declaration of* a Mans *Consent, to make him subject* to the Laws of any Government. There is a common distinction of an express and a tacit consent, which will concern our present Case. No body doubts but an *express Consent*, of any man, entring into any Society, makes him a perfect Member of that Society, a Subject of that Government. The difficulty is, what ought to be look'd upon as a *tacit Consent*, and how far it binds, *i.e.* how far any one shall be looked on to have consented, and thereby submitted to any

Government, where he has made no Expressions of it at all. And to this I say, that every Man, that hath any Possession, or Enjoyment, of any part of the Dominions of any Government, doth thereby give his *tacit Consent*, and is as far forth obliged to Obedience to the Laws of that Government, during such Enjoyment, as any one under it; whether this his Possession be of Land, to him and his Heirs for ever, or a Lodging only for a Week; or whether it be barely travelling freely on the Highway; and in Effect, it reaches as far as the very being of any one within the Territories of that Government. . .

The Majority having, as has been shew'd, upon Mens first uniting into Society, the whole power of the Community, naturally in them, may imploy all that power in making Laws for the Community from time to time, and Executing those Laws by Officers of their own appointing; and then the Form of the Government is a perfect *Democracy*: Or else may put the power of making Laws into the hands of a few select Men, and their Heirs or Successors; and then it is an *Oligarchy*: Or else into the hands of one Man, and then it is a *Monarchy*: If to him and his Heirs, it is an *Hereditary Monarchy*: If to him only for Life, but upon his Death the Power only of nominating a Successor to return to them; an *Elective Monarchy*. And so accordingly of these the Community may make compounded and mixed Forms of Government, as they think good. And if the Legislative Power be at first given by the Majority to one or more Persons only for their Lives, or any limited time, and then the Supream Power to revert to them again; when it is so reverted, the Community may dispose of it again anew into what hands they please, and so constitute a new Form of Government. For the *Form of Government depending upon the placing* the Supreme Power, which is the *Legislative*, it being impossible to conceive that an inferiour Power should prescribe to a Superiour, or any but the Supreme make Laws, according as the Power of making Laws is placed, such is the *Form of the Common-wealth*.

By *Common-wealth*, I must be understood all along to mean, not a Democracy, or any Form of Government, but *any Independent Community*.

The Second Treatise on Government

3   John Dryden, Right of Rebellion (1681)

Can people give away,
Both for themselves and sons their native sway?
Then they are left defenceless to the sword
Of each unbounded, arbitrary lord:
And laws are vain, by which we right enjoy,
If king's unquestion'd can those laws destroy.
Yet if the crowd be judge of fit and just,
And kings are only officers in trust,
Then this resuming covenant was declar'd
When kings were made, or is for ever barr'd.
If those who gave the sceptre could not tie
By their own deed their own posterity,
How then could Adam bind his future race?
How could his forfeit on mankind take place?
Or how could heavenly justice damn us all,
Who ne'er consented to our father's fall?
Then kings are slaves to those whom they command
And tenants to their people's pleasure stand.
Add, that the power for property allow'd
Is mischievously seated in the crowd:
For who can be secure of private right,
If sovereign sway may be dissolv'd by might?
Nor is the people's judgment always true:
The most may err as grossly as the few?
And faultless kings run down by common cry,
For vice, oppression, and for tyranny.
What standard is there in a fickle rout,
Which, flowing to the mark, runs faster out?
Nor only crowds but Sanhedrims may be
Infected with this public lunacy,
And share the madness of rebellious times,
To murder monarchs for imagin'd crimes.
If they may give and take whene'er they please,
Not kings alone (the Godhead's images,)
But government itself at length must fall
To nature's state, where all have right to all.
Yet grant our lords the people kings can make,
What prudent men a settled throne would shake?
For whatsoe'er their sufferings were before,
That change they covet makes them suffer more.

All other errors but disturb a state;
But innovation is the blow of fate.
If ancient fabrics nod, and threat to fall,
To patch their flaws, and buttress up the wall,
Thus far 'tis duty; but here fix the mark:
For all beyond it is to touch our ark.
To change foundations, cast the frame anew,
Is work for rebels, who base ends pursue;
At once divine and human laws control,
And mend the parts by ruin of the whole.
The tampering world is subject to this curse,
To physic their disease into a worse.

Absalom and Achitophel

4 David Hume, Of the Original Contract (1748)

As no party, in the present age, can well support itself without a
philosophical or speculative system of principles annexed to its
political or practical one, we accordingly find, that each of the
factions into which this nation is divided has reared up a fabric
of the former kind, in order to protect and cover that scheme of
actions which it pursues. The people being commonly very
rude builders, especially in this speculative way, and more
especially still when actuated by party-zeal, it is natural to
imagine that their workmanship must be a little unshapely, and
discover evident marks of that violence and hurry in which it
was raised. The one party, by tracing up government to the
Deity, endeavoured to render it so sacred and inviolate, that it
must be little less than sacrilege, however tyrannical it may
become, to touch or invade it in the smallest article. The other
party, by founding government altogether on the consent of the
people, suppose that there is a kind of *original contract*, by which
the subjects have tacitly reserved the power of resisting their
sovereign, whenever they find themselves aggrieved by that
authority, with which they have, for certain purposes, voluntarily intrusted him. These are the speculative principles of the two
parties, and these, too, are the practical consequences deduced
from them. . .

When we consider how nearly equal all men are in their

bodily force, and even in their mental powers and faculties, till cultivated by education, we must necessarily allow, that nothing but their own consent could, at first, associate them together, and subject them to any authority. The people, if we trace government to its first origin in the woods and deserts, are the source of all power and jurisdiction, and voluntarily, for the sake of peace and order, abandoned their native liberty, and received laws from their equal and companion. The conditions upon which they were willing to submit, were either expressed, or were so clear and obvious, that it might well be esteemed superfluous to express them. If this, then, be meant by the *original contract*, it cannot be denied, that all government is, at first, founded on a contract, and that the most ancient rude combinations of mankind were formed chiefly by that principle. . .

But philosophers, who have embraced a party (if that be not a contradiction in terms), are not contented with these concessions. They assert, not only that government in its earliest infancy arose from consent, or rather the voluntary acquiescence of the people; but also that, even at present, when it has attained its full maturity, it rests on no other foundation. They affirm, that all men are still born equal, and owe allegiance to no prince or government, unless bound by the obligation and sanction of *a promise*. And as no man, without some equivalent, would forego the advantages of his native liberty, and subject himself to the will of another, this promise is always understood to be conditional, and imposes on him no obligation, unless he meet with justice and protection from his sovereign. These advantages the sovereign promises him in return; and if he fail in the execution, he has broken, on his part, the articles of engagement, and has thereby freed his subject from all obligations to allegiance. Such, according to these philosophers, is the foundation of authority in every government, and such the right of resistance possessed by every subject.

But would these reasoners look abroad into the world, they would meet with nothing that, in the least, corresponds to their ideas, or can warrant so refined and philosophical a system. On the contrary, we find every where princes who claim their subjects as their property, and assert their independent right of sovereignty, from conquest or succession. We find also every where subjects who acknowledge this right in their prince, and suppose themselves born under obligations of obedience to a certain sovereign, as much as under the ties of reverence and duty to certain parents. . .

Almost all the governments which exist at present, or of which there remains any record in story, have been founded originally, either on usurpation or conquest, or both, without any pretence of a fair consent or voluntary subjection of the people. . .

The face of the earth is continually changing, by the increase of small kingdoms into great empires, by the dissolution of great empires into smaller kingdoms, by the planting of colonies, by the migration of tribes. Is there any thing discoverable in all these events but force and violence? Where is the mutual agreement or voluntary association so much talked of?. . .

Should it be said, that, by living under the dominion of a prince which one might leave, every individual has given a tacit consent to his authority, and promised him obedience; it may be answered, that such an implied consent can only have place where a man imagines that the matter depends on his choice. . .

Can we seriously say, that a poor peasant or artisan has a free choice to leave his country, when he knows no foreign language or manners, and lives, from day to day, by the small wages which he acquires? We may as well assert that a man, by remaining in a vessel, freely consents to the dominion of the master; though he was carried on board while asleep, and must leap into the ocean and perish, the moment he leaves her. . .

When we assert, that all lawful government arises from the consent of the people, we certainly do them a great deal more honour than they deserve.

'Of the Original Contract', in *Essays, Moral, Political and Literary*

5 Edmund Burke, The Contract of Eternal Society (1790)

One of the first and most leading principles on which the commonwealth and the laws are consecrated, is lest the temporary possessors and life-renters in it, unmindful of what they have received from their ancestors, or of what is due to their posterity, should act as if they were the entire masters; that they should not think it amongst their rights to cut off the entail, or commit waste on the inheritance, by destroying at their pleasure the whole original fabrick of their society; hazarding to leave to those who come after them a ruin instead of an habitation – and teaching these successors as little to respect their contrivances, as they had themselves respected the institutions of their fore-fathers. By this unprincipled facility of changing the state as often, and as much, and in as many ways, as there are floating fancies or fashions, the whole chain and continuity of the commonwealth would be broken. No one generation could link with the other. Men would become little better than the flies of a summer. . .

Society is indeed a contract. Subordinate contracts for objects of mere occasional interest may be dissolved at pleasure – but the state ought not to be considered nothing better than a partnership agreement in a trade of pepper and coffee, calico or tobacco, or some other such low concern, to be taken up for a little temporary interest, and to be dissolved by the fancy of the parties. It is to be looked on with other reverence; because it is not a partnership in things subservient only to the gross animal existence of a temporary and perishable nature. It is a partner-ship in all science; a partnership in all art; a partnership in every virtue, and in all perfection. As the ends of such a partnership cannot be obtained in many generations, it becomes a partner-ship not only between those who are living, but between those who are living, those who are dead, and those who are to be born. Each contract of each particular state is but a clause in the great primaeval contract of eternal society, linking the lower with the higher natures, connecting the visible and invisible world, according to a fixed compact sanctioned by the inviol-able oath which hold all physical and all moral natures, each in their appointed place. This law is not subject to the will of those, who by an obligation above them, and infinitely super-iour, are bound to submit their will to that law. The municipal corporations of that universal kingdom are not morally at liberty at their pleasure, and on their speculations of a con-tingent improvement, wholly to separate and tear asunder the bands of their subordinate community, and to dissolve it into an unsocial, uncivil, unconnected chaos of elementary principles. It is the first and supreme necessity only, a necessity that is not chosen, but chooses, a necessity paramount to deliberation, that admits no discussion, and demands no evidence, which alone can justify a resort to anarchy. This necessity is no exception to the rule; because this necessity itself is a part too of that moral and physical disposition of things, to which man must be obedient by consent of force: but if that which is only submission to necessity should be made the object of choice, the law is broken, nature is disobeyed, and the rebellious are outlawed, cast forth, and exiled, from this world of reason, and order, and peace, and virtue, and fruitful penitence, into the antagonist world of madness, discord, vice, confusion, and unavailing sorrow.

Reflections on the Revolution in France

6 Thomas Paine, The Need for Continuous Consent (1791)

There never did, there never will, and there never can, exist a Parliament, or any description of men, or any generation of men, in any country, possessed of the right or the power of binding and controuling posterity to the '*end of time*', or of commanding for ever how the world shall be governed, or who shall govern it; and therefore all such clauses, acts or declarations by which the makers of them attempt to do what they have neither the right nor the power to do, nor the power to execute, are in themselves null and void. Every age and generation must be as free to act for itself *in all cases* as the ages and generations which preceded it. The vanity and presumption of governing beyond the grave is the most ridiculous and insolent of all tyrannies. Man has no property in man; neither has any generation a property in the generations which are to follow. The Parliament or the people of 1688, or of any other period, had no more right to dispose of the people of the present day, or to bind or to controul them *in any shape whatever*, than the Parliament or the people of the present day have to dispose of, bind or controul those who are to live a hundred or a thousand years hence. Every generation is, and must be, competent to all the purposes which its occasions require. It is the living, and not the dead, that are to be accommodated. When man ceases to be, his power and his wants cease with him; and having no longer any participation in the concerns of this world, he has no longer any authority in directing who shall be its governors, or how its Government shall be organised, or how administered. . .

I am contending for the rights of the *living*, and against their being willed away, and controuled and contracted for, by the manuscript assumed authority of the dead; and Mr Burke is contending for the authority of the dead over the rights and freedom of the living. . .

Those who have quitted the world, and those who are not yet arrived at it, are as remote from each other as the utmost stretch of mortal imagination can conceive. What possible obligation, then, can exist between them; what rule or principle can be laid down that of two non-entities, the one out of existence and the other not in, and who never can meet in this world, the one should controul the other to the end of time?. . .

A greater absurdity cannot present itself to the understanding of man than what Mr Burke offers to his readers. He tells them, and he tells the world to come, that a certain body of men who existed a hundred years ago, made a law, and that there does not now exist in the Nation, nor ever will, nor ever can, a power to alter it. Under how many subtitles or absurdities has the divine right to govern been imposed on the credulity of mankind!. . .

It requires but a very small glance of thought to perceive that altho' laws made in one generation often continue in force through succeeding generations, yet that they continue to derive their force from the consent of the living. A law not repealed continues in force, not because it *cannot* be repealed, but because it *is not* repealed; and the non-repealing passes for consent. . .

Immortal power is not a human right, and therefore cannot be a right of Parliament. The Parliament of 1688 might as well have passed an act to have authorized themselves to live for ever, as to make their authority live for ever. . .

The circumstances of the world are continually changing, and the opinions of men change also; and as Government is for the living, and not for the dead, it is the living only that has any right in it. That which may be thought right and found convenient in one age may be thought wrong and found inconvenient in another. In such cases, Who is to decide, the living, or the dead?

The Rights of Man

B.   THE RIGHT TO VOTE

It is from the 1790s, influenced by the example of the French Revolution, that we see writers like Paine drawing explicitly radical conclusions from the traditional Whig theory that government is founded upon consent through the original contract. At the end of the first section we illustrated the debate between Burke and Paine as to whether that consent was permanent and binding across the generations, or subject to continual reaffirmation. Closely connected with this issue is the difference between the two as to whether men's 'natural rights' are retained in civil society. According to Burke (IV:7) these rights are necessarily surrendered to government, while Paine (IV:8) argues that they are retained, and indeed enhanced, in the form of 'civil rights'. The importance of this debate here is that it is primarily in terms of a natural and universal right to the vote that proponents of the various extensions of the franchise in the nineteenth and early twentieth centuries have put their case. It lies, for example, behind the demand for universal male suffrage in the People's Charter of 1837 (IV:9). But the conflict between the old idea of the representation of particular interests and the modern, egalitarian idea of the representation of all individuals in fact goes back a long way before the 1790s. We can see it at its most dramatic in the famous Putney Debates of 1647 (IV:10).

In the early nineteenth century, the utilitarians or 'philosophical radicals' explained this individualist basis of government in terms of individual interests. For them, society is no more than the aggregate of the individual interests of its members. Representative government is the means by which individuals ensure that their interests are pursued. John Stuart Mill (IV:11) turns Hobbes's theory on its head by arguing that the vote is a means of protection for the individual against government.

More generally influential than the utilitarians' hard-nosed picture of representative government as a giant calculating machine of individual self-interest has been a vaguer belief that the vote is a recognition of the moral worth of individuals. Thus the debates surrounding the various extensions of the franchise to different groups in society have frequently focussed on moral issues, on whether particular groups or classes are worthy of possession of the vote. Thus in George Eliot's 'Address to Working Men' (IV:12), written in the persona of the eponymous hero of her novel *Felix Holt*, we see an anxiety that the purely political, 'mechanical' reform of the franchise should be accompanied by a deeper, moral reformation. A different perspective on this issue is provided by John Stuart Mill's argument, in *Representative Government* (IV:13) that democracy improves the moral character of the people. A converse view – that it is the character of the people that determines the form of government – is put forward in Samuel Smiles's *Self-Help* (IV:14).

Historically, this connection between the vote and moral character can be seen in the close relationship in the nineteenth century between popular movements calling for extensions of the franchise to the working classes and women, and movements (often arising out of Protestant Non-conformity) calling for moral regeneration in the form of temperance, defence of family life and observation of the sabbath. In his autobiography, for example, the Chartist leader William Lovett pays particular attention to the importance of abstinence from alcohol (IV:15). The close connection between moral reform and popular political radicalism persisted right to the end of the century. Keir Hardie, often regarded as the founder of the Labour Party, first came to prominence as an advocate of temperance.

The idea that the vote constitutes a recognition of the moral worth of the individual can be seen clearly in the campaign for female suffrage. The demand that women have the vote was only one (albeit commonly regarded as the most important) of a number of objectives concerned with challenging society's placing of women in a different, inferior role to men. Feminism did not begin, or end, with the campaign for the vote. An early feminist text like Mary Wollstonecraft's *A Vindication of the Rights of Women* (IV:16) concentrates on the education of women and the improvement of character. But Harriet Taylor Mill (IV:17), writing sixty years later, makes the connection that was to prove so important to the campaign for the vote between the prejudice that assigned to women a separate 'feminine sphere' of activity and the denial to them of the vote. By 1912 this connection between denial of the vote and other forms of male prejudice is being made more angrily by the young Rebecca West (IV:18), directing her scorn at the Liberal leaders like Lloyd George who persisted in blocking women's suffrage. It was the moral aspect of the women's suffrage issue that made for the fervent, crusading character of militant 'suffragettes' such as the Pankhursts (IV:19), who resorted to civil disobedience in support of their campaign.

7   Edmund Burke, Attack on Natural Rights (1790)

If civil society be the offspring of convention, that convention must be its law. That convention must limit and modify all the descriptions of constitution which are formed under it. Every sort of legislature, judicial, or executory power, are its creatures. They can have no being in any other state of things; and how can any man claim, under the conventions of civil society, rights which do not so much as suppose its existence? Rights which are absolutely repugnant to it? One of the first motives to civil society, and which becomes one of its fundamental rules, *is that no man should be judge in his own cause*. By this each person has at once divested himself of the first fundamental right of uncovenanted man, that is, to judge for himself, and to assert his own cause. He abdicates all right to be his own governour. He inclusively, in a great measure, abandons the right of self-defence, the first law of nature. Men cannot enjoy the rights of an uncivil and of a civil state together. That he may obtain justice, he gives up his right of determining, what it is in points the most essential to him. That he may secure some liberty, he makes a surrender in trust of the whole of it. . .

Government is not made in virtue of natural rights. . . Government is a contrivance of human wisdom to provide for human *wants*. Men have a right that these wants should be provided for by this wisdom. Among these wants is to be reckoned the want, out of civil society, of a sufficient restraint upon their passions. Society requires not only that the passions of individuals should be subjected, but that even in the mass and body, as well as in the individuals, the inclinations of men should frequently be thwarted, their will controuled, and their passions brought into subjection. This can only be done *by a power out of themselves*; and not, in the exercise of its function, subject to that will and to those passions which it is its office to bridle and subdue. In this sense the restraints on men, as well as their liberties, are to be reckoned among their rights. But as the liberties and the restrictions vary with times and circumstances, and admit of infinite modifications, they cannot be settled upon any abstract rule; and nothing is so foolish as to discuss them upon that principle.

Reflections on the Revolution in France

8   Thomas Paine, Defence of Natural Rights (1791)

The illuminating and divine principle of the equal rights of man (for it has its origin from the Maker of man) relates, not only to the living individuals, but to generations of men succeeding each other. Every generation is equal in rights to the generations which preceded it, by the same rule that every individual is born equal in rights with his contemporary.

Every history of the creation, and every traditionary account, whether from the lettered or unlettered world, however they may vary in their opinion or belief of certain particulars, all agree in establishing one point, *the unity of man*; by which I mean that men are all of *one degree*, and consequently that all men are born equal, and with equal natural rights, in the same manner as if posterity had been continued by *creation* instead of *generation*, the latter being only the mode by which the former is carried forward; and consequently every child born into the world must be considered as deriving its existence from God. The world is as new to him as it was to the first man that existed, and his natural right in it is of the same kind. . .

Hitherto we have spoken only (and that but in part) of the natural rights of man. We have now to consider the civil rights of man, and to show how the one originates from the other. Man did not enter into society to become *worse* than he was before, not to have fewer rights than he had before, but to have those rights better secured. His natural rights are the foundation of all his civil rights. But in order to pursue this distinction with more precision, it will be necessary to mark the different qualities of natural and civil rights.

A few words will explain this. Natural rights are those which appertain to man in right of his existence. Of this kind are all the intellectual rights, or rights of the mind, and also all those rights of acting as an individual for his own comfort and happiness, which are not injurious to the natural rights of others. Civil rights are those which appertain to man in right of his being a member of society. Every civil right has for its foundation some natural right pre-existing in the individual, but to the enjoyment of which his individual power is not, in all cases, sufficiently competent. Of this kind are all those which relate to security and protection.

From this short view it will be easy to distinguish between that class of natural rights which man retains after entering into society and those which he throws into the common stock as a member of society.

The natural rights which he retains are all those in which the *power* to execute it is as perfect in the individual as the right itself. Among this class, as is before mentioned, are all the intellectual rights, or rights of the mind; consequently religion is one of those rights. The natural rights which are not retained, are all those in which, though the right is perfect in the individual, the power to execute them is defective. They answer not his purpose. A man, by natural right, has a right to judge in his own cause; and so far as the right of the mind is concerned, he never surrenders it. But what availeth it him to judge, if he has not power to redress? He therefore deposits this right in the common stock of society, and takes the arm of society, of which he is a part, in preference and in addition to his own. Society grants him nothing. Every man is a proprietor in society, and draws on the capital as a matter of right.

The Rights of Man

9 The People's Charter of 1837

1. A vote for every man twenty one years of age, of sound mind, and not undergoing punishment for crime.

2. THE BALLOT – To protect the elector in the exercise of his vote.

3. NO PROPERTY QUALIFICATION for members of Parliament – thus enabling the constituencies to return the man of their choice, be he rich or poor.

4. PAYMENT OF MEMBERS, thus enabling an honest tradesman, working man, or other person, to serve a constituency, when taken from his business to attend to the interests of the country.

5. EQUAL CONSTITUENCIES, securing the same amount of representation for the same number of electors – instead of allowing small constituencies to swamp the votes of larger ones.

6. ANNUAL PARLIAMENTS, thus presenting the most effectual check to bribery and intimidation, since though a constituency might be bought once in seven years (even with the ballot), no purse could buy a constituency (under a system of universal suffrage)

in each ensuing twelvemonth; and since members when elected for a year only, would not be able to defy and betray their constituents as now.

10   The Right to Vote (1647)

RAINBOROUGH: I think that the poorest he that is in England hath a life to live, as the greatest he; and therefore truly, sir, I think it's clear, that every man that is to live under a government ought first by his own consent to put himself under that government; and I do think that the poorest man in England is not at all bound in a strict sense to that government that he hath not had a voice to put himself under; and I am confident that, when I have heard the reasons against it, something will be said to answer those reasons, insomuch that I should doubt whether he was an Englishman or no, that should doubt of these things

IRETON: . . . For my part, I think it is no right at all. I think that no person hath a right to an interest or share in the disposing of the affairs of the kingdom, and in determining or choosing those that shall determine what laws we shall be ruled by here – no person hath a right to this, that hath not a permanent fixed interest in this kingdom, and those persons together are properly the represented of this kingdom, and consequently are [also] to make up the representers of this kingdom, who taken together do comprehend whatsoever is of real or permanent interest in the kingdom. And I am sure otherwise I cannot tell what any man can say why a foreigner coming in amongst us – or as many as will coming in amongst us, or by force or otherwise settling themselves here, or at least by our permission having a being here – why they should not as well lay claim to it as any other. We talk of birthright. Truly [by] birthright there is thus much claim. Men may justly have by birthright, by their very being born in England, that we should not seclude them out of England, that we should not refuse to give them air and place and ground, and the freedom of the highways and other things, to live amongst us – not any man that is born here, though by his birth there come nothing at all (that is part of the permanent interest of this kingdom) to him. That I think is due to a man by birth. But that by a man's being born here he shall have a share in that power that shall dispose of the lands here, and of all things here, I do not think it a sufficient ground. I am sure if we look upon that which is the utmost (within [any] man's view) of what was originally the constitution of this kingdom, upon that which is most radical and fundamental, and which if you take away, there is no man hath any land, any goods, [or] any civil interest, that is this: that those that choose the represeners for the making of laws by which this state and kingdom are to be governed, are the persons who, taken together, do comprehend the local interest of this kingdom; that is, the persons in whom all land lies, and those in corporations in whom all trading lies. This is the most fundamental constitution of this kingdom and [that] which if you do not allow, you allow none at all. This constitution hath limited and determined it that only those shall have voices in elections. . .

RAINBOROUGH: . . . I do hear nothing at all that can convince me, why any man that is born in England ought not to have his voice in election of burgesses. It is said that if a man have not a permanent interest, he can have no claim; and [that] we must be no freer than the laws will let us be, and that there is no [law in any] chronicle will let us be freer than that we [now] enjoy. Something was said to this yesterday. I do think that the main cause why Almighty God gave men reason, it was that they should make use of that reason, and that they should improve it for that end and purpose that God gave it them. And truly, I think that half a loaf is better than none if a man be hungry: [this gift of reason without other property may seem a small thing], yet I think there is nothing that God hath given a man that any [one] else can take from him. And therefore I say, that either it must be the Law of God or the law of man that must prohibit the meanest man in the kingdom to have this benefit as well as the greatest. I do not find anything in the Law of God, that a lord shall choose twenty burgesses, and a gentleman but two, or a poor man shall choose none: I find no such thing in the Law of Nature, nor in the Law of Nations.

The Putney Debates

11   John Stuart Mill, The Vote as a Means of Self-protection (1861)

The ideally best form of government, it is scarcely necessary to say, does not mean one which is practicable or eligible in all states of civilisation, but the one which, in the circumstances in which it is practicable and eligible, is attended with the greatest amount of beneficial consequences, immediate and prospective. A completely popular government is the only polity which can make out any claim to this character. It is pre-eminent in both the departments between which the excellence of a political constitution is divided. It is both more favourable to present good government, and promotes a better and higher form of national character, than any other polity whatsoever.

Its superiority in reference to present well-being rests upon two principles, of as universal truth and applicability as any general propositions which can be laid down respecting human affairs. The first is, that the rights and interests of every or any person are only secure from being disregarded when the person interested is himself able, and habitually disposed, to stand up for them. The second is, that the general prosperity attains a greater height, and is more widely diffused, in proportion to the amount and variety of the personal energies enlisted in promoting it.

Putting these two propositions into a shape more special to their present application; human beings are only secure from evil at the hands of others in proportion as they have the power of being, and are, self-*protecting*; and they only achieve a high degree of success in their struggle with Nature in proportion as they are self-*dependent*, relying on what they themselves can do, either separately or in concert, rather than on what others do for them.

The former proposition – that each is the only safe guardian of his own rights and interests – is one of those elementary maxims of prudence, which every person, capable of conducting his own affairs, implicitly acts upon, wherever he himself is interested. Many, indeed, have a great dislike to it as a political doctrine, and are fond of holding it up to obloquy, as a doctrine of universal selfishness. To which we may answer, that whenever it ceases to be true that mankind, as a rule, prefer themselves to others, and those nearest to them to those more remote, from that moment Communism is not only practicable, but the only defensible form of society; and will, when that time arrives, be assuredly carried into effect. For my own part, not believing in universal selfishness, I have no difficulty in admitting that Communism would even now be practicable among *the élite* of mankind, and may become so among the rest.

But as this opinion is anything but popular with those defenders of existing institutions who find fault with the doctrine of the general predominance of self-interest, I am inclined to think they do in reality believe that most men consider themselves before other people. It is not, however, necessary to affirm even thus much in order to support the claim of all to participate in the sovereign power. We need not suppose that when power resides in an exclusive class, that class will knowingly and deliberately sacrifice the other classes to themselves: it suffices that, in the absence of its natural defenders, the interest of the excluded is always in danger of being overlooked; and, when looked at, is seen with very different eyes from those of the persons whom it directly concerns.

Representative Government

12   George Eliot, The Need for Moral Improvement (1866)

FELLOW-WORKMEN, – I am not going to take up your time by complimenting you. It has been the fashion to compliment kings and other authorities when they have come into power, and to tell them that, under their wise and beneficent rule, happiness would certainly overflow the land. But the end has not always corresponded to that beginning. If it were true that we who work for wages had more of the wisdom and virtue necessary to the right use of power than has been shown by the aristocratic and mercantile classes, we should not glory much in that fact, or consider that it carried with it any near approach to infallibility.

In my opinion, there has been too much complimenting of that sort; and whenever a speaker, whether he is one of ourselves or not, wastes our time in boasting or flattery, I say, let us hiss him. If we have the beginning of wisdom, which is, to know a little truth about ourselves, we know that as a body we are neither very wise nor very virtuous. And to prove this, I will not point specially to our own habits and doings, but to the general state of the country. Any nation that had within it a majority of men – and we are the majority – possessed of much wisdom and virtue would not tolerate the bad practices, the commercial lying and swindling, the poisonous adulteration of goods, the retail cheating, and the political bribery which are carried on boldly in the midst of us. A majority has the power of creating a public opinion. We could groan and hiss before we had the franchise: if we had groaned and hissed in the right place, if we had discerned better between good and evil, if the multitude of us artisans, and factory hands, and miners, and labourers of all sorts, had been skilful, faithful, well-judging, industrious, sober – and I don't see how there can be wisdom and virtue anywhere without those qualities – we should have made an audience that would have shamed the other classes out of their share in the national vices. We should have had better members of Parliament, better religious teachers, honester tradesmen, fewer foolish demagogues, less impudence in infamous and brutal men; and we should not have had among us the abomination of men calling themselves religious while living in splendour on ill-gotten gains. I say, it is not possible for any society in which there is a very large body of wise and virtuous men to be as vicious as our society is – to have as low a standard of right and wrong, to have so much belief in falsehood, or to have so degrading, barbarous a notion of what pleasure is, or of what justly raises a man above his fellows. Therefore, let us have done with this nonsense about our being much better that the rest of our countrymen, or the pretence that that was a reason why we ought to have such an extension of the franchise as has been given to us. The reason for our having the franchise, as I want presently to show, lies somewhere else than in our personal good qualities, and does not in the least lie in any high betting chance that a delegate is a better man than a duke, or that a Sheffield grinder is a better man than any one of the firm he works for.

Felix Holt (Appendix A)

11 John Stuart Mill, Democracy as a Means of Improvement (1861)

If we ask ourselves on what causes and conditions good government in all its senses, from the humblest to the most exalted, depends, we find that the principal of them, the one which transcends all others, is the qualities of the human beings composing the society over which the government is exercised.

We may take, as a first instance, the administration of justice; with the more propriety, since there is no part of public business in which the mere machinery, the rules and contrivances for conducting the details of the operation, are of such vital consequence. Yet even these yield in importance to the qualities of the human agents employed. Of what efficacy are rules of procedure in securing the ends of justice, if the moral condition of the people is such that the witnesses generally lie, and the judges and their subordinates take bribes? Again, how can institutions provide a good municipal administration if there exists such indifference to the subject that those who would administer honestly and capably cannot be induced to serve, and the duties are left to those who undertake them because they have some private interest to be promoted? Of what avail is the most broadly popular representative system if the electors do not care to choose the best member of parliament, but choose him who will spend most money to be elected? How can a representative assembly work for good if its members can be bought, or if their excitability of temperament, uncorrected by public discipline or private self-control, makes them incapable of calm deliberation, and they resort to manual violence on the floor of the House, or shoot at one another with rifles?. . .

The first element of good government, therefore, being the virtue and intelligence of the human beings composing the community, the most important point of excellence which any form of government can possess is to promote the virtue and intelligence of the people themselves. . .

We may consider, then, as one criterion of the goodness of a government, the degree in which it tends to increase the sum of good qualities in the governed, collectively and individually; since, besides that their well-being is the sole object of government, their good qualities supply the moving force which works the machinery. This leaves, as the other constituent element of the merit of a government, the quality of the machinery itself; that is, the degree in which it is adapted to take advantage of the amount of good qualities which may at any time exist, and make them instrumental to the right purposes. . .

All government which aims at being good is an organisation of some part of the good qualities existing in the individual members of the community for the conduct of its collective affairs. A representative constitution is a means of bringing the general standard of intelligence and honesty existing in the community, and the individual intellect and virtue of its wisest members, more directly to bear upon the government, and investing them with greater influence in it, than they would in general have under any other mode of organisation; though, under any, such influence as they do have is the source of all good that there is in the government, and the hindrance of every evil that there is not. The greater the amount of these good qualities which the institutions of a country succeed in organising, and the better the mode of organisation, the better will be the government.

Representative Government

14   Samuel Smiles, Democracy as a Result of Improvement (1859)

'Heaven helps those who help themselves' is a well-tried maxim, embodying in a small compass the results of vast human experience. The spirit of self-help is the root of all genuine growth in the individual; and, exhibited in the lives of many, it constitutes the true source of national vigour and strength. Help from without is often enfeebling in its effects, but help from within invariably invigorates. Whatever is done *for* men or classes, to a certain extent takes away the stimulus and necessity of doing for themselves; and where men are subjected to over-guidance and over-government, the inevitable tendency is to render them comparatively helpless.

Even the best institutions can give a man no active help. Perhaps the most they can do is, to leave him free to develop himself and improve his individual condition. But in all times men have been prone to believe that their happiness and well-being were to be secured by means of institutions rather than by their own conduct. Hence the value of legislation as an agent in human advancement has usually been much over-estimated. To constitute the millionth part of a Legislature, by voting for one or two men once in three or five years, however conscientiously this duty may be performed, can exercise but little active influence upon any man's life and character. Moreover, it is every day becoming more clearly understood, that the function of Goverment is negative and restrictive, rather than positive and active; being resolvable principally into protection – protection of life, liberty, and property. Laws, wisely administered, will secure men in the enjoyment of the fruits of their labour, whether of mind or body, at a comparatively small personal sacrifice; but no laws, however stringent, can make the idle industrious, the thriftless provident, or the drunken sober. Such reforms can only be effected by means of individual action, economy, and self-denial; by better habits, rather than by greater rights.

The Goverment of a nation itself is usually found to be but the reflex of the individuals composing it. The Government that is ahead of the people will inevitably be dragged down to their level, as the Government that is behind them will in the long run be dragged up. In the order of nature, the collective character of a nation will as surely find its own level. The noble people will be nobly ruled, and the ignorant and corrupt ignobly. Indeed all experience serves to prove that the worth and strength of a State depend far less upon the form of its institutions than upon the character of its men. For the nation is only an aggregate of individual conditions, and civilization itself is but a question of the personal improvement of the men, women, and children of whom society is composed.

Self-Help

15   William Lovett, Temperance and the Working Man (1876)

Seeing, also, the great deterioration that is fast going on among the rising generation owing to most of their recreations and amusements being connected with public-houses, which have spread so extensively within these few years throughout the length and breadth of the land; and seeing, too, the great obstacles in the way of progress which the drinking habits of our people occasion, you should above all things aim to remedy this monstrous evil; and to secure rational and healthful amusements for the young, apart from the means of intoxication. Taking into account the physical and mental injury produced by the poisonous intoxicating compounds drunk by our people, the vast amount of social misery they occasion, and the great extent of vice and crime that can be clearly traced to their use,

you should not fail to consider and weigh the consequences of
this great evil, socially and politically, and the great waste of
capital it occasions. . . Who can fail to perceive that drunken-
ness is a great obstacle in the way of progress, socially and
politically? In your trade associations and unions, tipplers and
drunkards are the first to shirk their payments, to mar your
peaceful objects by their brawls and misconduct; the first to
desert your cause and go over to the enemy; and otherwise by
their drunken conduct, and neglect of home and children, to
bring disgrace upon the general body. *Politically*, they are even
worse enemies to progress, as their love of drink drowns all
regard for the welfare of their country; causes them to seize with
avidity the bribe of the enemy, and to be ready tools to fight, or
drown by noisy clamour, the best efforts for the improvement
of their country, for a paltry modicum of drink. These evils
should awaken the most thoughtful among you to a sense of
duty, and should induce you to band yourselves together
to discountenance in your fellows this love of drink, and to
join in all efforts for removing this great temptation from
among you.

Life and Struggles

16 Mary Wollstonecraft, The Education of Women (1792)

My own sex, I hope, will excuse me, if I treat them like rational
creatures, instead of flattering their *fascinating* graces, and
viewing them as if they were in a state of perpetual childhood,
unable to stand alone. I earnestly wish to point out in what true
dignity and human happiness consists – I wish to persuade
women to endeavour to acquire strength, both of mind and
body, and to convince them that the soft phrases, susceptibility
of heart, delicacy of sentiment, and refinement of taste, are
almost synonymous with epithets of weakness, and that those
beings who are only the objects of pity and that kind of love,
which has been termed its sister, will soon become objects of
contempt.

Dismissing, then, those pretty feminine phrases, which the
men condescendingly use to soften our slavish dependence, and
despising the weak elegancy of mind, exquisite sensibility, and

sweet docility of manners, supposed to be the sexual characteristics of the weaker vessel, I wish to shew that elegance is
inferior to virtue, that the first object of laudable ambition is to
obtain a character as a human being, regardless of the distinction
of sex; and that secondary views should be brought to this
simple touchstone. . .

The education of women has, of late, been more attended to
than formerly; yet they are still reckoned a frivolous sex, and
ridiculed or pitied by the writers who endeavour by satire or
instruction to improve them. It is acknowledged that they spend
many of the first years of their lives in acquiring a smattering of
accomplishments; meanwhile strength of body and mind are
sacrificed to libertine notions of beauty, to the desire of
establishing themselves, – the only way women can rise in the
world, – by marriage. And this desire making mere animals of
them, when they marry they act as such children may be
expected to act: – they dress; they paint, and nickname God's
creatures. Surely these weak beings are only fit for a seraglio! –
Can they be expected to govern a family with judgement, or
take care of the poor babes whom they bring into the world?

A Vindication of the Rights of Woman

17   Harriet Taylor Mill, The Enfranchisement of Women (1851)

That women have as good a claim as men have, in point of
personal right, to the suffrage, or to a place in the jury-box, it
would be difficult for any one to deny. It cannot certainly be
denied by the United States of America, as a people or as a
community. Their democratic institutions rest avowedly on the
inherent right of every one to a voice in the government. Their
Declaration of Independence, framed by the men who are still
their great constitutional authorities – that document which has
been from the first, and is now, the acknowledged basis of their
polity, commences with this express statement:

We hold these truths to be self-evident: that all men are created
equal; that they are endowed by their Creator with certain
inalienable rights; that among these are life, liberty, and the

pursuit of happiness; that to secure these rights, governments are instituted among men, deriving their just powers from the consent of the governed.

We do not imagine that any American democrat will evade the force of these expressions by the dishonest or ignorant subterfuge, that 'men', in this memorable document, does not stand for human beings, but for one sex only; that 'life, liberty, and the pursuit of happiness' are 'inalienable rights' of only one moiety of the human species; and that 'the governed', whose consent is affirmed to be the only source of just power, are meant for that half of mankind only, who, in relation to the other, have hitherto assumed the character of governors. The contradiction between principle and practice cannot be explained away. . .

When a prejudice, which has any hold on the feelings, finds itself reduced to the unpleasant necessity of assigning reasons, it thinks it has done enough when it has re-asserted the very point in dispute, in phrases which appeal to the pre-existing feeling. Thus, many persons think they have sufficiently justified the restrictions on women's field of action, when they have said that the pursuits from which women are excluded are *unfeminine*, and that the *proper sphere* of women is not politics or publicity, but private and domestic life.

We deny the right of any portion of the species to decide for another portion, or any individual for another individual, what is and what is not their 'proper sphere'. The proper sphere for all human beings is the largest and highest which they are able to attain to. What this is, cannot be ascertained, without complete liberty of choice. . . Let every occupation be open to all, without favour or discouragement to any, and employments will fall into the hands of those men or women who are found by experience to be most capable of worthily exercising them. There need be no fear that women will take out of the hands of men any occupation which men perform better than they. Each individual will prove his or her capacities, in the only way in which capacities can be proved – by trial; and the world will have the benefit of the best faculties of all its inhabitants. But to interfere beforehand by an arbitrary limit, and declare that whatever be the genius, talent, energy, or force of mind of an individual of a certain sex or class, those faculties shall not be exerted, or shall be exerted only in some few of the many modes in which others are permitted to use theirs, is not only an injustice to the individual, and a detriment to society, which loses what it can ill spare, but is also the most effectual mode of providing that, in the sex or class so fettered, the qualities which are not permitted to be exercised shall not exist. . .

The real question is, whether it is right and expedient that one-half of the human race should pass through life in a state of forced subordination to the other half. If the best state of human society is that of being divided into two parts, one consisting of persons with a will and a substantive existence, the other of humble companions to these persons, attached, each of them to one, for the purpose of bringing up *his* children, and making *his* home pleasant to him; if this is the place assigned to women, it is but kindness to educate them for this; to make them believe that the greatest good fortune which can befall them, is to be chosen by some man for this purpose; and that every other career which the world deems happy or honourable, is closed to them by the law, not of social institutions, but of nature and destiny.

When, however, we ask why the existence of one-half the species should be merely ancillary to that of the other – why each woman should be a mere appendage to a man, allowed to have no interests of her own, that there may be nothing to compete in her mind with his interests and his pleasure; the only reason which can be given is, that men like it. It is agreeable to them that men should live for their own sake, women for the sake of men: and the qualities and conduct in subjects which are agreeable to rulers, they succeed for a long time in making the subjects themselves consider as their appropriate virtues.

On the Enfranchisement of Women

18   Rebecca West, Male Prejudice (1912)

(*Rebecca West reports on an attack on suffragette protesters by the crowd at a rally for Lloyd George in Llanystumdwy.*)

This callousness should teach suffragettes two lessons. Firstly, that they cannot win their cause by mere virtuosic exhibitions of courage. Courage requires an audience of heroes. If Gladys Evans dies in Mountjoy Prison as a result of being forcibly fed, the public would stand it. There is no limit to what the public – the great mass of tired, weak souls, broken and killed by the capitalist struggle – will stand. It might make a certain amount of stir if that bloodthirsty stutterer, Mr J. L. Garvin, could so far subdue his natural loathing for suffragettes as to use them as a weapon against the Liberals. And the perception of this callousness should make us the more determined, if the more calm, to take a share in government. Since men take the assault of women so calmly we may judge that their self-sought task of the legislative protection of women will be done without zeal.

The second lesson is one for men. It never seems to strike men that a party which renounced the principle of liberty, when dealing with women, might renounce them when dealing with men. When Lewis Harcourt told the working women of Rossendale Valley that he would not give them votes because he did not believe they were as fit for self-government as his wife, it never struck the voters of Rossendale Valley that their member had confessed his disbelief in democracy.

It never struck them when the Government insulted women, gave them false promises, and shut them up in prison on faked charges and forcibly fed them, that this was not a firm with which an honest man would deal.

Then one morning the working men of England are dumb with amazement when they find that the Insurance Act is a fraud and the instrument of fraudulent societies, and a very ugly and deliberate device to break trade-unionism. Even since then they have voted for the Liberal at Crewe and Hanley and Cardiff and Midlothian. Perhaps now it will seem to them that a party led by a gentleman who turns his eyes up and thinks beautiful thoughts while his supporters light-heartedly hurl women over hedges can't be much good.

But this incident is of more than political interest. It is typical in the bitter thoughts which it must arouse in every woman of the disturbance in the relationship between men and women which this repression of the suffragette movement has brought about. It is a fact, minimised by the good nature of everyone concerned, that the present structure of society automatically compels women to be oppressed by men. The social liberty of a respectable woman is circumscribed by the vices of men. A woman who wishes to go about London alone by night or to look into shop windows in Bond Street in the afternoon encounters unpleasantness due to the accidents of the man-made social system. There is even an idea that women should regulate their dress according to men's lack of self-control rather than

their own comfort. The Vicar of Lee, for instance, is always
hoisting distress signals in the parish magazine (I presume, at the
spiritual state of his male parishioners) begging women not to
wear tight skirts because of their effect on men. He abstains
from considering the fact that it is more comfortable for a
woman to walk with two and a half yards of stuff hanging from
her hips than with five.

And at the back of these little, worrying interferences there is
the great economic grievance of women: that they are not given
equal pay for equal work, that they are not allowed equal
opportunities of education and profession.

The Young Rebecca. Writings of Rebecca West 1911–17

19 Christabel Pankhurst, The Suffragette Movement (1904)

Militancy really began on 20 February 1904, at a first Free Trade
Hall meeting with a protest of which little was heard and
nothing remembered – because it did not result in imprisonment!

The Free Trade League, a renaissance of the Anti-Corn Law
organization, had announced its initial meeting in the Free
Trade Hall to be addressed by Mr Winston Churchill. I applied
for a ticket and received one for the platform. This was excellent
for my purpose. Mr Churchill moved that 'this meeting affirms
its unshakable belief in the principles of Free Trade adopted
more than fifty years ago. . .', others had seconded and supported the resolution, when, as related by the *Manchester
Guardian*:

> Miss Pankhurst asked to be allowed to move an amendment
> with regard to Woman Suffrage. The Chairman said he was
> afraid he could not permit such an addition. It contained
> words and sentiments on a matter more or less contentious to
> which persons absolutely agreed on the question of Free Trade
> might have difficulty in giving their support. Miss Pankhurst
> seemed loth to give way, but finally, amid loud cries of
> 'Chair', she retired. The Chairman read the addition which
> Miss Pankhurst proposed to make to the resolution which

asked that the Representation of the People Acts should be so amended that the words importing the masculine gender should include women. He was sorry, he said, that he must adhere to his decision not to put it.

This was the first militant step – the hardest to me, because it was the first. To move from my place on the platform to the speaker's table in the teeth of the astonishment and opposition of will of that immense throng, those civic and county leaders and those Members of Parliament, was the most difficult thing I have ever done.

Something had been gained. Women's claim to vote had been imposed upon the attention of political leaders and the public, at one of the decisive political meetings of the century. The trouble was that the thought of woman suffrage quickly faded. I reproached myself for having given way too easily. Next time such a meeting was held, a mark should be made that could not disappear. Thus militancy had its origin in purpose.

We were now urging that the next Liberal Government, confidently predicted by Liberals themselves, should grant women the vote. . .

As the year 1905 went on, the Liberal Party was more clearly in the ascendant and the Liberal leaders counted upon early political office. Manchester – the Free Trade Hall – was again to be the scene of a rally at which the Liberal Party would utter their war cry for the General Election. Here was my chance! I would make amends for my weakness in not pressing that earlier amendment! Now there should be an act the effect of which would remain, a protest not of word but of deed. Prison this time! Prison would mean a fact that could not fade from the record, a proof of women's political discontent, a demonstration that the political subjection of women rested not on women's consent but on *force majeure* used to impose and enforce it. . .

Good seats were secured for the Free Trade Hall meeting. The question was painted on a banner in large letters, in case it should not be made clear enough by vocal utterance. How should we word it? 'Will you give woman suffrage?' – we rejected that form, for the word Suffrage suggested to some unlettered or jesting folk the idea of suffering. 'Let them suffer away!' – we had heard the taunt. We must find another wording and we did! It was so obvious and yet, strange to say, quite new. Our banner bore this terse device:

WILL YOU GIVE
VOTES
FOR WOMEN?

Thus was uttered for the first time the famous and victorious battle-cry: 'Votes for Women!'.

Unshackled. The Story of How We Won the Vote

V
Parties and Elections

In most people's minds at the present day, democracy is inextricably associated with party activity and elections dominated by party competition. Most too would accept party politics as at least a necessary evil, the necessary means towards desirable democratic goals. Despite this, distrust of political parties has permeated the historical discussion of representative institutions. This chapter will illustrate this persistent scepticism, but it will also trace the developing defence and acceptance of parties, in the first instance parties in Parliament and later mass extra-parliamentary parties. It will look also at the changing character of elections and at modern demands for further electoral reform.

A. AGAINST AND FOR PARTIES

In his *Social Contract*, Rousseau argued the incompatibility of political factions and democracy. Divisive political parties and party contention would, he thought, inhibit the emergence of a popular general will. This suspicion of factions was common also in eighteenth-century Britain. Factions, competing for control of government, whether in the context of court politics or parliamentary politics, were commonly seen as inevitably self-interested and sectarian. They were thought to produce a breed of politicians incapable of conceiving the general interest and unwilling to pursue it. The persistence of this distrust can be seen in the distaste which is still often attached to the phrase, 'party politics', and also in the attractiveness to many people of appeals for a 'national', non-party, government in moments of crisis. In both the world wars of the twentieth century, Britain abandoned party politics in favour of such 'national', coalition governments.

Attacks upon parties have taken all sorts of forms. On the side of ridicule are Jonathan Swift writing in the early eighteenth century and Hilaire Belloc writing in the early twentieth. Swift mocks the folly of party conflicts – high-heelers against low-heelers, big-enders against little-enders – but grimly notes the slaughter of Lilliputians that flowed from these meaningless disputes (V:1). Belloc, writing after an election in which a Liberal displaced a Conservative government, pithily hints at the lack of any difference but name between the parties (V:2).

Much earlier, Francis Bacon had more soberly urged on princes that, although they could and should not ignore the activities of factions within the state, they should try to remain independent of them (V:3). The same advice, not to try to govern through a party or faction, was given by Bolingbroke to his Patriot King (V:4). Both Bacon and Bolingbroke believed that rulers could not maintain an impartial pursuit of the general good if they relied on factional support and committed themselves to factional objectives. A similar argument was placed in a democratic context by Jeremy Bentham who, attacking the party battle of his day between Whigs and Tories as an empty struggle between the 'Ins' and 'Outs', argued that a truly democratic representative assembly would eschew party politics and thereby become capable of expressing the general interest of the people at large (V:5).

Maine's acid picture of the party politician has appealed to many in this century in Britain and elsewhere (V:6). The view of the party politician as morally corrupt and politically cowardly has been used as a stick with which to beat competitive party systems and as a means of support for authoritarian movements which assume that political probity and valour and truthfulness can flourish only in the absence of party attachments. The linking of a critique of pluralist party systems with support for authoritarian regimes has been made from another and different standpoint, the Marxist. John Strachey, writing in the 1930s from this perspective, thus combined an attack upon party competition in Britain and America with praise for the one-party system of the Soviet Union of his day (V:7).

Suspicion of parties, factions, party competition and party politicians has, then, been endemic in the British debate. Nevertheless, parties of one sort or another have operated within British politics since the end of the seventeenth century and, by the present day, it is generally accepted that the party battle is a necessary condition of representative democracy. The classic defence of parties, repeated many times since, was put by Burke in 1770 in his *Thoughts on the*

Cause of the Present Discontents (V:8). Burke was a spokesman for the Rockingham Whigs, a parliamentary group or 'connexion' which was out of power when he wrote this pamphlet. Much of the work relates to the politics of the time, but it does widen out into a general defence of parties in the context of the system of checks and balances created by the Glorious Revolution. In this defence, he had to face directly the distrust of factions, and more specifically the general suspicion that systematic opposition to the King's government smacked of treason. He had to face too the general admiration for the independence of connection of a politician like Chatham with his standard of 'Not men but measures'. The defence offered is complex, but essentially is based on three propositions; that the House of Commons existed as a control over the administration, that it could exercise such control only if it had within it political groups actively opposing administration with criticism and alternative policies, and that the serious politician will realize the need for combination with like-minded persons if he is to play any kind of effective political role. Audaciously, he tried to turn the distrust of faction on its head by attacking George III's administrations as government by factions.

By the early nineteenth century, much of the substance of Burke's argument had been generally accepted. The taint of treason that had clung to organized opposition to His Majesty's Government had disappeared, as can be seen by the approval in 1826 on all sides of the designation of the opposition as 'His Majesty's Opposition' (V:9). The incorporation of the Opposition into the formal structure of Parliament has been greatly extended since 1826. The position of Leader of the Opposition has, for instance, been formally recognized and is financed out of public funds, and the Opposition party, through its whips, plays a large part in the organization and conduct of parliamentary business. Whether or not Opposition parties now constitute an adequate check upon government is a controversial question, as has been seen in Chapter II.

1   Jonathan Swift, Parties in Lilliput (1726)

For, said he, as flourishing a condition as we appear to be in to foreigners, we labour under two mighty evils; a violent faction at home, and the danger of an invasion by a most potent enemy from abroad. As to the first, you are to understand, that for above seventy moons past, there have been two struggling parties in the empire, under the names of *Tramecksan* and

Slamecksan, from the high and low heels on their shoes, by which they distinguish themselves. It is alleged indeed, that the high heels are most agreeable to our ancient constitution: but however this be, his Majesty hath determined to make use of only low heels in the administration of the government and all offices in the gift of the crown, as you cannot but observe; and particularly, that his Majesty's imperial heels are lower at least by a *drurr* than any of his court; (*drurr* is a measure about the fourteenth part of an inch). The animosities between these two parties run so high, that they will neither eat nor drink, nor talk with each other. We compute the *Tramecksan*, or High-Heels, to exceed us in number; but the power is wholly on our side. We apprehend his Imperial Highness, the heir to the crown, to have some tendency towards the High-Heels; at least we can plainly discover one of his heels higher than the other, which gives him a hobble in his gait. Now, in the midst of these intestine disquiets, we are threatened with an invasion from the island of Blefuscu, which is the other great empire of the universe, almost as large and powerful as this of his Majesty. For as to what we have heard you affirm, that there are other kingdoms and states in the world, inhabited by human creatures as large as yourself, our philosophers are in much doubt, and would rather conjecture that you dropped from the moon, or one of the stars; because it is certain, that an hundred mortals of your bulk would, in a short time, destroy all the fruits and cattle of his Majesty's dominions. Besides, our histories of six thousand moons make no mention of any other regions, than the two great empires of Lilliput and Blefuscu. Which two mighty powers have, as I was going to tell you, been engaged in a most obstinate war for six and thirty moons past. It began upon the following occasion. It is allowed on all hands, that the primitive way of breaking eggs before we eat them, was upon the larger end: but his present Majesty's grandfather, while he was a boy, going to eat an egg, and breaking it according to the ancient practice, happened to cut one of his fingers. Whereupon the Emperor his father published an edict, commanding all his subjects, upon great penalties, to break the smaller end of their eggs. The people so highly resented this law, that our histories tell us there have been six rebellions raised on that account; wherein one emperor lost his life, and another his crown. These civil commotions were constantly fomented by the monarchs of Blefuscu; and when they were quelled, the exiles always fled for refuge to that empire. It is computed, that eleven thousand persons have, at several times, suffered death, rather than submit to break their eggs at the smaller end. Many hundred large volumes have been published upon this controversy: but the books of the Big-Endians have been long forbidden, and the whole party rendered incapable by law of holding employments. During the course of these troubles, the emperors of Blefuscu did frequently expostulate by their ambassadors, accusing us of making a schism in religion, by offending against a fundamental doctrine of our great prophet Lustrog, in the fifty-fourth chapter of the Brundecral (which is their Alcoran). This, however, is thought to be a mere strain upon the text: for the words are these; That all true believers shall break their eggs at the convenient end: and which is the convenient end, seems, in my humble opinion, to be left to every man's conscience, or at least in the power of the chief magistrate to determine. Now the Big-Endian exiles have found so much credit in the Emperor of Blefuscu's court, and so much private assistance and encouragement from their party here at home, that a bloody war hath been carried on between the two empires for six and thirty moons with various success; during which time we have lost forty capital ships, and a much greater number of smaller vessels, together with thirty thousand of our best seamen and soldiers; and the damage received by the enemy is reckoned to be somewhat greater than ours. However, they have now equipped a numerous fleet, and are just preparing to make a descent upon us; and his Imperial Majesty, placing great confidence in your valour and strength, hath commanded me to lay this account of his affairs before you.

Gulliver's Travels

2 Hilaire Belloc, On a General Election (n.d.)

The accursèd power which stands on Privilege
(and goes with Women, and Champagne and Bridge)
Broke – and Democracy resumed her reign:
(Which goes with Bridge, and Women and Champagne).

'On a General Election'

3   Francis Bacon, Government by Faction (1597)

Many have an opinion not wise, that for a prince to govern his estate or for a great person to govern his proceedings according to the respect of factions, is a principal part of policy: whereas contrariwise, the chiefest wisdom is either in ordering those things which are general, and wherein men of several factions do nevertheless agree, or in dealing with correspondence to particular persons, one by one. But I say not that the consideration of factions is to be neglected. Mean men, in their rising, must adhere; but great men, that have strength in themselves, were better to maintain themselves indifferent and neutral. Yet even in beginners, to adhere so moderately, as he be a man of the one faction which is most passable with the other, commonly giveth best way.

'Of Faction'

4   Lord Bolingbroke, Party as a Political Evil (1738)

To espouse no party, but to govern like the common father of his people, is so essential to the character of a PATRIOT KING, that he who does otherwise forfeits the title. It is the peculiar privilege and glory of this character, that princes who maintain it, and they alone, are so far from the necessity, that they are not exposed to the temptation, of *governing by a party*: which must always end in the government of a *faction*; the faction of the *prince* if he has ability, the faction of *his ministers* if he has not, and either one way or other in the oppression of the people. For *faction* is to *party* what the *superlative* is to the *positive*: *party* is a political evil, and *faction* is the worst of all *parties*.

The Idea of a Patriot King

5 Jeremy Bentham, A Radical Approach on Parties (1824)

The interests of the subject many being sacrificed to those of the ruling few on every occasion when the two compete, it is the constant object of study and endeavour on the part of the ruling few to preserve and extend the existing mass of abuse. Such, at any rate, is their constant propensity.

In the mass of abuse which it is their interest to defend, there is a portion from which they derive a direct and assignable profit, and also another portion from which they do not derive such profit. Now the mischievousness of the portion from which they do not derive any profit cannot be exposed except by bringing to light facts and observations which would apply also to that portion from which they do derive direct and particular profit. Thus it is that in every community all men who are in power, that is, the *Ins*, are constantly engaged by self-regarding interest in the maintenance of abuse in every shape in which they find it established.

But whatever the *Ins* have in possession, the *Outs* have in expectancy. Thus far, therefore, there is no distinction between the sinister interests of the *Ins* and those of the *Outs*, nor, consequently, in the fallacies which they employ in the support of their respective sinister interests.

The Handbook of Political Fallacies

6 Sir Henry Maine, The Corrupt Party Politician (1885)

Let us imagine some modern writer, with the unflinching perspicacity of a Machiavelli, analysing the great Party Hero – leader or agitator – as the famous Italian analysed the personage equally interesting and important in his day, the Tyrant or Prince. Like Machiavelli, he would not stop to praise or condemn on ethical grounds: 'he would follow the real truth of things rather than an imaginary view of them'. 'Many Party Heroes', he would say, 'have been imagined, who were never seen or known to exist in reality'. But he would describe them as they really were. Allowing them every sort of private virtue, he would deny that their virtues had any effect on their public conduct, except so far as they helped to make men believe their public conduct virtuous. But this public conduct he would find to be not so much immoral as non-moral. He would infer, from actual observation, that the party Hero was debarred by his position from the full practice of the great virtues of veracity, justice, and moral intrepidity. He could seldom tell the full truth; he could never be fair to persons other than his followers and associates; he could rarely be bold except in the interests of his faction. The picture drawn by him would be one which few living men would deny to be correct, though they might excuse its occurrence in nature on the score of moral necessity. And then, a century or two later, when Democracies were as much forgotten as the Italian Princedoms, our modern Machiavelli would perhaps be infamous and his work a proverb of immorality.

Popular Government

7 John Strachey, A Working Class Party (1936)

We have not yet described one of the most important of the political institutions of working class democracy. This institution plays an essential part both in the workers' rule over society as a whole during the period of the transition from capitalism to socialism and in the mobilization of the whole population for the continuous economic, social and cultural development of the community, once the foundations of socialism have been laid.

This instrument is a new type of political party. The working class, both in its struggles against capitalism and during its struggle to maintain and secure its own rule after the abolition of capitalism, is forced by the very conditions of these struggles to evolve a new type of political organization, known as a working class party. We say advisedly that this is a new type of political organization, for although it is described by the old term 'party', it has in reality very little resemblance to the familiar political parties of such countries as Britain and America. (It may, indeed, be a pity that some new term has not been devised to describe this new political entity. For to English and American ears the term party has come almost to imply the existence of another party, to carry with it the suggestion of electoral competition between organizations designed to catch the maximum number of votes in elections; and nothing could be much further than this from the conception of 'the party', as that conception has been developed in the international working class movement.)

The working class conception of a party, is on the contrary, that of an organization which comprises all the most active, intelligent, conscientious and politically conscious members of the working class. It is the essential political organization of the workers as a class, just as the Trade Unions are, as we saw, the essential economic and sectional organizations of the workers, as engineers, miners, spinners, weavers, or dockers. . .

A working class political party, of which the Russian Communist party is the first fully developed example, is naturally not wholly different from the political organizations which the capitalist class has always formed for the exercise of its rule. For the capitalist class habitually rules by means of one or more political parties, even though these capitalist parties are far less fully and consciously developed organizations for making effective the will of a given class than is a workers' party. The British governing class, for example, has always maintained and still maintains its rule quite as much by means of its political parties, or party, as by means of its king, law courts, parliaments and state apparatus.

The British capitalists have now, to all intents and purposes, followed the example of the Russian workers in creating one unified party for the expression of the will of their class. In the past in Britain, and even now in America, the capitalists have organized two or more political parties, usually representing sub-divisions of their class, with differing interests on particular points, to carry on their rule in alternating periods of office (e.g. the Conservative and Liberal parties in Great Britain, the Republican and Democratic parties in America).

The Theory and Practice of Socialism

8 Edmund Burke, In Defence of Parties (1770)

The house of commons was supposed originally to be *no part of the standing government of this country*. It was considered as a *controul*, issuing *immediately* from the people, and speedily to be resolved into the mass from whence it arose. . .

The virtue, spirit, and essence of a house of commons consists in its being the express image of the feelings of the nation. It was not instituted to be a controul *upon* the people, as of late it has been taught, by a doctrine of the most pernicious tendency. It was designed as a controul *for* the people. Other institutions have been formed for the purpose of checking popular excesses; and they are, I apprehend, fully adequate to their object. . .

He that supports every administration, subverts all government. The reason is this: The whole business in which a court usually takes an interest goes on at present equally well, in whatever hands, whether high or low, wise or foolish, scandalous or reputable; there is nothing therefore to hold it firm to any one body of men, or to any one consistent scheme of politicks. Nothing interposes, to prevent the full operation of all the caprices and all the passions of a court upon the servants of the publick. The system of administration is open to continual shocks and changes, upon the principles of the meanest cabal, and the most contemptible intrigue. Nothing can be solid and permanent. . .

Government may in a great measure be restored, if any considerable bodies of men have honesty and resolution enough never to accept administration, unless this garrison of *king's men*, which is stationed, as in a citadel, to controul and enslave it, be entirely broken and disbanded, and every work they have thrown up be levelled with the ground. . .

This cabal has, with great success, propagated a doctrine which serves for a colour to those acts of treachery; and whilst it receives any degree of countenance, it will be utterly senseless to look for a vigorous opposition to the court party. The doctrine is this: That all political connexions are in their nature factious, and as such ought to be dissipated and destroyed; and that the rule for forming administrations is mere personal ability, rated by the judgment of this cabal upon it, and taken by draughts from every division and denomination of publick men. . .

It is indeed in no way wonderful, that such persons should make such declarations. That connexion and faction are equivalent terms, is an opinion which has been carefully inculcated at all times by unconstitutional statesmen. The reason is evident. Whilst men are linked together, they easily and speedily communicate the alarm of any evil design. They are enabled to fathom it with common counsel, and to oppose it with united strength. Whereas, when they lie dispersed, without concert, order, or discipline, communication is uncertain, counsel difficult, and resistance impracticable. Where men are not acquainted with each other's principles, nor experienced in each other's talents, nor at all practised in their mutual habitudes and dispositions by joint efforts in business; no personal confidence, no friendship, no common interest, subsisting among them; it is evidently impossible that they can act a publick part with uniformity, perseverance, or efficacy. In a connexion, the most inconsiderable man, by adding to the weight of the whole, has his value, and his use; out of it, the greatest talents are wholly unserviceable to the publick. No man, who is not inflamed by vain-glory into enthusiasm, can flatter himself that his single, unsupported, desultory, unsystematick endeavours, are of power to defeat the subtle designs and united cabals of ambitious citizens. When bad men combine, the good must associate; else they will fall, one by one, an unpitied sacrifice in a contemptible struggle. . .

I do not wonder that the behaviour of many parties should have made persons of tender and scrupulous virtue somewhat out of humour with all sorts of connexion in politicks. I admit that people frequently acquire in such confederacies a narrow, bigotted, and proscriptive spirit; that they are apt to sink the idea of the general good in this circumscribed and partial interest. But where duty renders a critical situation a necessary one, it is our business to keep free from the evils attendant upon it. . .

Of such a nature are connexions in politicks; essentially necessary for the full performance of our publick duty, accidentally liable to degenerate into faction. Commonwealths are made of families, free commonwealths of parties also; and we may as well affirm, that our natural regards and ties of blood tend inevitably to make men bad citizens, as that the bonds of our party weaken those by which we are held to our country. . .

Party is a body of men united, for promoting by their joint endeavours the national interest, upon some particular principles in which they are all agreed. For my part, I find it impossible to conceive, that any one believes in his own politicks, or thinks them to be of any weight, who refuses to adopt the means of having them reduced into practice. It is the business of the speculative philosopher to mark the proper ends

of government. It is the business of the politician, who is the
philosopher in action, to find out proper means towards those
ends, and to employ them with effect. Therefore every honourable connexion will avow it is their first purpose, to pursue
every just method to put the men who hold their opinions into
such a condition as may enable them to carry their common
plans into execution, with all the power and authority of the
state. . .

It is an advantage to all narrow wisdom and narrow morals,
that their maxims have a plausible air; and, on a cursory view,
appear equal to first principles. They are light and portable.
They are as current as copper coin; and about as valuable. They
serve equally the first capacities and the lowest; and they are, at
least, as useful to the worst men as to the best. Of this stamp is
the cant of *Not men but measures*; a sort of charm by which many
people get loose from every honourable engagement. . .

Thoughts on the Cause of the Present Discontents

9   His Majesty's Opposition (1826)

The Chancellor of the Exchequer moved that the report of
the Committee of the whole House on the Civil List Act
be now received. Mr *Hobhouse* said, he would take that
opportunity. . .to enter his protest against that proceeding, and
to express his astonishment that his majesty's ministers should
have chosen that very peculiar time for proposing one of the
most uncalled for acts that could be conceived – that of making
an unnecessary addition to the burthens of the country, and to
the number of placement and pensioners now sitting in the
House of Commons. . . It was said to be very hard on his
majesty's ministers to raise objections to this proposition. For
his own part, he thought it was more hard on his majesty's
opposition [a laugh] to compel them to take this course. . . He
thought that his majesty's ministers had made use of the right
hon. gentleman's character in a way they ought not to have
done; namely for the purpose of carrying an improper
measure. . .

Mr Secretary *Canning* said. . .that the opportunity was not
selected by his majesty's government neither did the suggestion

emanate from them. It originated, not from his majesty's
government, but from those whom the hon. gentleman had
designated his majesty's opposition [a laugh]. . . If the government did not stir in this matter, some gentleman on the other
side of the House would take it up [hear]. . . He therefore
rebutted the charge of looking out to increase the number of
placemen in that House. . . But confessing that, in his opinion,
the influence of the Crown needed not in this respect to be
enlarged, he wished the House to look to the opposite
extreme. . . He knew of no law by which the Crown was at
present bound to select its ministers from either or both Houses
of Parliament. . .the king might send to any two private
gentlemen, offering to make one of them his secretary of state,
and the other his prime minister. . . He had, however, never
heard any gentleman say in that House that he thought such a
mode of conducting government a good one for the country.
The presence of government officers then became only a
question of degree, which was not to be met by any plan for
counting heads, but by the general views and immediate
character of the government itself. . . Though there was no rule
of law to require the Crown to choose its servants from
Parliament, was there not good sense in the practice? Was this
not a most useful check to the choosing of ministers upon a
system of mere favouritism?. . .

Mr *Tierney*. . .begged the House to consider the plain and
simple question which they were called upon to decide was this
– whether the salary of the President of the Board of Trade
should be £2,000 or £5,000 a year. . . What that had to do with
the influence of the Crown generally it might be for the right
hon. gentleman opposite to explain. He [Mr T] could not. . .
An hon. friend near him had called the opposition the 'king's
opposition'. The propriety of this appellation had been recognized by gentlemen on the other side; and indeed it could not be
disputed. From his personal experience, he could bear testimony to the truth of the designation. . . For years he had
opposed the measures of government, because he disapproved
of their principles; but when they changed their tone, had not
been backward in giving them his feeble support. My hon.
friend [continued Mr Tierney] could not have invented a better
phrase to designate us. . .for we are certainly to all intents and
purposes, a branch of his majesty's government. Its proceedings
for some time past have proved, that though the gentleman

opposite are in office, we are in power. The measures are ours but all the emoluments are theirs [cheers, and laughter].

. . . The right hon. gentleman. . .has declared that the government is in no want of such supporters as it may gain from this measure. I differ from him widely. I think that the government do want support. I never saw a session when they wanted it more. The right hon. gentleman may not be aware of the full extent of his obligations to this side of the House; but I can assure him, that if, as he asserts, he would not consent to stay in office with a pitiful majority of twenty, he would, without our support, have been long ago driven from his present honours. If we take away our support, out he must go tomorrow. . . I mean to consider the proposition as a compliment to the right hon. gentleman [Huskisson] for I am not convinced that his office ought permanently to be a cabinet office. . . I feel myself bound. . .to oppose this attempt to make the Presidency of the Board of Trade a substantive office. . . I am equally opposed to the miserable project for reducing the salary of the Treasurer of the Navy. . .in order that it may be given to somebody for support in this House. . .

The House divided Ayes 87 Noes 76. Majority for receiving the report 11. Mr Secretary *Canning* expressed his regret that the smallness of the majority would prevent him from persevering in a course which. . .he had conscientiously supported. . . As it seemed to be the wish of the House, they would consent to the union of the ancient office of Treasurer of the Navy with that of the President of the Board of Trade. . .

Mr *Tierney* rose. . .to assure his majesty's Government that they had, by this act, justly earned the approbation of 'his majesty's Opposition'.

Parliamentary Debates, N.S. (Hansard)

B. PARTIES AND ELECTIONS

There is a two-way relationship between electoral systems and party systems. On the one side, the nature of the electoral system – who has the vote, how constituencies are defined, how winners are decided – affects deeply the structure and behaviour and likely success of the parties in contention. At the same time, at any rate in the British case, it is governing parties that make decisions on electoral law and clearly those decisions are likely to be based at least in part on calculations of party advantage, although in the nineteenth century this was very far from an exact science. As a consequence, successive electoral reforms in the nineteenth century had profound effects on the party system and more recently those who had wished to restructure the party system have looked to electoral reform as a means.

The dramatic, and also the farcical, potential of elections made them a fertile source for nineteenth-century novelists. One of the best-known accounts of an election in English literature – Dickens's story of the Eatanswill election – throws light dramatically but exactly on the nature of parties and elections in the period before the 1832 Reform Act (V:10). Because of the variety of electoral arrangements in the parliamentary boroughs at this time, Eatanswill cannot be said to be typical. There were, for instance, some boroughs – the so-called rotten boroughs – where there were no electors and so no elections; MPs were nominated by the owners of the land on which the defunct boroughs had stood. In other boroughs, local notables, again generally landowners, could exert a decisive influence particularly since elections were open, in other words voters cast their notes unshielded by a secret ballot. But Eatanswill may be seen as a mirror of a large number of boroughs. The election is presented as a party contest between the Blues and the Buffs but there is no party organization in the borough. The candidates have simply declared their own attachments, the agents are their own personal agents, the electors are offered not party policies but beer and parasols, there is no intrusion of any sort of national party organization.

Elections of the Eatanswill sort implied that parties were what Burke envisaged and indeed advocated, purely parliamentary groupings of like-minded men. What happened over a long period was that these loose parliamentary 'connections', to use Burke's phrase, became more and more structured and disciplined parliamentary groups and developed more and more complex national and extra-parliamentary organizations, stretching down to the constituencies, involved in the nomination of candidates and working for a national party cause.

The 1832 Reform Act prompted some moves in these directions, although only slowly and falteringly. Given the decline in the Crown's ability to mount support in the Commons for its chosen ministers, party leaders had to try to create their own support; and, given the complexity of the property qualifications introduced by the Act, this required intervention from the centre to control the nomination of candidates and to create some organization at constituency level to monitor and manipulate the registration of voters on the electoral rolls. A glimpse into this emergent party world is given by Trollope in his novel, *Phineas Finn* (V:11). In some ways, the post-Reform Act world Trollope describes is not too different from the unreformed world. Loughshane is a small borough with a small electorate, like Eatanswill, but with a dominant local notable. Only quarrels within his family have altered political possibilities in the borough. Although Phineas Finn was born in Loughshane, his standing as a parliamentary candidate is fixed up in a London club. This is the scenario of mid-century politics, the use of political clubs – the Reform in this case, the Carlton in the case of the Tory connection – as a means of providing some central direction of local party activity. This loose and informal type of organization was gradually tightened and both Liberals and Conservatives developed national unions of local party committees.

It was, however, the 1867 Reform Act that was the main impetus to the formation of new types of party organization. The very considerable extension of the urban electorate achieved by that act required new methods of social and political discipline. As Ostrogorski, an acute and influential French observer, noted at the turn of the century, the breakdown of old hierarchies and social ties had been countered at least in the political sphere by the creation of extra-parliamentary, mass-membership parties incorporating and organizing the newly enfranchised electoral masses (V:12). By this time both the Liberal and the Conservative parties had constructed such a mass base, but these mass parties were the creation of pre-existing parliamentary groups and were called into existence as a means of winning elections, not as a means by which a mass membership could control party leadership or even influence its policies. A different conception of party was involved at least in the rhetoric of the newly formed socialist and labour parties that emerged around the turn of the century. As the programme of the Independent Labour Party showed, the party presented itself as consisting basically in the mass membership, united in a commitment to specific socialist objectives and seeking local and parliamentary representation solely as a way of attaining the ends of the party in the country at large (V:13).

Ostrogorski and others at the time he was writing feared that this new political order, a world of populist parties, might be unable to provide the stability and continuity being lost with the decay of older social disciplines. As has been seen, these fears were exaggerated and the emergence of mass parties has had in many ways the opposite effect of strengthening the dominance of the party leadership (and of the government when the party is in power).

There have been a number of different responses to these develop-ments. One has been demands for greater intra-party democracy. Another in recent years has been a revival of demands for electoral reform, more specifically for the introduction of an electoral process which would allow for the better representation in the Commons of opinions and movements outside the two major parties, a closer relationship between votes cast for particular parties and the number of seats they win. This has resulted in pressure for the replacement of the present system of single-member constituencies under the first-past-the-post rule (that is, that the candidate with the largest number of votes wins even if he or she does not have an absolute majority of the votes cast) by some form of proportional representation. Propo-sals of this sort were put forward sporadically during the nineteenth century, were examined by a Commons committee of inquiry in 1918 and have re-entered the political debate in the post-war era. A variety of arguments have been put forward in support – the unfairness and democratic illegitimacy of present arrangements, the need to provide minorities with means of self-expression and self-protection, and, an argument increasingly heard, the need to break the political duopoly of the major parties which has accommodated, even encouraged, the emergence of 'executive dictatorship'. This last complaint points to what many opponents of proportional repre-sentation see as one of the most pressing reasons for the retention of the present system, that it usually brings about a strong one-party government even when no one party has an absolute electoral majority. Recently, a British political scientist, Vernon Bogdanor, himself a supporter of proportional representation, has put forward the pros and cons of this system (V:14). It is interesting that what he suggests as the chief virtue of proportional representation, its encour-agement of power-sharing and consensual politics, was, as we have seen, anathema to Mrs Thatcher (see III:28).

10   Charles Dickens, The Eatanswill Election (1836/7)

It appears, then, that the Eatanswill people, like the people of many other small towns, considered themselves of the utmost and most mighty importance, and that every man in Eatanswill, conscious of the weight that attached to his example, felt himself bound to unite, heart and soul, with one of the two great parties that divided the town – the Blues and the Buffs.

Now the Blues lost no opportunity of opposing the Buffs, and
the Buffs lost no opportunity of opposing the Blues; and the
consequence was, that whenever the Buffs and Blues met
together at public meeting, Town-Hall, fair, or market, disputes and high words arose between them. With these dissensions it is almost superfluous to say that everything in
Eatanswill was made a party question. If the Buffs proposed
to new skylight the market-place, the Blues got up public
meetings, and denounced the proceeding; if the Blues proposed the erection of an additional pump in the High Street,
the Buffs rose as one man and stood aghast at the enormity.
There were Blue shops and Buff shops and Blue inns and Buff
inns; there was a Blue aisle and a Buff aisle, in the very church
itself.

Of course it was essentially and indispensably necessary that
each of these powerful parties should have its chosen organ and
representative: and, accordingly, there were two newspapers in
the town – the Eatanswill Gazette and the Eatanswill Independent; the former advocating Blue principles, and the latter
conducted on grounds decidedly Buff. Fine newspapers they
were. Such leading articles, and such spirited attacks! – 'Our
worthless contemporary, the Gazette' – 'That disgraceful and
dastardly journal, the Independent' – 'That false and scurrilous
print, the Independent' – 'That vile and slanderous calumniator,
the Gazette' – these, and other spirit-stirring denunciations were
strewn plentifully over the columns of each, in every number,
and excited feelings of the most intense delight and indignation
in the bosoms of the townspeople.

Mr Pickwick, with his usual foresight and sagacity, had
chosen a peculiarly desirable moment for his visit to the
borough. Never was such a contest known. The Honourable
Samuel Slumkey, of Slumkey Hall, was the Blue candidate; and
Horatio Fizkin Esq, of Fizkin Lodge, near Eatanswill, had been
prevailed upon by his friends to stand forward on the Buff
interest. The Gazette warned the electors of Eatanswill that the
eyes not only of England, but of the whole civilised world, were
upon them; and the Independent imperatively demanded to
know, whether the constituency of Eatanswill were the grand
fellows they had always taken them for, or base and servile
tools, undeserving alike of the name of Englishmen and the
blessings of freedom. Never had such a commotion agitated the
town before.

It was late in the evening, when Mr Pickwick and his companions, assisted by Sam, dismounted from the roof of the Eatanswill coach. Large blue silk flags were flying from the windows of the Town Arms Inn, and bills were posted in every sash, intimating, in gigantic letters, that the honourable Samuel Slumkey's Committee sat there daily. A crowd of idlers were assembled in the road, looking at a hoarse man in the balcony, who was apparently talking himself very red in the face in Mr Slumkey's behalf; but the force and point of whose arguments were somewhat impaired by the perpetual beating of four large drums which Mr Fizkin's committee had stationed at the street corner. There was a busy little man beside him, though, who took off his hat at intervals and motioned to the people to cheer, which they regularly did, most enthusiastically; and as the red-faced gentleman went on talking till he was redder in the face than ever, it seemed to answer his purpose quite as well as if anybody had heard him.

The Pickwickians had no sooner dismounted, than they were surrounded by a branch mob of the honest and independent, who forthwith set up three deafening cheers, which being responded to by the main body (for it's not at all necessary for a crowd to know what they are cheering about) swelled into a tremendous roar of triumph, which stopped even the red-faced man in the balcony.

'Hurrah!' shouted the mob in conclusion.

'One cheer more,' screamed the little fugleman in the balcony, and out shouted the mob again, as if lungs were cast iron, with steel works.

'Slumkey for ever!' roared the honest and independent.

'Slumkey for ever!' echoed Mr Pickwick, taking off his hat.

'No Fizkin!' roared the crowd.

'Certainly no!' shouted Mr Pickwick.

'Hurrah!' And then there was another roaring, like that of a whole menagerie when the elephant has rung the bell for the cold meat.

'Who is Slumkey?' whispered Mr Tupman.

'I don't know,' replied Mr Pickwick in the same tone. 'Hush. Don't ask questions. It's always best on these occasions to do what the mob do.'

'But suppose there are two mobs?' suggested Mr Snodgrass.

'Shout with the largest.' replied Mr Pickwick.

Volumes could not have said more.

They entered the house, the crowd opening right and left to let them pass, and cheering vociferously. The first object of consideration was to secure quarters for the night.

'Can we have beds here?' inquired Mr Pickwick, summoning the waiter.

'Don't know, sir,' replied the man; 'afraid we're full, sir – I'll inquire, sir.' Away he went for that purpose, and presently returned, to ask whether the gentlemen were 'Blue'.

As neither Mr Pickwick nor his companions took any vital interest in the cause of either candidate, the question was rather a difficult one to answer. In this dilemma Mr Pickwick bethought himself of his new friend, Mr Perker.

'Do you know a gentleman of the name of Perker?' inquired Mr Pickwick.

'Certainly, sir; honourable Mr Samuel Slumkey's agent.'

'He is Blue, I think?'

'Oh yes, sir.'

'Then we are Blue,' said Mr Pickwick; but observing that the man looked rather doubtful at this accommodating announcement, he gave him his card, and desired him to present it to Mr Perker forthwith, if he should happen to be in the house. The waiter retired; and re-appeared almost immediately with a request that Mr Pickwick would follow him, led the way to a large room on the first floor, where, seated at a long table covered with books and papers, was Mr Perker.

'Ah – ah, my dear sir,' said the little man, advancing to meet him; 'very happy to see you, my dear sir, very. Pray sit down. So you have carried your intention into effect. You have come down here to see an election – eh?'

Mr Pickwick replied in the affirmative.

'Spirited contest, my dear sir,' said the little man.

'I am delighted to hear it,' said Mr Pickwick, rubbing his hands. 'I like to see sturdy patriotism, on whatever side it is called forth; – and so it's a spirited contest?'

'Oh yes,' said the little man, 'very much so indeed. We have opened all the public-houses in the place, and left our adversary nothing but the beer-shops – masterly stroke of policy that, my dear sir, eh?' – the little man smiled complacently, and took a large pinch of snuff.

'And what are the probabilities as to the result of the contest?' inquired Mr Pickwick.

'Why doubtful, my dear sir; rather doubtful as yet,' replied the little man. 'Fizkin's people have got three-and-thirty voters in the lock-up coach-house at the White Hart.'

'In the coach-house!' said Mr Pickwick, considerably astonished by this second stroke of policy.

'They keep 'em locked up there till they want 'em,' resumed the little man. 'The effect of that is, you see, to prevent our getting at them; and even if we could, it would be of no use, for they keep them very drunk on purpose. Smart fellow Fizkin's agent – very smart fellow indeed.'

Mr Pickwick stared, but said nothing.

'We are pretty confident, though,' said Mr Perker, sinking his voice almost to a whisper. 'We had a little tea-party here, last night – five-and-forty women, my dear sir – and gave every one of 'em a green parasol when she went away.'

'A parasol!' said Mr Pickwick.

'Fact, my dear sir, fact. Five-and-forty green parasols, at seven and sixpence a-piece. All women like finery – extraordinary the effect of those parasols. Secured all their husbands, and half their brothers – beats stockings, and flannel, and all that sort of thing hollow. My idea, my dear sir, entirely. Hail, rain, or sunshine, you can't walk half a dozen yards up the street, without encountering half a dozen green parasols.'

The Pickwick Papers

11 Anthony Trollope, Parliamentary Parties (1869)

At the end of the three years Phineas was called to the Bar, and immediately received a letter from his father asking minutely as to his professional intentions. His father recommended him to settle in Dublin, and promised the one hundred and fifty pounds for three more years, on condition that this advice was followed. He did not absolutely say that the allowance would be stopped if the advice were not followed, but that was plainly to be implied. That letter came at the moment of a dissolution of Parliament. Lord de Terrier, the Conservative Prime Minister, who had now been in office for the almost unprecedentedly long period of fifteen months, had found that he could not face continued majorities against him in the House of Commons, and had dissolved the House. Rumour declared that he would have much preferred to resign, and betake himself once again to the easy glories of opposition; but his party had naturally been obdurate with him, and he had resolved to appeal to the country. When Phineas received his father's letter, it had just been suggested to him at the Reform Club that he should stand for the Irish borough of Loughshane.

This proposition had taken Phineas Finn so much by surprise that when first made to him by Barrington Erle it took his breath away. What! he stand for Parliament, twenty-four years old, with no vestige of property belonging to him, without a penny in his purse, as completely dependent on his father as he was when he first went to school at eleven years of age! And for Loughshane, a little borough in the county Galway, for which a brother of that fine old Irish peer, the Earl of Tulla, had been sitting for the last twenty years, – a fine, high-minded represent-ative of the thorough-going Orange Protestant feeling of Ireland! And the Earl of Tulla, to whom almost all Loughshane belonged, – or at any rate the land about Loughshane, – was one of his father's staunchest friends! Loughshane is in county Galway, but the Earl of Tulla usually lived at his seat in county Clare, not more than ten miles from Killaloe, and always confided his gouty feet, and the weak nerves of the old countess, and the stomachs of all his domestics, to the care of Dr Finn. How was it possible that Phineas should stand for Loughshane? From whence was the money to come for such a contest? It was a beautiful dream, a grand idea, lifting Phineas almost off the earth by its glory. When the proposition was first made to him in the smoking-room at the Reform Club by his friend Erle, he was aware that he blushed like a girl, and that he was unable at the moment to express himself plainly, – so great was his astonishment and so great his gratification. But before ten minutes had passed by, while Barrington Erle was still sitting over his shoulder on the club sofa, and before the blushes had altogether vanished, he had seen the improbability of the scheme, and had explained to his friend that the thing could not be done. But to his increased astonishment, his friend made nothing of the difficulties. Loughshane, according to Barrington Erle, was so small a place, that the expense would be very little. There were altogether no more than 307 registered electors. The inhabitants were so far removed from the world, and were so ignorant of the world's good things, that they knew nothing about bribery. The Hon. George Morris, who had sat for the last twenty years, was very unpopular. He had not been near the borough since the last election, he had hardly done more than show himself in Parliament, and had neither given a shilling in the town nor got a place under Government for a single son of Loughshane. 'And he has quarrelled with his brother,' said Barrington Erle. 'The devil he has!' said Phineas. 'I thought they always swore by each other.' 'It's at each other they swear now,' said Barrington; 'George has asked the Earl for more money, and the Earl has cut up rusty.' Then the negotiator went on to explain that the expenses of the election would be defrayed out of a certain fund collected for such purposes, that Loughshane had been chosen as a cheap place, and that Phineas Finn had been chosen as a safe and promising young man. As for qualification, if any question were raised, that should be made all right. An Irish candidate was wanted, and a Roman Catholic. So much the Loughshaners would require on their own account when instigated to dismiss from their service that thorough-going Protestant, the Hon George Morris. Then 'the party', – by which Barrington Erle probably meant the great man in whose service he himself had become a politician, – required that the candidate should be a safe man, one who would support 'the party', – not a cantankerous, red-hot semi-Fenian, running about to meetings at the Rotunda, and such-like, with views of his own about tenant-right and the Irish Church. 'But I have views of my own,' said Phineas, blushing again. 'Of course you have, my dear boy,' said Barrington, clapping him on the back. 'I shouldn't come to you unless you had views. But your views and ours are the same, and you're just the lad for Galway. You mightn't have such an opening again in your life, and of course you'll stand for Loughshane.' Then the conversation was over, the private secretary went away to arrange some other little matter of the kind, and Phineas Finn was left alone to consider the proposition that had been made to him.

Phineas Finn

12   M. Ostrogorski, Mass Membership Parties (1902)

The advent of democracy shattered the old framework of political society. The hierarchy of classes and their internal cohesion were destroyed, and the time-honoured social ties which bound the individual to the community were severed. As the old fabric had to be replaced by a new one, the problem was to find out how the individual could be reunited to society, in what new organization both could be incorporated, so as to assure form and permanency to their existence. The supremacy accorded to numbers in the State complicated matters by raising the question how the promiscuous crowd of old and young, of learned and unlearned, of rich and poor, who were all declared collectively arbiters of their political destinies, would be able to discharge their new function of 'sovereign'. The representative form of government adopted by modern democracies simplifies the problem in appearance only without touching its essence, for after all national representation proceeds from the great mass of the people.

Without, perhaps, having considered this problem in its general aspect, or having defined all its factors, some modern democracies have endeavoured to solve it amidst the march of events and in a somewhat empirical fashion. This solution consists in a methodical organization of the electoral masses, by extra-constitutional means and in the form of disciplined and permanent parties. The experiment has been carried to considerable lengths in the Anglo-Saxon countries of Europe and America, and the experience gained incontestably possesses great importance. Under what conditions has it been inaugurated? What has been its progress and development, and its influence on political life? Does it bring us nearer the possibility of embracing the political society which issued from the democratic revolution in a new synthesis? In a word, what are the results which it has given or which it holds out? The answer to these questions will be as interesting to the historian as to the political thinker and the thinking politician. . .

In this respect the England of our days presents incomparable advantages. Hardly two generations back she was still an aristocratic and feudal society; at the present moment she is completely drawn into the democratic current, with no inclination to retrace her steps or to wrangle about the results obtained. Compressed into a more limited space of time and uninterrupted in its progress, the democratic evolution of England pursues its course before the spectator, working out its logical development under his eyes and presenting an orderly sequel of premise and conclusion.

This is especially the case with the problem which we propose to study. We shall begin with England for this reason, and, in accordance with the plan sketched out, start by considering the unity of the old English society with its spontaneous connection and, so to speak, organic cohesion; we shall take note of its disintegration and then deal with the endeavours to restore unity to it in the sphere of politics; this will bring us eventually to the attempts to create a methodical organization of the electoral masses.

Democracy and the Organisation of Political Parties

13 A Democratic Socialist Party (1906–7)

NAME:

'The Independent Labour Party'.

MEMBERSHIP:

Open to all Socialists who endorse the principles and policy of the Party, are not members of either the Liberal or Conservative Party, and whose application for membership is accepted by a Branch.

Any member expelled from membership of a Branch of the ILP shall not be eligible for membership of any other Branch without having first submitted his or her case for adjudication of the NAC.

OBJECT:

The object of the Party is to establish the Socialist State, when land and capital will be held by the community and used for the well-being of the community, and when the exchange of commodities will be organized also by the community, so as to secure the highest possible standard of life for the individual. In giving effect to this object it shall work as part of the International Socialist movement.

METHOD:

The Party, to secure its objects, adopts:–

1. *Educational Methods*, including the publication of Socialist literature, the holding of meetings, etc.
2. *Political Methods*, including the election of its members to local and national administrative and legislative bodies.

The Programme of the Independent Labour Party

14 V. Bogdanor, Proportional Representation (1984)

Attitudes to proportional representation tend to reflect radically different views of society and divergent conceptions of the democratic process. Those who favour proportional representation may be accused of taking a rather optimistic view of British society, which they believe to be fundamentally harmonious and fraternal. They do not deny the existence of conflict but believe that it is exaggerated by Britain's political institutions and especially the party system, which tends to the manufacture of conflict where none exists. Many advocates of proportional representation look longingly towards Scandinavia and West Germany, where conflict is contained in a political system which breeds conciliation and agreement. In such countries political stability is combined with social progress and efficient government. Supporters of proportional representation are said to make the optimistic assumption that if only the diverse interests in British society received fair representation, if only all the voices were heard, then consensus and agreement will be the result.

Opponents of proportional representation accuse reformers of being hopelessly idealistic. For them conflict is endemic in British society, and the party battle is but a reflection of real and substantial disagreement between different social groups. Because such disagreement exists, the proportional representation of different interests in Parliament or Government will lead not to consensus agreement but to immobilism. Nothing will be decided and Britain will drift and stagnate, rather like Italy. Britain will become a country without government. For there is a genuine ideological division in Britain between advocates of a market economy and supporters of socialism, and it is for the electorate to choose between them. The only way in which Britain can be governed effectively, indeed governed at all, is by maintaining an electoral system which artificially creates a majority Government, ensuring that voters are presented with clear alternatives and forced to choose between competing priorities. Whatever its theoretical defects, therefore, the British electoral system provides the only method by which a divided society can be governed and strong decisions taken. Proportional representation, on the other hand, allows the electorate to avoid making choices, and so the country is prevented from following a clear path. It provides the worst of both worlds – consensus politics, the absence of clear direction and the sacrifice of all convictions in the interest of consensus.

Such would be the view not only of Margaret Thatcher but also of Neil Kinnock, Tony Benn and Enoch Powell, in agreement on this if on little else. It is the logical consequence of the Westminster model of government, but it is to take an essentially over-simplified view of politics to imagine that political alternatives can be confined to two ideologies – free-market liberalism and socialism – whose roots lie in the nineteenth century and which have little to offer in the way of solutions to the problems of a modern industrial society.

Advocates of proportional representation put forward a radical alternative to the Westminster model. They believe that democracy involves not the victory of one side over another in a battle fought between obsolete ideologies but a process of negotiation and agreement. The central strength of proportional representation is that it makes for the sharing of power at governmental level. This inculcates attitudes which spread outwards into society so that power in the economy and in industry also comes to be shared. Advocates of proportional representation tend to see it as a political concomitant, and indeed prerequisite, of power-sharing policies in the economic and social sphere – incomes policy, worker participation in industry and the restoration of a tripartite framework of co-operation between Government, industry and labour.

What Is Proportional Representation?

VI
Democracy and Freedom

People often talk as though democracy and freedom were synonymous. Phrases such as 'democratic freedoms' and 'liberal democracy' have become political clichés. Yet at both a theoretical and a practical level, the relationship between democracy and freedom is in fact controversial and complex. The aim of this chapter is to illustrate some of the conflicts and connections between the two. The first section considers the relationship between democracy and liberalism at a philosophical level. The second, on Bills of Rights and the rule of law, is concerned with how freedoms are (or, as some argue, are *not*) protected in Britain. The third section deals with one particular freedom that is of great importance in a democracy – freedom of expression – while the fourth illustrates a preoccupation of many writers since the 1930s: the relationship between democracy and totalitarianism.

A.   LIBERALISM AND DEMOCRACY

Historically, ideas of democracy and liberty have not always coincided. Western democracy is customarily traced back to fifth-century Athens, yet neither the Ancient Greeks nor Romans seem to have had notions of legally guaranteed 'rights' in the modern sense. Conversely, feudal societies of the European Middle Ages embodied in their political systems the idea of particular guaranteed 'liberties' for particular groups, yet none of them could be described as democratic. Eighteenth-century Britain could hardly be described as a democracy. And finally, many regimes in the twentieth century have had pretensions to democracy that have had no pretension to liberalism. Practically every modern dictator, from Hitler to Mao, has described his rule as being 'for the good of the people' or embodying 'the will of the people'.

Philosophically, the conflict between liberty and democracy has been encapsulated in the idea of the 'tyranny of the majority', a phrase made famous by John Stuart Mill in his *On Liberty* (1859) (VI:1). A hundred years after Mill published his essay, the philosopher and historian Isaiah Berlin elaborated on this by drawing a distinction between 'Two Concepts of Liberty' (VI:2) – one being a 'negative' idea of liberty that draws an area of non-interference around the individual, and the other being a 'positive' concept of liberty. And implicit in it was a warning of the illiberal twist that could be given to democracy.

One might illustrate the practical implications of this philosophical distinction between liberty and democracy by asking, for example, whether it is 'democratic' for the power of an elected assembly to be limited by a written constitution which it is powerless to overturn. If democracy is defined simply as 'the rule of the people' or 'the rule of the majority', then the answer must be 'No'. But what happens if an elected assembly without constitutional restrictions, elected by 'democratic' procedures, decides by majority vote to deprive a minority (or an individual) of its right to the vote, or to free speech, or to life itself? Is that 'democratic'? Put in these terms, it is clear that democracy must mean more than simply 'the rule of the majority'. Certain freedoms – freedom of expression, freedom of association, etc. – would seem to be essential for ensuring that democracy does not destroy itself.

In this sense it is not contradictory to talk of 'democratic freedoms'. Yet within the area of that common ground, tensions between the demands of liberty and those of democracy will persist. The novelist E. M. Forster, for example, gives 'Two Cheers for Democracy' (VI:3) because it provides the best guarantee of certain freedoms. But he does not give it three. As a liberal and an individualist, the third cheer is reserved for the private and singular.

1 John Stuart Mill, The Tyranny of the Majority (1859)

In political and philosophical theories, as well as in persons, success discloses faults and infirmities which failure might have concealed from observation. The notion, that the people have no need to limit their power over themselves, might seem axiomatic, when popular government was a thing only dreamed about, or read of as having existed at some distant period of the past. Neither was that notion necessarily disturbed by such temporary aberrations as those of the French Revolution, the worst of which were the work of a usurping few, and which, in any case, belonged, not to the permanent working of popular institutions, but to a sudden and convulsive outbreak against monarchical and aristocratic despotism. In time, however, a democratic republic came to occupy a large portion of the earth's surface, and made itself felt as one of the most powerful members of the community of nations; and elective and responsible government became subject to the observations and criticisms which wait upon a great existing fact. It was now perceived that such phrases as 'self-government,' and 'the power of the people over themselves,' do not express the true state of the case. The 'people' who exercise the power are not always the same people with those over whom it is exercised; and the 'self-government' spoken of is not the government of each by himself, but of each by all the rest. The will of the people, moreover, practically means the will of the most numerous or the most active *part* of the people; the majority, or those who succeed in making themselves accepted as the majority; the people, consequently *may* desire to oppress a part of their number; and precautions are as much needed against this as against any other abuse of power. The limitation, therefore, of the power of government over individuals loses none of its importance when the holders of power are regularly accountable to the community, that is, to the strongest party therein. This view of things, recommending itself equally to the intelligence of thinkers and to the inclination of those important classes in European society to whose real or supposed interests democracy is adverse, has had no difficulty in establishing itself; and in political speculations 'the tyranny of the majority' is now generally included among the evils against which society requires to be on its guard.

Like other tyrannies, the tyranny of the majority was at first, and is still vulgarly, held in dread, chiefly as operating through the acts of the public authorities. But reflecting persons perceived that when society is itself the tyrant – society collectively over the separate individuals who compose it – its means of tyrannising are not restricted to the acts which it may do by the hands of its political functionaries. Society can and does execute its own mandates; and if it issues wrong mandates instead of right, or any mandates at all in things with which it ought not to meddle, it practises a social tyranny more formidable than many kinds of political oppression, since, though not usually upheld by such extreme penalties, it leaves fewer means of escape, penetrating much more deeply into the details of life, and enslaving the soul itself. Protection, therefore, against the tyranny of the magistrate is not enough; there needs protection also against the tyranny of the prevailing opinion and feeling; against the tendency of society to impose, by other means than civil penalties, its own ideas and practices as rules of conduct on those who dissent from them; to fetter the development, and, if possible, prevent the formation, of any individuality not in harmony with its ways, and compels all characters to fashion themselves upon the model of its own. There is a limit to the legitimate interference of collective opinion with individual independence: and to find that limit, and maintain it against encroachment, is as indispensable to a good condition of human affairs, as protection against political despotism.

Essay on Liberty

2 Isaiah Berlin, Individual Liberty and Democratic Rule (1958)

I am normally said to be free to the degree to which no man or body of men interferes with my activity. Political liberty in this sense is simply the area within which a man can act un-obstructed by others. . .

This is what the classical English political philosophers meant when they used this word. They disagreed about how wide the area could or should be. They supposed that it could not, as things were, be unlimited, because if it were, it would entail a state in which all men could boundlessly interfere with all other men; and this kind of 'natural' freedom would lead to social chaos in which men's minimum needs would not be satisfied; or else the liberties of the weak would be suppressed by the strong. Because they perceived that human purposes and activities do not automatically harmonize with one another, and because (whatever their official doctrines) they put high value on other goals, such as justice, or happiness, or culture, or security, or varying degrees of equality, they were prepared to curtail freedom in the interests of other values and, indeed, of freedom itself. For without this, it was impossible to create the kind of association that they thought desirable. Consequently, it is assumed by these thinkers that the area of men's free action must be limited by law. But equally it is assumed, especially by such libertarians as Locke and Mill in England, and Constant and Tocqueville in France, that there ought to exist a certain minimum area of personal freedom which must on no account be violated; for if it is overstepped, the individual will find himself in an area too narrow for even that minimum development of his natural faculties which alone makes it possible to pursue, and even to conceive, the various ends which men hold good or right or sacred. It follows that a frontier must be drawn between the area of private life and that of public authority. . .

'Freedom' in this sense is not, at any rate logically, connected with democracy or self-government. Self-government may, on the whole, provide a better guarantee of the preservation of civil liberties than other regimes, and has been defended as such by libertarians. But there is no necessary connexion between individual liberty and democratic rule. The answer to the question 'Who governs me?' is logically distinct from the question 'How far does government interfere with me?' It is in this difference that the great contrast between the two concepts of negative and positive liberty, in the end, consists. For the 'positive' sense of liberty comes to light if we try to answer the question, not 'What am I free to do or be?', but 'By whom am I ruled?' or 'Who is to say what I am, and what I am not, to be or do?' The connexion between democracy and individual liberty is a good deal more tenuous than it seemed to many advocates of both. The desire to be governed by myself, or at any rate to participate in the process by which my life is to be controlled, may be as deep a wish as that of a free area for action, and perhaps historically older. But it is not a desire for the same thing. . .

The 'positive' sense of the word 'liberty' derives from the wish on the part of the individual to be his own master. I wish my life and decisions to depend on myself, not on external forces of whatever kind. I wish to be the instrument of my own, not of other men's, acts of will. I wish to be a subject, not an object; to be moved by reasons, by conscious purposes, which are my own, not by causes which affect me, as it were, from outside. I wish to be somebody, not nobody; a doer – deciding, not being decided for, self-directed and not acted upon by external nature or by other men as if I were a thing, or an animal, or a slave incapable of playing a human role, that is, of conceiving goals and policies of my own and realizing them. This is at least part of what I mean when I say that I am rational, and that it is my reason that distinguishes me as a human being from the rest of the world. I wish, above all, to be conscious of myself as a thinking, willing, active being bearing responsibility for my choices and able to explain them by references to my own ideas and purposes. I feel free to the degree that I believe this to be true, and enslaved to the degree that I am made to realize that it is not. . .

To understand why things must be as they must be is to will them to be so. Knowledge liberates not by offering us more open possibilities amongst which we can make our choice, but by preserving us from the frustration of attempting the impossible. To want necessary laws to be other than they are is to be prey to an irrational desire – a desire that what must be X should also be not X. To go further, and believe these laws to be other than what they necessarily are, is to be insane. That is the metaphysical heart of rationalism. The notion of liberty contained in it is not the 'negative' conception of a field (ideally) without obstacles, a vacuum in which nothing obstructs me, but the notion of self-direction or self-control. I can do what I will with my own. I am a rational being; whatever I can demonstrate to myself as being necessary, as incapable of being otherwise in a rational society – that is, in a society directed by rational minds, towards goals such as a rational being would have – I cannot, being rational, wish to sweep out of my way. I assimilate it into my substance as I do the laws of logic, of mathematics, of physics, the rules of art, the principles that govern everything of which I understand, and therefore will, the rational purpose, by which I can never be thwarted, since I cannot want it to be other than it is.

This is the positive doctrine of liberation by reason. Socialized forms of it, widely disparate and opposed to each other as they are, are at the heart of many of the nationalist, communist, authoritarian and totalitarian creeds of our day. It may, in the course of its evolution, have wandered far from its rationalist moorings. Nevertheless, it is this freedom that, in democracies and in dictatorships, is argued about, and fought for, in many parts of the earth today.

'Two Concepts of Liberty'

3   E. M. Forster, Two Cheers for Democracy (1951)

Democracy is. . .less hateful than other contemporary forms of government, and to that extent it deserves our support. It does start from the assumption that the individual is important, and that all types are needed to make a civilisation. It does not divide its citizens into the bossers and the bossed – as an efficiency-regime tends to do. The people I admire most are those who are sensitive and want to create something or discover something, and do not see life in terms of power, and such people get more of a chance under a democracy than elsewhere. They found religions, great or small, or they produce literature and art, or they do disinterested scientific research, or they may be what is called 'ordinary people', who are creative in their private lives, bring up their children decently, for instance, or help their neighbours. All these people need to express themselves; they cannot do so unless society allows them liberty to do so, and the society which allows them most liberty is a democracy.

Democracy has another merit. It allows criticism, and if there is not public criticism there are bound to be hushed-up scandals. That is why I believe in the Press, despite all its lies and vulgarity and why I believe in Parliament. Parliament is often sneered at because it is a Talking Shop. I believe in it *because* it is a talking shop. I believe in the Private Member who makes himself a nuisance. He gets snubbed and is told that he is cranky or ill-informed, but he does expose abuses which would otherwise never have been mentioned, and very often an abuse gets put right just by being mentioned. Occasionally, too, a well-meaning public official starts losing his head in the cause of efficiency, and thinks himself God Almighty. Such officials are particularly frequent in the Home Office. Well, there will be questions about them in Parliament sooner or later, and then they will have to mind their steps. Whether Parliament is either a representative body or an efficient one is questionable, but I value it because it criticises and talks, and because its chatter gets widely reported.

So Two Cheers for Democracy: one because it admits variety and two because it permits criticism. Two cheers are quite enough: there is no occasion to give three.

Two Cheers for Democracy

B. BILLS OF RIGHTS AND THE RULE OF LAW

In the first section of this chapter we touched on the question of whether it is 'democratic' for the actions of an elected Parliament to be circumscribed by constitutionally entrenched freedoms or 'rights'. It is a question that goes to the heart of the debate about Britain's 'unwritten constitution'.

It has sometimes been argued that Britain does have a bill of rights. In particular, people have pointed to the Magna Carta of 1215 (VI:4) and the Bill of Rights of 1689 (VI:5). Four and a half centuries of social and political change separate these two documents, but they have certain features in common that cause one to hesitate to describe them as 'Bills of Rights' as the term is usually understood nowadays. In the first place, neither is a general statement of the rights of all Englishmen (still less of all human beings). They are a detailed list of specific grievances and their remedies. In this sense they are very different from the French Declaration of the Rights of Man (1789) or the United Nations Declaration of Human Rights (1946). Second, neither Magna Carta nor the Bill of Rights of 1689 has any special constitutional status. As ordinary statutes (Magna Carta was incorporated in the first or Great Roll of Statutes of 1297), they could (and have) been superseded by subsequent statute law. Third, both are concerned with restricting the powers of the Crown rather than with defining and asserting the rights of citizens. Rather than some universal declaration of rights, the 1689 Bill should be seen as the culmination of the struggle between Crown and Parliament that had dominated much of the seventeenth century. And finally, both documents are conservative, being phrased in terms of the restoration and reaffirmation of existing or customary rights, rather than in terms of the founding of a new political order.

It is often argued that we in Britain do not need a bill of rights because our freedoms are adequately protected by the principle of the 'rule of law'. The most famous and influential statement of this principle comes in A. V. Dicey's *The Law of the Constitution* (1885) (VI:6). Dicey's claims about the 'rule of law' have often been challenged and recently the notion of the rule of law has been called into question by the comments of a leading judge in the 'Spycatcher' case (VI:7).

Recent disquiet about whether civil liberties are adequately protected by the principle of the 'rule of law' has led to a debate as to whether Britain should have its own Bill of Rights, or should incorporate the European Convention on Human Rights into British law. (See the comments of Lord Scarman, I:6 above). The final two extracts in this section provide different perspectives on this issue. K. D. Ewing and C. A. Gearty (VI:8) argue that to call for a Bill of Rights is a simplistic and inadequate response to what they see as 'the crisis facing civil liberties in Britain'. (Ewing and Gearty's arguments echo some of the theoretical arguments about democracy as against liberty that we saw in the first section.) Ferdinand Mount (VI:9), in favour of a Bill of Rights, deals with the specific argument that an entrenched Bill of Rights is impossible under the British system because of the principle that no Parliament can bind its successors.

4 Magna Carta (1215)

JOHN, by the grace of God King of England, Lord of Ireland, Duke of Normandy and Aquitaine, and Count of Anjou, to his archbishops, bishops, abbots, earls, barons, justices, foresters, sheriffs, stewards, servants, and to all his officials and loyal subjects, Greeting. . .

TO ALL FREE MEN OF OUR KINGDOM we have also granted, for us and our heirs for ever, all the liberties written out below, to have and to keep for them and their heirs, of us and our heirs:. . .

(20) For a trivial offence, a free man shall be fined only in proportion to the degree of his offence, and for a serious offence correspondingly, but not so heavily as to deprive him of his livelihood. In the same way, a merchant shall be spared his merchandise, and a husbandman the implements of his hus-bandry, if they fall upon the mercy of a royal court. None of these fines shall be imposed except by the assessment on oath of reputable men of the neighbourhood. . .

(39) No free man shall be seized or imprisoned, or stripped of his rights or possessions, or outlawed or exiled, or deprived of his standing in any other way, nor will we proceed with force against him, or send others to do so, except by the lawful judgement of his equals or by the law of the land.

(40) To no one will we sell, to no one deny or delay right or justice.

(41) All merchants may enter or leave England unharmed and without fear, and may stay or travel within it, by land or water, for purposes of trade, free from all illegal exactions, in accordance with ancient and lawful customs. This, however, does not apply in time of war to merchants from a country that

is at war with us. Any such merchants found in our country at the outbreak of war shall be detained without injury to their persons or property, until we or our chief justice have discovered how our own merchants are being treated in the country at war with us. If our own merchants are safe they shall be safe too.

Magna Carta

5   Bill of Rights (1689)

Whereas the late King James the Second, by the assistance of divers evil counsellors, judges, and ministers employed by him, did endeavour to subvert and extirpate the protestant religion, and the laws and liberties of this kingdom,

1.   By assuming and exercising a power of dispensing with and suspending of laws, and the execution of laws, without consent of parliament.

2.   By committing and prosecuting divers worthy prelates, for humbly petitioning to be excused from concurring to the said assumed power.

3.   By issuing and causing to be executed a commission under the great seal for erecting a court called, The court of commissioners for ecclesiastical causes.

4.   By levying money for and to the use of the crown, by pretence of prerogative, for other time, and in other manner, than the same was granted by parliament.

5.   By raising and keeping a standing army within this kingdom in time of peace, without consent of parliament, and quartering soldiers contrary to law.

6.   By causing several good subjects, being protestants, to be disarmed at the same time when papists were both armed and employed, contrary to law.

7.   By violating the freedom of election of members to serve in parliament.

8.   By prosecutions in the court of King's bench, for matters and causes cognizable only in parliament; and by divers other arbitrary and illegal causes.

9.   And whereas of late years, partial, corrupt, and unqualified persons have been returned and served on juries in trials, and particularly divers jurors in trials for high treason, which were not freeholders.

10. And excessive bail hath been required of persons committed in criminal cases, to elude the benefit of the laws made for the liberty of the subjects.

11. And excessive fines have been imposed; and illegal and cruel punishments inflicted.

12. And several grants and promises made of fines and forfeitures, before any conviction or judgement against the persons, upon whom the same were to be levied.

All which are utterly and directly contrary to the known laws and statutes, and freedom of this realm.

And whereas the said late King James the Second having abdicated the government, and the throne being thereby vacant, his highness the prince of Orange (whom it hath pleased Almighty God to make the glorious instrument of delivering this kingdom from popery and arbitrary power) did (by the advice of the lords spiritual and temporal, and divers principal persons of the commons) cause letters to be written to lords spiritual and temporal, being protestants; and other letters to the several counties, cities, universities, boroughs, and cinque-ports, for the choosing of such persons to represent them, as were of right to be sent to parliament, to meet and sit at Westminster upon the two and twentieth day of January, in this year one thousand six hundred eighty and eight, in order to such an establishment, as that their religion, laws, and liberties might not again be in danger of being subverted: upon which letters, elections have been accordingly made.

And thereupon the said lords spiritual and temporal, and commons, pursuant to their respective letters and elections, being now assembled in a full and free representative of this nation, taking into their most serious consideration the best means for attaining the ends aforesaid; do in the first place (as their ancestors in like case have usually done) for the vindicating and asserting their ancient rights and liberties, declare:

1. That the pretended power of suspending of laws, or the execution of laws, by regal authority, without consent of parliament, is illegal.

2. That the pretended power of dispensing with laws, or the execution of laws, by regal authority, as it hath been assumed and exercised of late, is illegal.

3. That the commission for erecting the late court of commissioners for ecclesiastical causes, and all other commissions and courts of like nature are illegal and pernicious.

4. That levying money for or to the use of the crown, by pretence of prerogative, without grant of parliament, for longer time, or in other manner than the same is or shall be granted, is illegal.

5. That it is the right of the subjects to petition the King, and all commitments and prosecutions for such petitioning are illegal.

6. That the raising or keeping a standing army within the kingdom in time of peace, unless it be with consent of parliament, is against law.

7. That the subjects which are protestants, may have arms for their defence suitable to their conditions, and as allowed by law.

8. That election of members of parliament ought to be free.

9. That the freedom of speech, and debates or proceedings in parliament ought not to be impeached or questioned in any court or place out of parliament.

10. That excessive bail ought not to be required, nor excessive fines imposed; nor cruel and unusual punishments inflicted.

11. That jurors ought to be duly impanelled and returned, and jurors which pass upon men in trials for high treason ought to be freeholders.

12. That all grants and promises of fines and forfeitures of particular persons before conviction, are illegal and void.

13.   And that for redress of all grievances, and for the amending, strengthening, and preserving of the laws, parliaments ought to be held frequently.

And they do claim, demand, and insist upon all and singular
the premises, as their undoubted rights and liberties; and that no
declarations, judgments, doings or proceedings, to the prejudice
of the people in any of the said premises, ought in any wise to be
drawn hereafter into consequence or example.

Bill of Rights

6   A. V. Dicey, The Rule of Law (1885)

When we say that the supremacy or the rule of law is a
characteristic of the English constitution, we generally include
under one expression at least three distinct though kindred
conceptions.

We mean, in the first place, that no man is punishable or can
be lawfully made to suffer in body or goods except for a distinct
breach of law established in the ordinary legal manner before the
ordinary Courts of the land. In this sense the rule of law is
contrasted with every system of government based on the
exercise by persons in authority of wide, arbitrary, or discretionary powers of constraint.

Modern Englishmen may at first feel some surprise that the
'rule of law' (in the sense in which we are now using the term)
should be considered as in any way a peculiarity of English
institutions, since, at the present day it may seem to be not so
much the property of any one nation as a trait common to every
civilised and orderly state. Yet, even if we confine our observation to the existing condition of Europe, we shall soon be
convinced that the 'rule of law' even in this narrow sense is
peculiar to England, or to those countries which like the United
States of America, have inherited English traditions. In almost
every continental community the executive exercises far wider
discretionary authority in the matter of arrest, of temporary
imprisonment, of expulsion from its territory and the like, than
is either legally claimed or in fact exerted by the government in
England; and a study of European politics now and again
reminds English readers that wherever there is discretion there
is room for arbitrariness, and that in a republic no less than

under a monarchy discretionary authority on the part of the government must mean insecurity for legal freedom on the part of its subjects. . .

We mean in the second place, when we speak of the 'rule of law' as a characteristic of our country, not only that with us no man is above the law, but (what is a different thing) that here every man, whatever be his rank or condition, is subject to the ordinary law of the realm and amenable to the jurisdiction of the ordinary tribunals.

In England the idea of legal equality, or of the universal subjection of all classes to one law administered by the ordinary Courts, has been pushed to its utmost limit. With us every official, from the Prime Minister down to a constable or a collector of taxes, is under the same responsibility for every act done without legal jurisdiction as any other citizen. The Reports abound with cases in which officials have been brought before the Courts, and made, in their personal capacity, liable to punishment, or to the payment of damages for acts done in their official character but in excess of their lawful authority. A colonial governor, a secretary of state, a military officer, and all subordinates, though carrying out the commands of their official superiors, are as responsible for any act which the law does not authorise as is any private and unofficial person. Officials, such for example as soldiers or clergymen of the Established Church, are, it is true, in England as elsewhere, subject to laws which do not affect the rest of the nation, and are in some instances amenable to tribunals which have no jurisdiction over their fellow-countrymen; officials, that is to say, are to a certain extent governed under what may be termed official law. But this fact is in no way inconsistent with the principle that all men are in England subject to the law of the realm; for though a soldier or a clergyman incurs from his position legal liabilities from which other men are exempt, he does not (speaking generally) escape thereby from the duties of an ordinary citizen. . .

There remains yet a third and a different sense in which the 'rule of law' or the predominance of the legal spirit may be described as a special attribute of English institutions. We may say that the constitution is pervaded by the rule of law on the ground that the general principles of the constitution (as for example the right to personal liberty, or the right of public meeting) are with us the result of judicial decisions determining the rights of private persons in particular cases brought before the Courts; whereas under many foreign constitutions the security (such as it is) given to the rights of individuals results or appears to result, from the general principles of the constitution. . .

There is in the English constitution an absence of those declarations or definitions of rights so dear to foreign constitutionalists. Such principles, moreover, as you can discover in the English constitution are, like all maxims established by judicial legislation, mere generalisations drawn either from the decisions or dicta of judges, or from statutes which, being passed to meet special grievances, bear a close resemblance to judicial decisions, and are in effect judgements pronounced by the High Court of Parliament. To put what is really the same thing in a somewhat different shape, the relation of the rights of individuals to the principles of the constitution is not quite the same in countries like Belgium, where the constitution is the result of a legislative act, as it is in England, where the constitution itself is based upon legal decisions. In Belgium, which may be taken as a type of countries possessing a constitution formed by a deliberate act of legislation, you may say with truth that the rights of individuals to personal liberty flow from or are secured by the constitution. In England the right to individual liberty is part of the constitution, because it is secured by the decisions of the Courts, extended or confirmed as they are by the Habeas Corpus Acts. If it be allowable to apply the formulas of logic to questions of law, the difference in this matter between the constitution of Belgium and the English constitution may be described by the statement that in Belgium individual rights are deductions drawn from the principles of the constitution, whilst in England the so-called principles of the constitution are inductions or generalisations based upon particular decisions pronounced by the Courts as to the rights of given individuals.

The Law of the Constitution

7 K. D. Ewing and C. A. Gearty, Breaches of the Rule of Law (the 'Spycatcher' Case) (1990)

Of some public concern are the remarks expressed by Sir John Donaldson, who, as Master of the Rolls, is the senior member of the Court of Appeal, a mantle which he inherited from Lord Denning. Two points in particular may be mentioned here. The first is the suggestion that it was appropriate in some circumstances for the security service to commit criminal offences. Indeed, the Master of the Rolls went so far as to suggest that it was 'absurd' to claim that every breach of the law by the security service amounted to a 'wrongdoing'! Thus,

> Let us suppose that the service has information which suggests that a spy may be operating from particular premises. It needs to have confirmation. It may well consider that, if he proves to be a spy, the interests of the nation are better served by letting him continue with his activities under surveillance. . . What is the Service expected to do? A secret search of the premises is the obvious answer.

This possible criminal activity, dismissed merely as 'covert invasions of privacy', was likened to the emergency services who break the law by speeding to the site of an emergency. Happily, however, he could never conceive of physical violence coming into the category of excusable criminal conduct. Nevertheless such comments so publicly expressed so soon after the tercentenary of the Bill of Rights by one of our most senior judges is somewhat surprising. . .

One of the hallmarks of a democratic and civilized society is that government is conducted in accordance with the rule of law. One of the hallmarks of a totalitarian society is that state officials have unrestrained power. Dicey, no radical by a long chalk, pointed out in a passage well known to all first year students of constitutional law that the rule of law 'excludes the idea of any exemption of officials or others from the duty of obedience to the law which governs other citizens or from the jurisdiction of the ordinary tribunals'.

Freedom under Thatcher: Civil Liberties in Modern Britain

8 K. D. Ewing and C. A. Gearty, A New Bill of Rights – the Case Against (1990)

Perhaps the reform which has been most frequently proposed in recent years in response to the growing threat to political freedom is the introduction of a bill of rights. Such a document would list the political freedoms which are cherished in many liberal democracies. These would include freedom of association and peaceful assembly, freedom of expression (including freedom of the press), and freedom of conscience and religion. Parliament would not be permitted to pass laws which violated the terms of the bill of rights, while existing legislation would be capable of challenge if it contravened the guaranteed freedoms. . .

The movement in favour of formally incorporating the European Convention [on Human Rights] (or an equivalent document) into domestic law has been growing rapidly since the early 1970s. . . There are, however, major difficulties associated with such an initiative. . .

The first problem is a technical problem of constitutional law which perhaps ought not to be exaggerated. But equally it cannot be ignored or dismissed. . . The doctrine of parliamentary sovereignty. . .means that one Act of Parliament cannot bind Parliament in the future if the subsequent Parliament should wish to change the law. It also goes further than this. If an Act of Parliament is impliedly inconsistent with an earlier one, the courts have a duty to uphold and give effect to the one most recently passed. If this doctrine were applied to an incorporated European Convention or a bill of rights, it would mean that earlier legislation inconsistent with the Convention would be repealed (expressly or impliedly) to the extent of the inconsistency. But it would also mean that the Convention or the bill of rights could not govern future legislation and that the Government would be free through its control of Parliament to secure the passage of legislation which contravened the terms of the bill of rights. The duty of the courts would be to uphold the legislation despite the fact that it contravened the incorporated European Convention. Indeed they would be required to do so even if the later measure was only implicitly inconsistent with the bill of rights, without there being an expressed intention to deviate from its terms. . .

Even if the knotty legal problems can be unravelled, there is a further difficulty with entrenchment. This is whether such an initiative can be justified as a matter of political principle and democratic theory. Three problems arise here. The first is that it would involve conferring the ultimate sovereign power upon a group of people who are appointed and not elected. The final political decision on major questions would be made by people who have no mandate to make such decisions. This in itself would be a cause for great concern. Any such concerns, however, pale in light of the fact that appointment to these key positions is by the Prime Minister. Senior judges in Britain (including all the members of the House of Lords) are appointed without any parliamentary scrutiny or approval. . .

Related to this is a second problem that these appointed people who make the major political decisions are not account-able in any way for what they do with this quite enormous power. Once appointed, judges have security of tenure until death or retirement, and although there are procedures for the removal of senior judges, these have never been used in modern times. Judges are thus given the power to disrupt decisions and adjustments made by the process of persuasion, compromise, and agreement in the political arena. Difficult ethical, social, and political questions would be subject to judicial preference rather than the shared or compromised community morality. . .

The third and perhaps the most bizarre problem of principle is that not only would we be giving the final say on the big political questions to people who are appointed rather than elected, and to people who are not accountable for their decisions, but we would do so without any clear idea of what we expect of them. We would be giving to these people the freedom to determine the limits and scope of their own power. . .

The judges are free not only to determine how actively they will intervene, they are free to determine which constitutional freedoms they are willing to read broadly, and they are also free to determine which groups and interests they are willing to defend. It is open to question whether the ultimate political power should depend in this way on the whims, prejudices, and vision of a handful of citizens. . .

Our third concern is that in the hands of the English judges a bill of rights would make very little difference to the condition of political freedom in this country. . .

Many of the restrictions on political freedom which have taken place in the 1980s have not been as a result of legislation but have been judge-made initiatives authorizing the extension of executive power. Some of the most significant restrictions on the freedom of assembly, freedom of movement, and the freedom of the press were imposed by the courts, not by Parliament. The harsh reality is that we need to be protected by

Parliament from the courts, as much as we need to be protected
from the abuse of executive power.

Freedom under Thatcher: Civil Liberties in Modern Britain

9   Ferdinand Mount, A Written Constitution and Parliamentary Sovereignty (1992)

In their obsession with the principle that no Parliament has the
power to bind its successor, old parliamentary hands have lost
sight of the equally important principle that Parliament must act
according to law. In fact, the latter principle must be prior,
since, in exercising its power to overturn its predecessor's acts,
each Parliament has to respect the law and custom which that
predecessor has bequeathed to it. If the first Parliament passes a
Bill stating that all Bills of a constitutional type (including the
Bill itself and any Bill to repeal or amend the Bill itself) must in
future secure a two-thirds majority in both Houses in order to
become law, that law will bind the second Parliament until it is
repealed; and the repeal Bill will itself require a two-thirds
majority. No doubt a wilful second Parliament might try to find
ways round the dilemma by asserting – in defiance of the
original Bill's wording – that the repeal Bill was not itself a
constitutional Bill within the meaning of the Act by finding
some other defect. But, if it was felt that liberty was at stake,
then the public uproar would prevent the rascals from getting
away with it.

This is not a far-fetched legal quibble. It is, in practice, the
habitual protection of any written constitution. Suppose that a
majority in the US Congress wanted to do away with the old
laborious procedure for amending the American Constitution –
which under Article V of that Constitution involves securing
the amendment's passage in three-quarters of the state legislatures or by Conventions in three-quarters of the states (after the
amendment has been passed by two-thirds majorities in both
Houses or applied for by two-thirds of the state legislatures) –
and proposed to substitute the 'streamlined', 'flexible' procedure of a simple majority in both Houses of Congress. There
is nothing to prevent Congress from attempting this 'reform',

except that the attempt would have to be made through the existing laborious procedures and would ignominiously fail.

Parliament is the master of its own procedure, but it is, at the same time, the servant of its own procedure. The point is blissfully simple, and obvious to anyone who has ever served on any rules committee: the rules can only be changed according to the rules as they stand.

I do not think that even constitutional lawyers are fully seized of the seriousness with which Parliament treats its own procedures. After all, as the saying goes, procedure is the only constitution that MPs – or the rest of us, come to that – have got. Religious adherence to the rules as they stand is not simply the enthusiasm of a few pettifoggers. It is the heart and soul of parliamentary practice and 'parliamentary sovereignty' necessarily implies 'Parliament as duly constituted and as acting in accordance with its own procedures'. . .

In this procedural sense, far from it being the case that 'no parliament can bind its successor', *every parliament cannot help binding its successor*; the binding is what defines its successor as a true parliament and endows its decisions with proper authority.

The British Constitution Now: Recovery or Decline?

C. FREEDOM OF EXPRESSION

In Section A we saw how liberty and democracy are not always synonymous. The most famous defence of free speech in English literature, Milton's *Areopagitica* (VI:10), argues against censorship purely in terms of the importance of human reason and knowledge for its own sake, without reference to it being a 'democratic right'. But the ability to argue publicly and to express a wide variety of views, and also to have access to a variety of views and sources of information, is particularly important to a democratic system. Modern discussions of the importance of free speech such as that by A. D. Lindsay (VI:11) tend to be framed in these democratic terms.

There is probably no society on earth that has ever countenanced an absolute, unlimited freedom of expression. In Britain there are laws not only against libel and slander, but also against obscenity, against incitement to racial hatred (and, in Northern Ireland, against incitement to religious hatred), against misleading advertising (the

Trades Description Act) and against publication of material that might endanger national security (through the Official Secrets Act and also through the 'D Notice' system, under which material to be published or broadcast is voluntarily submitted to a committee and the publisher advised if any of it might endanger national security).

Apart from restrictions on grounds of 'national security', the most controversial area of censorship is that of material deemed obscene. (The most important legislation in this area is the Obscene Publications Act (1959).) Until 1968, the live theatre was censored by the Lord Chamberlain's office. Richard Crossman's diary (VI:12) gives us an interesting glimpse of the Cabinet discussions that led to the abolition of this system.

The most celebrated 'free speech' issue of recent times has been the 'Rushdie Affair', arising from the offence taken by many Muslims in Britain to certain passages in Salman Rushdie's novel, *The Satanic Verses*. Part of the anger of the Muslim community arose from the fact that although there exists a (rarely invoked) blasphemy law, it applies only to the Christian religion. To make the law fairer, it has been variously proposed that the law of blasphemy be abolished completely, that it be extended to cover all religions (which raises the question of how one would define a 'religion') or that it is replaced by a law against incitement to religious hatred such as already exists in Northern Ireland. Two different perspectives on the 'Rushdie Affair' are given here, from Shabbir Akhtar (VI:13) and from Salman Rushdie himself (VI:14).

The converse of 'freedom of expression' is 'freedom of information'. There has always been a debate about how 'open' government should be and how far its proceedings should be publicized. The terms in which the publication of parliamentary speeches was opposed in the eighteenth century (VI:15) – as offending the 'dignity' of the House – was echoed in debates over the televising of Parliament in the 1980s. (Freedom of reporting debates in the press was established in 1771.) In 1803 William Cobbett began publishing *Parliamentary Debates*, and this was taken over by Hansard in 1812. From 1855 Hansard received a subsidy from public funds. Televising of Parliament began in 1988. Other deliberations, such as those within Cabinet, are by convention held in private, though even this convention is often broken by 'leaks'. The most notorious obstacle to 'open' government in Britain till 1989 was Section 2 of the 1911 Official Secrets Act. In theory, this section made it a criminal offence for any civil servant to communicate any information, no matter how trivial and no matter to whom, without authority. Although this section was never, of course, enforced in all its extraordinary scope, its very existence was widely acknowledged to contravene the principle of open government. In 1989 the 1911 Act was replaced by a more precisely worded Official Secrets Act which identified particular areas of government activity such as defence and intelligence to which it applied. But since the 1911 Act had never anyway been enforced in full, some critics have questioned whether the 1989 Act, although removing an anomaly, does in practice amount to a liberalization of the law.

The issue of 'open government' is only one aspect of freedom of information. The other is the press itself. Essential to a democracy is a press that provides citizens with a wide spectrum of opinion. The press (or 'the media', including TV and radio) is not a neutral transmitter of information, but an independent actor with its own considerable power (the 'Fourth Estate', as it began to be called in the nineteenth century). Robert Southey, writing in 1807 (VI:16), gives an early example of how the press has often been the mere tool of politicians wishing to manipulate public opinion. The same sort of cynicism is exhibited in the twentieth century in a short poem by Humbert Wolfe (VI:17). In recent decades, concern about the media has centred on concentration of ownership and the ability of proprietors to interfere with editorial independence (VI:18). This was the major theme of Howard Brenton and David Hare's 1985 play, *Pravda* (VI:19).

10   John Milton, The Killing of Books (1644)

I deny not but that it is of greatest concernment in the church and commonwealth to have a vigilant eye how books demean themselves, as well as men, and thereafter to confine, imprison, and do sharpest justice on them as malefactors. For books are not absolutely dead things, but do contain a potency of life in them to be as active as that soul was whose progeny they are; nay, they do preserve as in a vial the purest efficacy and extraction of that living intellect that bred them. I know they are as lively, and as vigorously productive, as those fabulous dragon's teeth; and being sown up and down, may chance to spring up armed men. And yet, on the other hand, unless wariness be used, as good almost kill a man as kill a good book:

who kills a man kills a reasonable creature, God's image; but he who destroys a good book, kills reason itself, kills the image of God, as it were in the eye. Many a man lives a burden to the earth; but a good book is the precious life-blood of a master spirit, embalmed and treasured up on purpose to a life beyond life. 'Tis true, no age can restore a life, whereof, perhaps, there is no great loss; and revolutions of ages do not oft recover the loss of a rejected truth, for the want of which whole nations fare the worse. We should be wary, therefore, what persecution we raise against the living labors of public men, how we spill that seasoned life of man preserved and stored up in books; since we see a kind of homicide may be thus committed, sometimes a martyrdom; and if it extend to the whole impression, a kind of massacre, whereof the execution ends not in the slaying of an elemental life, but strikes at that ethereal and fifth essence, the breath of reason itself, slays an immortality rather than a life.

Areopagitica

11   Lord Lindsay, Democracy and Discussion (1929)

Now surely, if we reflect upon it, what matters most in the tiny democratic societies which we feel to be thoroughly satisfactory forms of government is what comes out of the free give and take of discussion. When men who are serving a common purpose meet to pool their experience, to air their difficulties and even their discontents, there comes about a real process of collective thinking. The narrowness and one-sidedness of each person's point of view are corrected, and something emerges which each can recognize as embodying the truth of what he stood for, and yet (or rather therefore) is seen to serve the purpose of the society better than what any one conceived for himself. That is of course an ideal. Such perfect agreement is not often reached. But it is an ideal which is always to some extent realized when there is open and frank discussion. And any one with experience of the effectiveness of discussion in a small democratic society must recognize how valuable is the contribution of those who are not easily convinced but can stand up resolutely for their own point of view. Where discussion of that kind prevails, we recognize that democracy is not a makeshift or a compromise or a means of keeping people quiet by the production of a sham unanimity, or a process of counting heads to save the trouble of breaking them, but the ideal form of government.

Observe further that the moment we take discussion seriously, we are committed to the view that we are concerned not primarily to obtain or register consent, but to find something out. . . Modern science is a great realm of co-operative thinking where discoveries are made originally by the work of isolated individuals, but where they are tested and enlarged by criticism and discussion. Every scientific discoverer knows that what he most wants to know is not what can be said for, but what can be said against his theory. What he most wants is an opposition. The example of scientific co-operative thinking may remind us that democratic discussion is entirely compatible with leadership and with any amount of difference in the weight of the contributions made by different members. Democracy assumes that each member of the community has something to contribute if it can be got out of him. It does not for a moment assume that what each member contributes is of equal value.

Now if, with all this in mind, we approach the problem created by the large scale of political democracy, we shall say that what matters is not that the final decision of government should be assented to by every one, but that every one should have somehow made his contribution to that decision. There cannot possibly be one enormous discussion, but there may be smaller areas of discussion, and the results of these may be conveyed by the representative to a further discussion, and so on. If we examine the means by which non-political democratic societies which have grown beyond the area of a discussion group try to keep the society democratic, we find the process of representation at its best. A comparatively large voluntary society, with a membership running into thousands, can keep the real spirit of democracy provided that its primary units of discussion – its branches or lodges – are vigorous and alive. If that condition is fulfilled, representatives of branches may then meet by districts for common discussion, and representatives of district meetings may meet for discussion at the General Council of the whole society. . .

Political representative democracy of course falls far short of such an ideal. For one thing, its primary units, the constituencies, are far too large for effective discussion; and not nearly enough attention has been paid to the limits of effective discussion in the organization of representative assemblies. But in spite of these obvious defects modern representative government when it is successful does make possible an immense deal of real and effective discussion.

The Essentials of Democracy

12 R. H. S. Crossman, Theatre Censorship (1967)

To Downing Street for morning prayers. The only subject the P.M. wanted to talk about was theatre censorship. There had just been published a report from a very representative committee which unanimously recommended the abolition of the functions of the Lord Chamberlain as censor of the living drama. This Roy Jenkins had very much wanted to accept but the P.M. told John and me this would be a terrible mistake and he also let us know that he'd sent George Wigg to the Home Affairs Committee to warn them against accepting it. I had had to leave the Committee just when George Wigg was starting to speak and hadn't realized that he was the P.M.'s emissary: indeed, I thought he'd gone there with a brief from Arnold Goodman, who was a member of the original departmental committee. Harold's explanation was very elaborate, I think because he was a little embarrassed. 'I've received representations from the Palace,' he said. 'They don't want to ban all plays about live persons but they want to make sure that there's somebody who'd stop the kind of play about Prince Philip which would be painful to the Queen. Of course,' he hurriedly added, 'they're not denying that there should be freedom to write satirical plays, take-offs, caricatures: what they want to be able to ban are plays devoted to character assassinations and they mention, as an example, 'Mrs Wilson's Diary'.

I pricked up my ears. 'Mrs Wilson's Diary' is, of course, one of the most popular features of *Private Eye* and there were ideas about putting it on the stage. When I asked him, Harold told me that he had been shown the text of the play, which made him out a complete mugwump and gave a picture of George Brown's drinking and swearing and using four-letter words. My first reaction was to tell him that he could hardly keep censorship of the live theatre and leave television and radio free. He had a quick reply. 'That'll all be lined up now,' he said, 'because Charlie Hill has already cleaned up ITV and he'll do the same to BBC now I'm appointing him chairman.' It was obvious from the way he talked that he wanted the censorship as much as the Queen. Indeed he wanted it so much that he'd put it on Thursday's Cabinet agenda.

Cabinet once again. Theatre censorship, as Harold promised, was the first item on the agenda. Despite George Wigg, the Home Affairs Committee had recommended acceptance of the committee's report. One of its main arguments was that one could hardly forbid the portrayal of living persons in the live theatre when it was not prohibited on television. Here Harold had equipped himself with an effective reply, namely an assurance from Charlie Hill that the powers vested in the Governors of the BBC were quite adequate to ensure that character assassination was altogether forbidden.

I had been expecting a great confrontation between Harold and the man he detests and whose influence he really hates in the Cabinet. Faced with the P.M.'s unexpected coup Roy was quite firm, cool and collected. He said of course he would consider this and the matter must certainly go back to Home Affairs for reconsideration. But he added that it would be extremely difficult to evolve any way of controlling the live theatre which didn't mean the reintroduction of censorship and more discrimination against it in comparison with television and radio. The Prime Minister seemed content with this and when I intervened to suggest that we needn't rush the Bill he indicated that it should be given high priority and he hoped that Roy would be able to satisfy him on this point. The agreement reached, as recorded in the Cabinet minutes, runs: 'In neither medium would ordinary political satire be forbidden but there should be safeguards against the theatre being used deliberately to discredit or create political hostility towards public political figures.'

The Crossman Diaries; entries for Wednesday, 26 July and
Thursday, 27 July 1967

13 Shabbir Akhtar, Religious Faith and Censorship (1989)

Had the voice of mockery in *The Satanic Verses* been even slightly more subdued, there would have been grounds for restraint and forbearance. But an authentic Muslim is bound to feel intolerably outraged by the book's claims, for Rushdie writes with all the knowledge of an insider. This is not to deny his right to explore, in fiction, the great parameters of life, sexuality, mortality and the existence (or non-existence) of deity. But Muslims must and do take issue with his choice of idiom and the temper it serves. His treatment is uniformly supercilious and dismissive; his reservations are shallow, playful, predictable, unoriginal. One looks in vain in his unprincipled prose for the reverent yet iconoclastic doubt which might set the agenda for the Islamic Enlightenment. There is nothing in *The Satanic Verses* which helps to bring Islam into a fruitful confrontation with modernity, nothing that brings it into thoughtful contact with contemporary secularity and ideological pluralism. Rushdie's scepticism fails to teach the ignorant, disturb the orthodox, agitate and educate the indifferent. Sceptics there have been and always will be. What matters is the quality and integrity of their reservations.

Let me introduce an autobiographical note here. Ever since the publication of *The Satanic Verses* in September 1988, my name has been associated with the campaign for its withdrawal. . . I believe that *The Satanic Verses* is a calculated attempt to vilify and slander Muhammad. It is my conviction that while freedoms of belief, expression, conscience, and dissent are rightly valued in a liberal democratic society, it is immoral to defend, in the name of these freedoms, wanton attacks on established religious (and indeed humanist) traditions. There is all the difference in the world between sound historical criticism that is legitimate and ought to be taken seriously, on the one hand, and scurrilous imaginative writing which should be resolutely rejected and withdrawn from public circulation.

Be Careful with Muhammed! The Salman Rushdie Affair

14　Salman Rushdie, Religious Faith and Free Speech (1991)

Throughout human history, the apostles of purity, those who have claimed to possess a total explanation, have wrought havoc among mere mixed-up human beings. Like many millions of people, I am a bastard child of history. Perhaps we all are, black and brown and white, leaking into one another, as a character of mine once said, *like flavours when you cook.*

The argument between purity and impurity, which is also the argument between Robespierre and Danton, the argument between the monk and the roaring boy, between primness and impropriety, between the stultifications of excessive respect and the scandals of impropriety, is an old one; I say, let it continue. Human beings understand themselves and shape their futures by arguing and challenging and questioning and saying the unsayable; not by bowing the knee, whether to gods or to men.

The Satanic Verses is, I profoundly hope, a work of radical dissent and questioning and reimagining. It is not, however, the book it has been made out to be, that book containing 'nothing but filth and insults and abuse' that has brought people out on to the streets across the world.

That book simply does not exist.

This is what I want to say to the great mass of ordinary decent, fair-minded Muslims, of the sort I have known all my life, and who have provided much of the inspiration of my work: to be rejected and reviled by, so to speak, one's own characters is a shocking and painful experience for any writer. I recognize that many Muslims have felt shocked and pained, too. Perhaps a way forward might be found through the mutual recognition of that mutual pain. Let us attempt to believe in each other's good faith.

Imaginary Homelands – Essays and Criticism 1981–91

15   The Reporting of Parliament (1738)

The Speaker informed the House, that it was with some concern he saw a practice prevailing, which a little reflected upon the dignity of that House: what he meant was the inserting an Account of their Proceedings in the printed News Papers, by which means the Proceedings of the House were liable to very great misrepresentations. . .

Mr Pulteney said: '. . .It is absolutely necessary a stop should be put to the practice which has so justly been complained of: I think no appeals should be made to the public with regard to what is said in this assembly, and to print or publish the

Speeches of gentlemen in this House, even though they were
not misrepresented, looks very like making them accountable
without doors for what they say within. . .'

. . . It was unanimously resolved: 'That it is a high indignity
to, and a notorious breach of the Privilege of, this House, for
any News-Writer, in Letters or other Papers,. . .to give therein
any Account of the Debates, or other Proceedings of this
House, or any Committee thereof, as well during the Recess, as
the sitting of Parliament; and that this House will proceed with
the utmost severity against such offenders.'

Parl. Hist., x, 800, 13 April, 1738

16 Robert Southey, A Partisan Press (1807)

Of those papers for which there is the greatest sale, from four to
five thousand are printed. It is not an exaggerated calculation to
suppose that every paper has five readers, and that there are
250,000 people in England who read the news every day and
converse upon it. In fact, after the 'How do you do?' and the
state of the weather, the news is the next topic in order of
conversation and sometimes it even takes place of cold, heat,
rain or sunshine. You will judge then that the newspapers must
be a powerful political engine. The ministry have always the
greater number under their direction, in which all their measures are defended, their successes exaggerated, their disasters
concealed or palliated, and the most flattering prospects constantly held out to the people. This system was carried to a great
length during the late war. If the numbers of the French who
were killed in the ministerial newspapers were summed up, they
would be found equal to all the males in the country, capable of
bearing arms. Nor were these manufacturers of good news
contented with slaying their thousands; in the true style of
bombast, they would sometimes assert that a Republican army
had been not merely cut to pieces, – but annihilated. On the
other hand, the losses of the English in their continental
expeditions were as studiously diminished. Truth was indeed
always to be got at by those who looked for it; the papers in the
opposite interest told all which their opponents concealed, and
magnified on their side to gratify their partisans. The English
have a marvellous faculty of believing what they wish, and

nothing else; for years and years did they believe that France was on the brink of ruin; now the government was to be overthrown for want of gunpowder, now by famine, now by the state of their finances. . . A staunch ministerialist believes every thing which his newspaper tells him, and takes his information and his opinions with the utmost confidence from a paragraph-writer, who is paid for falsifying the one and misleading the other.

Letters from England

17   Humbert Wolfe, The British Journalist (n.d.)

You cannot hope
    to bribe or twist,
thank God! the
    British journalist.

But, seeing what
    the man will do
unbribed, there's
    no occasion to.

18   E. P. Thompson, The Decline of Political Heresy (1980)

One hundred years ago – from the standpoint of formal democracy – we were an under-developed country. But within this limited democracy political heresy abounded and was often surprisingly effective. The minority had direct access to its own means of communication. The cost of launching a newspaper was not prohibitive. From the press, the public meeting, or the chapel, a determined minority could conduct a sustained propaganda, on the issues which it selected and according to its own strategy.

Today orthodox political thought assumes the viability of our formal democratic procedures. But these procedures are becoming more and more empty of real content, public life more enervated, and controversy more muffled. We all know some of the reasons for this drift – the centralized control over the major media of communication; the power of the party machine, together with the gross conforming idiocy of two-party parliamentary routines; the manipulation of opinion by the techniques of the salesman – the brand-image, persuasion by association, the play upon status anxieties. . . 'Get on, get ahead, get up!' say the advertisers. 'The Opportunity State', says the Conservative Party. 'Equality of Opportunity', says the official Labour echo. In this orchestration of competitive values, how is incipient heresy to be heard at all? To say that our aim should be, not equality of opportunity within an acquisitive society, but, a society of equals; that we need, not more ladders, but, more generous patterns of community life; to say these things is simply to proclaim one's political irrelevance.

Writing by Candlelight

19   Howard Brenton and David Hare, The Making of the News (1985)

The Newsroom of The Victory. *It is nine o'clock. The first edition is due in fifteen minutes. There is a calm and orderly atmosphere. Various journalists are sitting working at their desks or filing copy.*
From The Bystander *we recognize* SUZIE FONTAINE *but she has become more fashionable in her appearance. At the centre of the room sits* DOUG FANTOM, *the night editor. He is a man in his forties, wiry, tough, with his shirt sleeves rolled up.*
      (*A* JOURNALIST *passes through the room with sheaves of paper.*)
JOURNALIST: Last copy please. First edition due in fifteen minutes.
      (*A* JOURNALIST *yawns.* DOUG FANTOM *is sitting back with his legs on the desk reading some copy. At the side* LARRY PUNT, *a nervous young reporter, is sneaking glances at him. When* FANTOM *eventually speaks it is to himself.*)
FANTOM: For my sins, for my sins. (*He calls out.*) Whose is this?
      (LARRY PUNT *approaches at once.*)
LARRY: Oh, its mine.
FANTOM: It's a very nice story, Larry. Well done.
LARRY: Thank you.
FANTOM: Have you been to Loch Fergus?
LARRY: Well . . . yes, Mr Fantom. I was there just after it happened. Doesn't that show?

FANTOM: Let's see, let's read this out.

(*Without comment he hands the copy to* LARRY.)

LARRY: 'Women who have recently formed a peace camp outside the gates for the plant on Loch Fergus where the building of the new Fork-Lightning missile is soon to begin, were yesterday recovering from a surprise attack by two hundred policemen in the early hours of Tuesday morning.

The police mounted their attack in full riot gear and destroyed the camp in twenty-five minutes. Twenty-seven women were charged with various alleged minor offences and subsequently spent the night in cells at Loch Fergus police station.

Commenting on the surprise attack Mrs Mary Kingham, a thirty-four-year-old mother of two, said "I was dragged by the hair from my sleeping bag and pulled across the road, where I was thrown violently into the back of a van while being abused by a masked policeman".'

(LARRY *pauses a moment and looks at* FANTOM *who makes no reaction.*)

'Last night two women were still being detained with serious injuries in Loch Fergus General Hospital.'

(FANTOM *nods judiciously.*)

FANTOM: Yes, well, that's good, that makes things very clear.

LARRY: Thank you.

FANTOM: The only quibble I have is that we must remember the first rule of reporting: to distinguish between what's been told to you and what you actually saw. Did you actually see them being pulled by their hair?

LARRY: No. But I did meet the women. There was blood. The hair had been torn away from the scalp.

FANTOM: Yes. To be supercilious, Larry, a woman of that type. . . It is possible she tore her own hair out.

LARRY: Yes. And kicked herself in the groin.

FANTOM: Quite.

(*The two men look at each other without humour. There is a short silence.*)

This is just a professional exercise. To maintain standards, that's all.

(LARRY *hands the copy back to him, silently.* FANTOM *puts it on the desk in front of him and takes a Mont Elanc fountain pen.*)

Women. What sort of women? (*He writes.*) Middle-aged women. Peace. Camp. Peace on this paper is always in inverted commas. You'll find that in the style book. Peace *camp*, Camp? Camp implies facilities, showers, toilets, camps are things you take the family to in Brittany. Call it a peace – inverted commas – squat. Better. 'Middle-aged women who squatted illegally. . .' Better. Do police really 'Mount an attack'? Surely they're defending *us*? Society? Themselves? So it's 'Police defending themselves'. 'In full riot gear'? That's an allegation. Out. (*He makes a great mark across the paper.*) 'Destroyed'? No. Cleared the site. In twenty-five minutes. . .that's 'Quickly and efficiently'. In spite of. . . What? How do women fight? Kicking and scratching, that kind of thing? This Mary Kingham. Do we know she's still with her husband? Left her children I suppose, to squat all over the road.

LARRY: There's no proof of that.

FANTOM: No. Abused by a what? (*He smiles up at* LARRY *good naturedly*.) Quote 'A masked policeman'? What is this, South America, Larry? Come on. (*He scores a line through the paper.*) Then you try to end it with this stuff about Loch Fergus General Hospital. I'm not sure it works. Did you go there?

LARRY: Yes, I went there. They're very badly wounded.

(FANTOM *looks at him then strikes the last line out.*)

FANTOM: The piece is too long. OK. Well done, Larry. You're coming along.

Pravda. A Fleet Street Comedy

D.   DEMOCRACY AND TOTALITARIANISM

A theme of this chapter has been the ways in which liberty and democracy can diverge. In the twentieth century, and especially since the 1930s, this thought has taken the form of a fear of 'totalitarian democracy'. Observers have noted how Hitler used democratic machinery to gain power, how he increased his power with such devices as plebiscites, and how he maintained himself in power through the skilful use of mass propaganda. (At the end of the last section we illustrated fears that the media can be used not to enlighten but to manipulate public opinion.) The concept of 'totalitarian democracy' has more of a European than a specifically British resonance, but it has been powerfully expressed by British writers. In particular, George Orwell is associated with the unmasking of totalitarian political techniques. In *Animal Farm* (VI:20), we see the pig Snowball manipulating democratic machinery to gain power.

20   George Orwell, Animal Farm (1941)

On Sundays there was no work. Breakfast was an hour later than usual, and after breakfast there was a ceremony which was observed every week without fail. First came the hoisting of the flag. Snowball had found in the harness-room an old green tablecloth of Mrs Jones's and had painted on it a hoof and a horn in white. This was run up the flagstaff in the farmhouse garden every Sunday morning. The flag was green, Snowball explained, to represent the green fields of England, while the hoof and horn signified the future Republic of the Animals which would arise when the human race had been finally overthrown. After the hoisting of the flag all the animals trooped into the big barn for a general assembly which was known as the Meeting. Here the work of the coming week was planned out and resolutions were put forward and debated. It was always the pigs who put forward the resolutions. The other animals understood how to vote, but could never think of any resolutions of their own. Snowball and Napoleon were by far the most active in the debates. But it was noticed that these two were never in agreement: whatever suggestion either of them made, the other could be counted on to oppose it. Even when it was resolved – a thing no one could object to in itself – to set aside the small paddock behind the orchard as a home of rest for animals who were past work, there was a stormy debate over the correct retiring age for each class of animal. The Meeting always ended with the singing of 'Beasts of England', and the afternoon was given up to recreation. . .

In January there came bitterly hard weather. The earth was like iron, and nothing could be done in the fields. Many meetings were held in the big barn, and the pigs occupied themselves with planning out the work of the coming season. It had come to be accepted that the pigs, who were manifestly cleverer than the other animals, should decide all questions of farm policy, though their decisions had to be ratified by a majority vote. This arrangement would have worked well enough if it had not been for the disputes between Snowball and Napoleon. These two disagreed at every point where disagreement was possible. If one of them suggested sowing a bigger acreage with barley, the other was certain to demand a bigger acreage of oats, and if one of them said that such a field was just right for cabbages, the other would declare that it was useless for anything except roots. Each had his own following, and there were some violent debates. At the Meetings Snowball often won over the majority by his brilliant speeches, but Napoleon was better at canvassing support for himself in between times. He was especially successful with the sheep. Of late the sheep had taken to bleating 'Four legs good, two legs bad' both in and out of season, and they often interrupted the Meeting with this. It was noticed that they were especially liable to break into 'Four legs good, two legs bad' at crucial moments in Snowball's speeches. . .

The whole farm was deeply divided on the subject of the windmill. Snowball did not deny that to build it would be a difficult business. Stone would have to be quarried and built up into walls, then the sails would have to be made and after that there would be need for dynamos and cables. (How these were to be procured, Snowball did not say.) But he maintained that it could all be done in a year. And thereafter, he declared, so much labour would be saved that the animals would only need to work three days a week. Napoleon, on the other hand, argued that the great need of the moment was to increase food production, and that if they wasted time on the windmill they would all starve to death. The animals formed themselves into two factions under the slogans, 'Vote for Snowball and the three-day week' and 'Vote for Napoleon and the full manger'. Benjamin was the only animal who did not side with either faction. He refused to believe either that food would become more plentiful or that the windmill would save work. Windmill or no windmill, he said, life would go on as it had always gone on – that is, badly. . .

At last the day came when Snowball's plans were completed. At the Meeting on the following Sunday the question of whether or not to begin work on the windmill was to be put to the vote. When the animals had assembled in the big room, Snowball stood up and, though occasionally interrupted by bleating from the sheep, set forth his reasons for advocating the building of the windmill. Then Napoleon stood up to reply. He said very quietly that the windmill was nonsense and that he advised nobody to vote for it, and promptly sat down again; he had spoken for barely thirty seconds, and seemed almost indifferent as to the effect he produced. At this Snowball sprang to his feet, and shouting down the sheep, who had begun bleating again, broke into a passionate appeal in favour of the windmill. Until now the animals had been about equally divided in their sympathies, but in a moment Snowball's eloquence had carried them away. In glowing sentences he painted a picture of Animal Farm as it might be when sordid labour was lifted from the animals' backs. His imagination had now run far beyond chaff-cutters and turnip-slicers. Electricity, he said, could operate threshing machines, ploughs, harrows, rollers and reapers and binders, besides supplying every stall with its own electric light, hot and cold water, and an electric heater. By the time he had finished speaking, there was no doubt as to which way the vote would go. But just at this moment Napoleon stood up and, casting a peculiar sidelong look at Snowball, uttered a high-pitched whimper of a kind no one had ever heard him utter before.

At this there was a terrible baying sound outside, and nine enormous dogs wearing brass-studded collars came bounding into the barn. They dashed straight for Snowball, who only sprang from his place just in time to escape their snapping jaws. In a moment he was out of the door and they were after him. Too amazed and frightened to speak, all the animals crowded through the door to watch the chase. Snowball was racing across the long pasture that led to the road. He was running as only a pig can run, but the dogs were close on his heels. Suddenly he slipped and it seemed certain they had him. Then he was up again, running faster than ever, then the dogs were gaining on him again. One of them all but closed his jaws on Snowball's tail, but Snowball whisked it free just in time. Then he put on an extra spurt and, with a few inches to spare, slipped through a hole in the hedge and was seen no more.

Animal Farm

VII
Nations and Empire

Democracy means 'rule by the people'. But who constitutes a 'people'? In ancient Athens, citizenship was limited to a minority of the population, excluding women, slaves and foreigners. In Chapters III and IV we saw how in Britain during the nineteenth and early twentieth centuries the franchise was gradually extended until the vast majority of the adult population possessed the vote. But this process does not exhaust the problem of who should be included in 'the people'. Is a 'people' necessarily homogeneous in its language, religion, culture and race? What happens if there exists a minority permanently at odds with the majority in any of these respects? Can their rights and interests be protected within a system of majority rule, or should they be considered a separate 'people', entitled to their own democracy? And once this division into separate 'nations' has begun, where does it end?

Nationalist and democratic movements have been intertwined over the past two hundred years. In nineteenth-century Europe, liberalism was associated with calls for national unity against the remnants of feudal particularism (in Germany and Italy) or with the emancipation of subject peoples or nations from old Empires such as the Hapsburg and Ottoman. More recently, nationalism has been associated in the 'Third World' with the desire for self-determination among the former subjects of the old European empires. In twentieth-century Europe, from the carnage of the First World War, through Nazism and fascism to the recent troubles in the former Soviet Union and Yugoslavia, we have seen the darker side of nationalism.

The aim of this chapter is to illustrate the importance of these issues for debates about democracy within Britain. No book on democracy in Britain would be complete without some consideration of nationalism and race. Britain is a multi-national state, incorporating peoples from the four historic nations of England, Ireland, Scotland and Wales. At different times, and to varying degrees, there have been nationalist movements among the 'Celtic' peoples of Ireland, Scotland and Wales that have demanded freedom from English domination. This 'territorial' dimension to British democracy has been a central strand in British history, and continues to be a significant fact of British politics, particularly with reference to the seemingly intractable problem of Northern Ireland. In addition, for more than three hundred years Britain was the centre of a large overseas Empire, a fact that had important ramifications not only for the 'subjects' of the British Empire in Asia, Africa and the Caribbean, but also for British society itself. One important legacy of Empire is the issue of race in British society.

A. Nations

One basic question that often puzzles foreigners about Britain is what exactly to call it. The British Isles? Great Britain? The United Kingdom? What do these various terms refer to, and how do they relate to those other geographical, national and cultural designations – 'England', 'Scotland', 'Wales' and 'Ireland'? This confusion over names – which goes to the heart of the 'territorial dimension' of British politics – is wittily discussed in Bernard Crick's essay, 'An Englishman Considers his Passport' (VII:1). Supporters of the notion of 'Britain' would argue that there is nothing inherently wrong with such historically generated anomalies, and that there is no reason why a state should not incorporate more than one nation. Writing in 1862, the historian Lord Acton (VII:2) attacks nationalism (or the 'modern theory of nationality', as he refers to it) for assuming that the state should be identified with just one nation or 'people', and defends multi-national states such as Britain and the Austrian Hapsburg Empire.

An Irish or Scottish or Welsh nationalist's reply to Lord Acton would be that, although what he says may be true in theory, in practice the British state has not been a voluntary association of nations on an equal footing, but a cloak for the domination of one state (England) over the others. Many of the extracts that follow, illustrating the specific histories of Irish, Scottish and Welsh nationalisms, express this basic viewpoint and use it to argue for some form of national self-determination.

The most important of the three 'nationalisms', in terms of its impact on the politics of Britain as a whole, has been the Irish. The bitterness and deep-rootedness of the conflict over Ireland owes a good deal to its partly religious nature: the majority of the population of Ireland are Roman Catholic, and for a large part of their history were deprived of civil rights by their Protestant 'Anglo-Irish' rulers. Catholic 'Emancipation' – enabling Catholics to enter Parliament and hold civil and military offices – was only achieved in 1829. Although the protracted and sometimes violent struggles for Irish 'Home Rule' eventually resulted in the creation of the Irish Free State in December 1921 (renamed the 'Republic of Ireland' under the 1937 constitution), it was achieved at the price of partitioning off the six counties of 'Northern Ireland' (or 'Ulster') with their Protestant majority. (Much of this Protestant population of Northern Ireland was the product of the so-called 'plantations' of the seventeenth century, when Protestant immigrants from Scotland and Ireland were encouraged to settle by the government.) Northern Ireland was granted devolved government within the United Kingdom, but by the 1960s there were strong protests from the Catholic minority of Northern Ireland at what they perceived as abuses of their civil rights by the Protestant majority. In 1969 the British army was sent into Northern Ireland – initially to protect Catholics – and in 1972 the devolved government of Northern Ireland was dissolved and direct rule from Westminster imposed. Over 3,000 people have been killed in the Northern Irish 'Troubles' since 1969, and all attempts to reach a political solution have failed. Catholic nationalists (or 'Republicans') demand greater links, or unity, with the Irish Republic, while Protestant 'Unionists' (or 'Loyalists') wish to retain the link with the United Kingdom and fear being swallowed up in a predominantly Catholic united Ireland.

Although the modern (post-French Revolution) character of nationalism has been stressed up to now, there is an older, pre-democratic origin to the desire for national self-determination. For example, in his *Drapier's Letters* (VII:3) of 1724 (so called because of the pseudonym under which he wrote them) the great satirist Jonathan Swift argues for the legislative independence of the Irish Parliament. It would be wholly misleading to describe Swift – who was an Irish Protestant and a Tory – as a nationalist in the modern sense, for his argument is based not on nationality but on the principle that 'government without the consent of the governed is the very definition of slavery'. The implicit weakness of Swift's argument lay in the fact that the Irish Parliament represented only the Protestant minority of the island.

In Ireland as in other parts of Europe, news of the French Revolution inspired movements advocating republicanism and political reform. (As elsewhere, Thomas Paine's *Rights of Man* was a bestseller; seven Irish editions were published between 1791 and 1792.) The most important of these was the Society of United Irishmen, founded in Belfast in 1791. Drawing its initial support mainly from Protestants, the United Irishmen began as a movement for parliamentary reform, but by 1798 it had become a secret society with deep roots in the Catholic peasantry, calling for the establishment of a republic. In that year the movement was violently suppressed. One result of the political ferment of the 1790s was the union of the English and Irish Parliaments (1800). The author of the 'Declaration of the Society of United Irishmen' (VII:4) was probably Theobald Wolfe Tone, who (though a Protestant) is often regarded as the founder of modern Irish nationalism.

Tone and the United Irishmen provided a potent example to the Irish nationalists of the late nineteenth century. There were celebrations in 1898 to mark the centenary of the United Irishmen's uprising, organized primarily by the Irish Republican Brotherhood (or 'Fenians'), the most influential nationalist organization of that period. Successive Home Rule Bills introduced into the Westminster Parliament (1886, 1893 and 1912) foundered on the opposition of English political interests and Ulster Unionists. But it was external events (the outbreak of the First World War) that created the conditions for the 'Easter Rising' of 1916. As Chairman of the Provisional Government of the Irish Republic, Patrick Pearse read the Proclamation of Independence (VII:5) from the steps of the General Post Office in Dublin. The Rising was suppressed, and Pearse, along with the other signatories of the Declaration, was court-martialled and executed shortly after. From the above it can be seen that although the causes of the present 'Troubles' in Northern Ireland date back most obviously to the partition of 1921, they also have deep roots in more than three hundred years of Irish history. Seamus Heaney, whose background is Northern Irish Catholic, gives a vivid snapshot of the misery and disruption caused to the people of Northern Ireland by the Troubles (VII:6), while John Hewitt (who, along with Heaney, was a prominent figure in the Northern Irish literary renaissance of the past thirty years) provides the perspective of a writer from the Protestant community (VII:7).

Conflict between the historic kingdoms of England and Scotland stretches back hundreds of years. One of the most potent literary texts for modern Scottish nationalists has been the Declaration of Arbroath, an appeal written in Latin in 1320 by the Scottish barons to the Pope, who had refused to recognize Robert the Bruce as King of Scotland and Scottish independence of England. In the famous

passage quoted here (VII:8) the barons pledge their loyalty to Robert
the Bruce and make an eloquent plea for liberty.

The two kingdoms were united under a single ruler in 1603, when
James VI of Scotland acceded to the English throne, but the term
'United Kingdom' (see VII:1) refers to the Act of Union of 1707,
under which the Scottish Parliament agreed to an amalgamation of
the two kingdoms. The 1707 Act of Union remains the constitutional
basis of the relationship between Scotland and England, although
there has been considerable administrative devolution since the
nineteenth century. (In 1887 the Scottish Office was created, taking
on the functions that in England are the responsibility of the Home
Office.) In addition, Scotland has retained its distinctive educational,
legal, religious and cultural traditions.

Modern Scottish nationalism does not have the violent history of
its Irish counterpart, but calls for independence or, less ambitiously,
some form of legislative devolution have been a persistent theme in
British politics. We saw above, with reference to the United
Irishmen, the galvanizing effect that the French Revolution had in
encouraging advocates of republicanism and political reform. Henry
Cockburn (VII:9), recalling the events surrounding the Sedition
Trials of 1793–4, describes a similar process in Scotland. The
principal defendant in these trials – which are regarded as a landmark
in Scottish legal and political history – was Thomas Muir, a radical
lawyer and a leader of the 'Friends of the People' in Scotland. He was
charged with having excited disaffection, circulated Paine's *Rights of
Man*, and read and defended the Address of the United Irishmen (see
VII:4) at a convention of the Friends of the People. He was sentenced
to fourteen years' transportation to the new penal colony at Botany
Bay, Australia.

Support for Scottish 'Home Rule' was the enthusiasm of only a
tiny minority for most of the nineteenth century. The majority of the
country voted Liberal, and traditional symbols of Scottishness like
the wearing of tartan kilts were domesticated and became little more
than costumes of aristocratic affectation. Queen Victoria established a
summer residence at Balmoral in the Highlands. Interest in the idea of
Home Rule revived towards the end of the century, largely as a spin-
off of attempts to get an Irish Home Rule Bill through Parliament. A
Scottish Home Rule Association was formed in 1886. But although
the Scottish Liberals came out in favour of Home Rule, the Liberal
leadership didn't take up the issue with any enthusiasm, regarding
Ireland as the priority.

Keir Hardie, the 'father' of the Labour Party, was Scottish, as was the first Labour Prime Minister (1922–4 and 1929–31), Ramsay MacDonald. (The leadership of the present-day Labour Party continues to be dominated by Scotsmen.) Scottish voters have consistently been to the Left of their English counterparts. The turning point in this respect was the 1922 election, which signalled a shift from the Liberals to Labour in Scotland. Earlier, in 1919, Communist influence in the industrial area of Clydeside was demonstrated when strikes and demonstrations led to the government putting troops on to the streets to suppress what they perceived as a potentially revolutionary situation. The most prominent figure of 'Red Clydeside', John Maclean (VII:10), went on to attempt (unsuccessfully) to create a Scottish Workers' Republican Party which would combine Marxism and Scottish nationalism.

Both Keir Hardie and Ramsay MacDonald began as advocates of Home Rule, but this failed to produce any positive moves when Labour gained power. Frustration with this inaction led to the formation of the National Party of Scotland in 1928 (acquiring its contemporary name, the Scottish National Party, in 1934). Meanwhile, there was occurring a significant renaissance in Scottish literary life (which had been largely dormant since the 'Scottish Enlightenment' of the late eighteenth century). C. M. Grieve (better known by his pen-name, Hugh MacDiarmid), the leading figure of this revival, was an ardent nationalist and socialist (VII:11). But MacDiarmid was opposed by another leading figure in the Scottish literary revival, Edwin Muir, who expressed scepticism about the notion of a Scottish identity (VII:12). Muir's origins serve as a reminder that Scotland itself is by no means homogenous; he came from the Orkney Islands, which have their own Scandinavian cultural connections through their distant Viking past.

Desire for Scottish independence, or for legislative devolution, became a significant force in British politics in the 1970s. Despite defeat for the idea of national assemblies in referenda held in Scotland and Wales in 1979, devolution is advocated by both Labour and Liberal Democrat parties in Scotland. Scottish Nationalists call for complete independence. In the late 1980s calls for a Scottish assembly began to be heard once more and a cross-party Constitutional Convention (boycotted by the Conservatives and Scottish Nationalists) was organized to explore possibilities and put forward proposals.

Desire for political separation from the United Kingdom has been a much less powerful force in Wales than in Ireland or Scotland, but nationalist feeling has made itself felt through such cultural issues as education, religion and, above all, the preservation of the Welsh language. The political union of England and Wales dates back to 1536, but at the beginning of the nineteenth century the vast majority of Welsh people still spoke Welsh rather than English. (By 1901 the proportion of Welsh speakers had fallen to 50 per cent. In 1981 the figure was 19 per cent.) From about 1885 there was a revival of national consciousness in Wales. The most important issue of the time was disestablishment of the Church in Wales (VII:13), an importance that reflected the prominence of Protestant Non-conformity. Nationalist sentiment was also channelled into the campaign for a National University. As in Scotland, there was a massive shift in the first two decades from the Liberals to Labour. (One might also note the number of important figures in the leadership of the Labour movement who have been Welsh, or sat for Welsh seats – Aneurin Bevan, Michael Foot and Neil Kinnock, for example.) Plaid Cymru, the Welsh Nationalist Party, was formed in 1925, and at first its objectives were focussed on protection of the Welsh language rather than political self-government. The most prominent figure in the early history of Welsh nationalism was Saunders Lewis, who leapt to public attention in 1936, when he and two others took part in the burning of an RAF bombing school at Pen-y-Berth in North Wales (VII:14). At the end of the Second World War, with the Labour Party (which showed less interest in Welsh self-government than the Liberals had done) in the ascend-ancy, Welsh nationalism seemed virtually dead as a political force. But in the 1960s there was a significant revival in nationalist feeling, particularly among the young, and again focussed around the language issue. In 1966 Plaid Cymru gained a seat in Parliament for the first time. In the late 1970s, responding to this increased nationalist sentiment, the Labour Party moved (albeit not unanim-ously) towards supporting devolution, but in the 1979 referendum only 12 per cent of the electorate voted in favour of a Welsh assembly, with 46.5 per cent against. If political nationalism remains weak in Wales, a desire to preserve 'Welshness' remains a potent cultural force. In 1982 a Welsh TV channel was created. More pessimistically, a major literary figure of present-day Wales, R. S. Thomas, expresses bitter gloom about the prospects of preserving a national identity against English economic and cultural encroachment (VII:15).

1   Bernard Crick, An Englishman's Passport (1988)

I am a citizen of a state with no agreed colloquial name. Our passports call us citizens of 'The United Kingdom of Great Britain and Ireland'. But what does one reply when faced by that common existential question of civilised life, which is neither precisely legal nor precisely philosophical, found in foreign hotel registers, 'Nationality?'.

If that question is meant to establish legal citizenship, then 'British' is correct, although that is the least used name colloquially for people as distinct from goods. . . The majority write 'English'. The overwhelming majority of UK passport holders are, of course, 'English', but I have a suspicion that many of them write 'English' not as an assertion of nationality, as do those who write Irish, Scottish or Welsh, but out of a common but mistaken belief that 'English' is the adjective corresponding to 'citizen of the United Kingdom of Great Britain and Northern Ireland'. . .

Even in documents more elaborate than a passport we English are very confused when we try to name our state. The Central Office of Information publishes an annual handbook on the UK which has all kinds of useful information in it, and has a wide circulation abroad. The title of it is bizarrely (though no one notices or complains) the name of a former Roman province, which has no modern legal or precise geographical meaning: *Britain*. The current Preface of *Britain* states:

> Care should be taken when studying British statistics to note whether they refer to England, to England and Wales. . .to Great Britain, which comprises England, Wales and Scotland, or to the United Kingdom (which is the same as Britain, that is Great Britain and Northern Ireland) as a whole.

Indeed. But is 'Britain' usually understood to be 'the same as' the United Kingdom as a whole? When I say 'Britain' I mean, contrary to the C.O.I., the 'mainland' only, and say 'Great Britain' when I want to include Northern Ireland. Perhaps usage varies. In the O.E.D. early usages of Britain all refer to the island or the mainland of the archipelago. And O.E.D's summary of early modern usage is confused: 'The proper name of the whole island, containing England, Wales and Scotland, with

their dependencies; more fully called Great Britain; now used
for the British state or Empire as a whole.' That 'more fully' is
as a dictionary entry politically very question-begging and pre-
emptive. 'Britain' and 'Great Britain' are as often used to refer to
different entities. Ulster Loyalists are always careful to proclaim
their (conditional) loyalty to 'Great Britain' or 'The United
Kingdom'; they rightly suspect that loose talk of 'Britain' can
often mean the mainland alone, and thus prove a device to
distance them, ultimately to separate them.

The fundamental problem is not, of course, even as simple as
that of maintaining or recovering a true view of Great Britain as
a multi-national society and, in many respects, a quasi-federal
polity. . .

An often forgotten aspect of the problem of national interrela-
tions in the British Isles is a lack of clarity on the part of the
English as to what constitutes their own national identity. There
are very few serious studies of English character, still less
of English dilemmas about identity. . . Considering that the
English are not lacking in self-esteem and, what A. L. Lowell
once called, 'a certain effortless sense of superiority', this is
strange – but true. If you doubt this, try to compile a
bibliography or look at any subject-catalogue in a great library:
subheadings will show shelf-loads of books on Irish, Scottish
and Welsh nationalism or national identity, not to mention
French, German and American, etc. etc.; but very few, and then
mostly rubbishy, on England and Englishness.

Why this massive silence? Why did the bulldog not bark even
in the good old days when it could really bite? The explanation
could lie in a very obvious factor. It is the simple presuppositions that we usually miss. Consider what historically, since at
least the accession of James I and James VI to the two thrones,
has been the main preoccupation of English politics: holding the
United Kingdom together. . .

For the English to have developed a strident literature of
English nationalism, such as arose, often under official patronage, everywhere else in Europe, and in Ireland and Scotland,
eventually in Wales, would have been divisive. From political
necessity English politicians tried to develop a United Kingdom
nationalism and, at least explicitly and officially, to identify
themselves with it, wholeheartedly. . .

When King James VI of Scotland had been proclaimed King
in England it was not, as often said, as 'James I of England' but

as 'James I, King of Great Britain'. And that same formula was used throughout the Act or Treaty of Union in 1707, almost a pretence that 'England' as a separate entity had gone out of business, whereas in 1603 a separate kingdom of Scotland was plainly acknowledged and in 1707 a formidable list of Scottish rights set down, including the establishment of the Presbyterian Church (which many Scots at the time saw as the real national, popular and representative institution rather than the aristocratically dominated and corrupt Parliament). Throughout the eighteenth century English governments and courts, especially after the great scare of 1745, made conscious and strenuous efforts to establish 'British' as the general description, and to replace 'Scottish' and 'English' with 'North British' and 'South British'. Some Ministerial hacks even tried 'West British' for Irish, or at least for loyal Irish.

'An Englishman Considers His Passport'

2   Lord Acton, In Defence of Multi-National States (1878)

In pursuing the outward and visible growth of the national theory we are prepared for an examination of its political character and value. The absolutism which has created it denies equally that absolute right of national unity which is a product of democracy, and that claim of national liberty which belongs to the theory of freedom. These two views of nationality, corresponding to the French and to the English systems, are connected in name only, and are in reality the opposite extremes of political thought. In one case, nationality is founded on the perpetual supremacy of the collective will, of which the unity of the nation is the necessary condition, to which every other influence must defer, and against which no obligation enjoys authority, and all resistance is tyrannical. The nation is here an ideal unit founded on the race, in defiance of the modifying action of external causes, of tradition, and of existing rights. It overrules the rights and wishes of the inhabitants, absorbing their divergent interests in a fictitious unity; sacrifices their several inclinations and duties to the higher claim of nationality, and crushes all natural rights and all established liberties for the purpose of vindicating itself. . . Connected with this theory in nothing except in the common enmity of the absolute state, is the theory which represents nationality as an essential, but not a supreme element in determining the forms of the State. It is distinguished from the other, because it tends to diversity and not to uniformity, to harmony and not to unity; because it aims not at an arbitrary change, but at careful respect for the existing conditions of political life, and because it obeys the laws and results of history, not the aspirations of an ideal future. While the theory of unity makes the nation a source of despotism and revolution, the theory of liberty regards it as the bulwark of self-government, and the foremost limit to the excessive power of the State. Private rights, which are sacrificed to the unity, are preserved by the union of nations. No power can so efficiently resist the tendencies of centralisation, of corruption, and of absolutism, as that community which is the vastest that can be included in a State, which imposes on its members a consistent similarity of character, interest, and opinion, and which arrests the action of the sovereign by the influence of a divided patriotism. The presence of different nations under the same sovereignty is similar in its effect to the independence of the Church in the State. It provides against the servility which flourishes under the shadow of a single authority, by balancing interests, multiplying associations, and giving to the subject the restraint and support of a combined opinion. In the same way it promotes independence by forming definite groups of public opinion, and by affording a great source and centre of political sentiments, and of notions of duty not derived from the sovereign will. Liberty provokes diversity, and diversity preserves liberty by supplying the means of organisation. All those portions of law which govern the relations of men with each other, and regulate social life, are the varying result of national custom and the creation of private society. In these things, therefore the several nations will differ from each other; for they themselves have produced them, and they do not owe them to the State which rules them all. This diversity in the same State is a firm barrier against the intrusion of the government beyond the political sphere. . .

If we take the establishment of liberty for the realisation of moral duties to be the end of civil society, we must conclude that those states are substantially the most perfect which, like the British and Austrian Empires, include various distinct nationalities without oppressing them. Those in which no mixture of races has occurred are imperfect; and those in which its effects have disappeared are decrepit. A State which is incompetent to satisfy different races condemns itself; a State which labours to neutralise, to absorb, or to expel them, destroys its own vitality; a State which does not include them is destitute of the chief basis of self-government. The theory of nationality, therefore, is a retrograde step in history.

Essays on Freedom and Power

3 Jonathan Swift, The Independence of Ireland (1724)

Those who who come over hither to us from *England*, and some *weak* People among ourselves, whenever, in Discourse, we make mention of *Liberty* and *Property*, shake their Heads, and tell us, that *Ireland* is *a depending Kingdom*; as if they would seem, by this Phrase, to intend, that the People of *Ireland* is in some State of Slavery or Dependance, different from those of England: Whereas, *a depending Kingdom* is a *modern Term of Art*; unknown, as I have heard, to all antient *Civilians*, and *Writers upon Government*; and *Ireland* is, on the contrary, called in some Statutes an *Imperial Crown*, as held only from God; which is as high a Style, as any Kingdom is capable of receiving. Therefore by this Expression, *a depending Kingdom*, there is no more understood, than that by a Statute made here, in the 33d Year of Henry VIII, *The King and his Successors, are to be Kings Imperial of this Realm, as united and knit to the Imperial Crown of* England. I have looked over all the *English* and *Irish* Statutes, without finding any Law that makes *Ireland depend* upon *England*; any more than *England* doth upon *Ireland*. We have, indeed, obliged ourselves to have *the same King with them*; and consequently they are obliged to have *the same King with us*. For the Law was made by *our own Parliament*; and our Ancestors then were not such *Fools (whatever they were in the preceding Reign)* to bring themselves under I know not what *Dependance*, which is now talked of, without any Ground of *Law, Reason,* or *common Sense*.

LET whoever think otherwise, I *M. B. Drapier*, desire to be excepted. For I declare, next under God, I *depend* only on the

King my Sovereign, and on the Laws of my own Country, And
I am so far from *depending* upon the People of *England*, that, if
they should ever *rebel* against my Sovereign, (which GOD
forbid) I would be ready at the first Command from his Majesty
to take Arms against them; as some of *my* Countrymen did
against *theirs* at *Preston*. And, if such a Rebellion should prove so
successful as to fix the *Pretender* on the Throne of *England*; I
would venture to transgress that *Statute* so far, as to lose every
Drop of my Blood, to hinder him from being *King* of *Ireland*.

IT is true, indeed, that within the Memory of Man, the
Parliaments of *England* have *sometimes* assumed the Power of
binding this Kingdom, by Laws enacted there; wherein they
were, at first, openly opposed (as far as *Truth, Reason*, and *Justice*
are capable of *opposing*) by the famous Mr *Molineaux*, an *English*
Gentleman born here; as well as by several of the greatest
Patriots, and *best Whigs* in *England*; but the *Love and Torrent* of
Power prevailed. Indeed, the Arguments on both Sides were
invincible. For in *Reason*, all *Government* without the Consent of
the *Governed*, is the *very Definition of Slavery*: But in *Fact, Eleven
Men well armed, will certainly subdue one single Man in his Shirt*.
But I have done. For those who have used *Power* to cramp
Liberty, have gone so far as to resent even the *Liberty* of
Complaining; although a Man upon the Rack, was never known
to be refused the Liberty of *roaring* as loud as he thought fit.

The Drapier's Letters, Letter IV,
'To The Whole People of Ireland'

4 Wolfe Tone, The Society of United Irishmen (1791)

In the present great era of reform, when unjust Governments
are falling in every quarter of Europe; when religious persecution is compelled to abjure her tyranny over conscience; when
the rights of men are ascertained in theory, and that theory
substantiated by practice; when antiquity can no longer defend
absurd and oppressive forms, against the common sense and
common interests of mankind; when all government is acknowledged to originate from the people, and to be so far only
obligatory as it protects their rights and promotes their welfare:

We think it our duty, as Irishmen, to come forward, and state
what we feel to be our heavy grievance, and what we know to
be its effectual remedy.

WE HAVE NO NATIONAL GOVERNMENT; we are
ruled by Englishmen, and the servants of Englishmen, whose
object is the interest of another country, whose instrument is
corruption, and whose strength is the weakness of Ireland; and
these men have the whole of the power and patronage of the
country, as means to seduce and to subdue the honesty and the
spirit of her representatives in the legislature. Such an extrinsic
power, acting with uniform force in a direction too frequently
opposite to the true line of our obvious interests, can be resisted
with effect solely by unanimity, decision, and spirit in the
people; qualities which may be exerted most legally, constitutionally, and efficaciously, by that great measure essential to the
prosperity and freedom of Ireland, AN EQUAL REPRE-
SENTATION OF ALL THE PEOPLE IN PARLIA-
MENT. . .

Impressed with these sentiments, we have agreed to form an
association, to be called 'THE SOCIETY OF UNITED IRISH-
MEN:' And we do pledge ourselves to our country, and
mutually to each other, that we will steadily support, and
endeavor, by all due means, to carry into effect, the following
resolutions:

First, Resolved, That the weight of English influence in the
Government of this country is so great, as to require a cordial
union among ALL THE PEOPLE OF IRELAND, to maintain
that balance which is essential to the preservation of our
liberties, and the extension of our commerce.

Second, That the sole constitutional mode by which this
influence can be opposed, is by a complete and radical reform of
the representation of the people in Parliament.

Third, That no reform is practicable, efficacious, or just,
which shall not include *Irishmen* of every religious persuasion.

Satisfied, as we are, that the intestine divisions among
Irishmen have too often given encouragement and impunity to
profligate, audacious, and corrupt Administrations, in measures
which, but for these divisions, they durst not have attempted:
we submit our resolutions to the nation, as the basis of our
political faith.

We have gone to what we conceive to be the root of the evil;
we have stated what we conceive to be the remedy. With a

Parliament thus reformed, everything is easy; without it, nothing can be done: and we do call on and most earnestly exhort our countrymen in general to follow our example, and to form similar societies in every quarter of the kingdom, for the promotion of constitutional knowledge, the abolition of bigotry in religion and politics, and the equal distribution of the rights of man through all sects and denominations of Irishmen. The people, when thus collected, will feel their own weight, and secure that power which theory has already admitted as their portion, and to which, if they be not aroused by their present provocations to vindicate it, they deserve to forfeit their pretensions FOR EVER.

'Declaration and Resolutions of the Society of United Irishmen
of Belfast'

5   The Proclamation of the Irish Republic (1916)

*The Provisional Government of the Irish Republic
to the People of Ireland*

Irishmen and Irishwomen: In the name of God and of the dead generations from which she receives her old tradition of nationhood, Ireland, through us, summons her children to her flag and strikes for her freedom.

Having organized and trained her manhood through her secret revolutionary organization, the Irish Republican Brotherhood, and through her open military organizations, the Irish Volunteers, and the Irish Citizen Army, having patiently perfected her discipline, having resolutely waited for the right moment to reveal itself, she now seizes that moment, and, supported by her exiled children in America and by gallant allies in Europe, but relying in the first on her own strength, she strikes in full confidence of victory.

We declare the right of the people of Ireland to the ownership of Ireland, and to the unfettered control of Irish destinies, to be sovereign and indefeasible. The long usurpation of that right by a foreign people and government has not extinguished the right, nor can it ever be extinguished except by the destruction of the Irish people. In every generation the Irish people have asserted their right to national freedom and sovereignty; six times during the past three hundred years they have asserted it in arms. Standing on that fundamental right and again asserting it in arms in the face of the world, we hereby proclaim the Irish republic as a sovereign independent state, and we pledge our lives and the lives of our comrades-in-arms to the cause of its freedom, of its welfare, and of its exaltation among the nations.

The Irish republic is entitled to, and hereby claims, the allegiance of every Irishman and Irishwoman. The republic guarantees religious and civil liberty, equal rights and equal opportunities to all its citizens, and declares its resolve to pursue the happiness and prosperity of the whole nation and of all its parts, cherishing all the children of the nation equally, and oblivious of the differences carefully fostered by an alien government, which have divided a minority from the majority in the past.

Until our arms have brought the opportune moment for the establishment of a permanent national government, representative of the whole people of Ireland and elected by the suffrages of all her men and women, the Provisional Government, hereby constituted, will administer the civil and military affairs of the republic in trust for the people. We place the cause of the Irish republic under the protection of the Most High God, whose blessing we invoke upon our arms, and we pray that no one who serves that cause will dishonour it by cowardice, inhumanity, or rapine. In this supreme hour the Irish nation must, by its valour and discipline, and by the readiness of its children to sacrifice themselves for the common good, prove itself worthy of the august destiny to which it is called.

Signed on behalf of the provisional government,

Thomas J. Clarke, Sean MacDiarmada, Thomas MacDonagh, P. H. Pearse, Eamonn Ceannt, James Connolly, Joseph Plunkett

Issued 24 April 1916

6 Seamus Heaney, Christmas in Belfast, 1971

People keep asking what it's like to be living in Belfast and I've found myself saying that things aren't too bad in our part of the

town: a throwaway consolation meaning that we don't expect
to be caught in crossfire if we step into the street. It's a
shorthand that evades unravelling the weary twisted emotions
that are rolled like a ball of hooks and sinkers in the heart. I am
fatigued by a continuous adjudication between agony and
injustice, swung at one moment by the long tail of race and
resentment, at another by the more acceptable feelings of pity
and terror. We live in the sickly light of TV screens, with a pane
of selfishness between ourselves and the suffering. We survive
explosions and funerals and live on among the families of the
victims, those blown apart and those in cells apart.

And we have to live with the Army. This morning I was
stopped on the Falls Road and marched to the nearest police
barracks, with my three-year-old son, because my car tax was
out of date. My protests grew limp when the officer in charge
said: 'Look, either you go to the police up the road or we take
you now to Holywood' – their own ground. It hasn't been
named martial law but that's what it feels like. Everywhere
soldiers with cocked guns are watching you – that's what
they're here for – on the streets, at the corners of streets, from
doorways, over the puddles on demolished sites. At night, jeeps
and armoured cars groan past without lights; or road-blocks are
thrown up, and once again it's delays measured in hours,
searches and signings among the guns and torches. As you drive
away, you bump over ramps that are specially designed to
wreck you at speed and maybe get a glimpse of a couple of
youths with hands on their heads being frisked on the far side of
the road. Just routine. Meanwhile up in the troubled estates
street-lights are gone, accommodating all the better the night-
sights of sniper and marksman.

If it is not army blocks, it is vigilantes. They are very
efficiently organized, with barricades of new wood and watch-
men's huts and tea rotas, protecting the territories. If I go round
the corner at ten o'clock to the cigarette machine or the chip
shop, there are the gentlemen with flashlights, of mature years
and determined mien, who will want to know my business.
How far they are in agreement with the sentiments blazoned on
the wall at the far end of the street I have not yet enquired. But
'Keep Ulster Protestant' and 'Keep Blacks and Fenians out of
Ulster' are there to remind me that there are attitudes around
here other than defensive ones. All those sentry boxes where tea
and consultation are taken through the small hours add up to yet

another slogan: 'Six into Twenty-Six won't go.' I walk back –
'Good-night now, sir' – past a bank that was blown up a couple
of months ago and a car showroom that went three weeks ago.
Nobody was killed. Most of the windows between the sites are
boarded up still. Things aren't too bad in our part.

There are few enough people on the roads at night. Fear has
begun to tingle through the place. Who's to know the next
target on the Provisional list? Who's to know the reprisals won't
strike where you are? The bars are quieter. If you're carrying a
parcel you make sure it's close to you in case it's suspected of
being about to detonate. In the Queen's University staff
common-room, recently, a bomb-disposal squad had defused a
bundle of books before the owner had quite finished his drink in
the room next door. Yet when you think of the corpses in the
rubble of McGurk's Bar such caution is far from risible.

Then there are the perils of the department stores. Last
Saturday a bomb scare just pipped me before I had my socks and
pyjamas paid for in Marks and Spencer, although there were
four people on the Shankill Road who got no warning. A
security man cornered my wife in Robinson and Cleaver – not
surprisingly, when she thought of it afterwards. She had a
timing device, even though it was just an old clock from an
auction, lying in the bottom of her shopping bag. A few days
previously someone else's timing device had given her a scare
when an office block in University Road exploded just as she
got out of range. . .

Instead of the Christmas tree, which will be deliberately
absent from many homes, people will put the traditional candle
in the window. I am reminded of Louis MacNeice, 'born to the
Anglican order, banned for ever from the candles of the Irish
poor'; and of W. R. Rodgers, whose *Collected Poems* have
appeared in time for Christmas; and of John Hewitt, that
Ulsterman of Planter stock whose poetry over the years has
been an exploration of the Ulster Protestant consciousness. All
three men were born to a sense of 'two nations' and part of their
imaginative effort was a solving of their feelings towards
Ireland, a new answer to the question that Macmorris asked
Fluellen in the Globe Theatre almost four hundred years ago:
'What is my nation?' As Northern Protestants, they each in
different ways explored their relationship to the old sow that
eats her farrow. They did not hold apart and claim kin with a
different litter. Although, in fact, I have never seen farrow eaten

by a sow in my life: what usually happens is that the young pigs
eat one another's ears.

Preoccupations. Selected Prose 1968–78

7   John Hewitt, Once Alien Here (1942)

Once alien here my fathers built their house,
claimed, drained, and gave the land the shapes of use,
and for their urgent labour grudged no more
than shuffled pennies from the hoarded store
of well-rubbed words that had left their overtones
in the ripe England of the mounded downs.

The sullen Irish limping to the hills
bore with them the enchantments and the spells
that in the clans' free days hung gay and rich
on every twig of every thorny hedge,
and gave the rain-pocked stone a meaning past
the blurred engraving of the fibrous frost.

So I, because of all the buried men
in Ulster clay, because of rock and glen
and mist and cloud and quality of air
as native in my thought as any here,
who now would seek a native mode to tell
our stubborn wisdom individual,
yet lacking skill in either scale of song,
the graver English, lyric Irish tongue,
must let this rich earth so enhance the blood
with steady pulse where now is plunging mood
till thought and image may, identified,
find easy voice to utter each aright.

'Once Alien Here', *The Collected Poems of John Hewitt*

8   The Declaration of Arbroath – The Letter of the Scottish Barons to the Pope (1320)

Unto him, as the man through whom salvation has been
wrought in our people, we are bound both of right and by his

service rendered, and are resolved in whatever fortune to cleave, for the preservation of our liberty. Were he to abandon the enterprise begun, choosing to subject us or our kingdom to the king of the English or to the English people, we would strive to thrust him out forthwith as our enemy and the subverter of right, his own and ours, and take for our king another who would suffice for our defence; for so long as an hundred remain alive we are minded never a whit to bow beneath the yoke of English dominion. It is not for glory, riches or honours that we fight: it is for liberty alone, the liberty which no good man relinquishes but with his life.

9 Henry Cockburn, The Edinburgh Sedition Trials (1793–4)

Everything rung, and was connected, with the Revolution in France; which, for above 20 years, was, or was made, the all in all. Everything, not this or that thing, but literally everything, was soaked in this one event.

Yet we had wonderfully few proper Jacobins; that is, persons who seriously wished to introduce a republic into this country, on the French precedent. There were plenty of people who were called Jacobins; because this soon became the common nick-name which was given, not only to those who had admired the dawn of the French liberation, but to those who were known to have any taste for any internal reform of our own. There was a short period, chiefly in 1793 and 1794, during which this imputation was provoked by a ridiculous aping of French forms and phraseology, and an offensive vaunting of the superior excellence of everything in that country. But the folly, which only appeared in a few towns, was very soon over, cured by time, by the failure of the French experiment, and by the essential absurdity of the thing itself; and it had never been patronised by a single person of sense and public character or influence. Firm, but mild and judicious, treatment, and a little reliance on the tendency of time to abate epidemic follies, would have made the British Constitution popular, and the proceedings in France odious, everywhere. Scotch Jacobinism did not exist. But Scotch Toryism did, and with a vengeance. . .

By far the most frightful, and the justest, idea of the spirit of those times is to be found in the proceedings of the Supreme Criminal Court in the Sedition Trials of 1793 and 1794. . .

They were political prosecutions, during a period of great political excitement; and therefore, however faction might have raged, everything done by the Court ought to have been done calmly, impartially, and decorously. The general prevalence of public intemperance was the very circumstance that ought to have impressed more deeply upon judges the duty of steady candour, and of that judicial humanity which instinctively makes every right-minded occupier of the judgement seat interpose between a prisoner and prejudice. . . But I fear that no impartial censor can avoid detecting, throughout the whole course of the trials, not mere casual indications of bias, but absolute straining for convictions. . .

When the verdicts were returned, the Court had to exercise a discretionary power in fixing upon the sentence; which discretion ranged, as these judges decided, from one hour's imprisonment to transportation for life. Assuming transportation to be lawful, it was conceded not to be necessary, and it was not then, nor at any time, used in England as a punishment of sedition. At that period it implied a frightful voyage of many months, great wretchedness in the new colony, an almost complete extinction of all communication with home, and such difficulty in returning, that a man transported was considered as a man never to be seen again. Nevertheless, transportation for a first offence was the doom of every one of these prisoners. . .

These trials sunk deep not merely into the popular mind, but into the minds of all men who thought. It was by these proceedings, more than by any other wrong, that the spirit of discontent justified itself throughout the rest of that age. It was to them that peaceful reformers appealed for the practical answer to those, who pretended to uphold our whole Scotch system as needing no change. . .

Such was the public condition of Edinburgh in 1800, and for the preceding ten years. It was a condition of great pain and debasement, the natural consequence of bad times operating on defective political institutions. . .

This was the first time that Scotland had ever been agitated by discussions upon general principles of liberty.

Memorials of his Time

10 John Maclean, A Scottish Workers' Republic (1920)

For some time past the feeling has been growing that Scotland should strike out for national independence, as well as Ireland and other lands. This has recently been strengthened by the English government's intention to rely mainly on Scottish troops to murder the Irish race.

Genuine Scotsmen recently asked themselves the question: 'Are we Scots to be used as the bloody tools of the English against our brother Celts of Erin?' And naturally the instinctive response was – No!

Again, the land seizures by Highland crofters are arousing the blood of Highlandmen driven south to the Clyde Valley for work. Especially the filthy tactics of Lord Leverhulme (an English capitalist), who has dismissed Stornoway wage-slaves as a means of beating the Lewis raiders who seized the farms of Coll and Gress. Divide and conquer again!

Scottish students of history now realise that Edinburgh lawyers and politicians sold Scottish independence in 1707, although most blame has fallen on the Earl of Stair. Many of us are convinced that ever since 1707 the Edinburgh kings' and queens' counsels and politicians have been in the regular pay of London to keep Scotland as the base tool of the English government. These scoundrels in the eighteenth century helped to ruin Burns, the peasants' and people's poet.

The 'rebellions' of 1715 and 1745 were natural reactions against the treacherous deed of 1707, but these unfortunate outbursts but gave the English the excuse and chance to subdue the Highland chiefs and then corrupt them with an English education at Oxford and Cambridge.

Since 1790 the chiefs became Englishmen in outlook, and used their clansmen to defend English capitalism against the revolution started in Paris in 1789. Since the Napoleonic wars the Highland regiments have been used to defend the stolen lands of England all over the globe, and have largely helped to extend the English empire.

Whilst doing this, the Dukes of Sutherland and Argyll and other chiefs proceeded with the English landlord policy of land clearances. The friends of the fighters were chased off their native heath into the lowlands or out to Canada and Australia.

Now the reaction is beginning – inspired by Ireland and

Russia. Scotland must again have independence, but not to be
ruled by traitor kings or chiefs, lawyers and politicians. The
communism of the clans must be re-established on a modern
basis. (Bolshevism, to put it roughly, is but the modern
expression of the communism of the *mir*.) Scotland must
therefore work itself into a communism embracing the whole
country as a unit. The country must have but one clan, as it
were – a united people working in co-operation and co-
operatively, using the wealth that is created.

We can safely say, then: back to communism and forward to
communism.

'All Hail, the Scottish Workers' Republic!'

11   Hugh MacDiarmid, The Absence of Scottish Nationalism (1927)

Scotland is unique among European nations in its failure to
develop a nationalist sentiment strong enough to be a vital
factor in its affairs – a failure inconsistent alike with our
traditional love of country and reputation for practicality. The
reason probably lies in the fact that no comprehensive-enough
agency has emerged; and the common-sense of our people has
rejected one-sided expedients incapable of addressing the
organic complexity of our national life. For it must be recognized that the absence of Scottish nationalism is, paradoxically
enough, a form of Scottish self-determination. If that self-
determination, which, in the opinion of many of us, has reduced
Scottish arts and affairs to a lamentable pass, is to be induced to
take a different form and express itself in a diametrically
opposite direction to that which it has taken for the past two
hundred and twenty years, the persuading programme must
embody considerations of superior power to those which have
so long ensured the opposite process. Scottish opinion is
anachronism-proof in matters of this kind. The tendency
inherent in the Union, to assimilate Scotland to England, and
ultimately to provincialize the former – the stage which has been
so unexpectedly but unmistakably arrested at the eleventh hour
– has, as a matter of fact, not yet been effectively countered by
the emergence of any principle demanding a reversed tendency.
That is why, despite the persistence in Scotland of an entirely

different psychology, the desire to retain and develop distinctive traditions in arts and affairs, and the fairly general recognition that the political, economic and social consequences of the Union have never been by any means wholly favourable to Scottish interests and have latterly, in many ways, become decreasingly so to a very alarming degree, there has nevertheless been at most little more than a passive resistance to complete assimilation masked by an external acquiescence. This is because Home Rule has been conceived for the most part, even by its advocates, merely as a measure of devolution – a continuance of substantially the same thing as prevails at Westminster; not something fundamentally different and answering to the unexpressed needs of the Scottish spirit. It is this passive resistance which accounts, for example, for the comparative paucity and poverty of distinctively Scottish literature since the Union. Only that fringe of the Scottish genius amenable to Anglicization has continued to find expression; the rest has, practically, 'held its tongue', and, to a large extent its powers of expression have atrophied. A similar phenomenon manifests itself in our schools. Many teachers tell me that the children's abilities to express themselves, and, behind that, to think, are largely suppressed by official insistence upon the use of 'correct English'. They actually think, and could express themselves a great deal more readily and effectively, in dialect. This tenacity of Scots in the life of our people is extraordinary. Observe the way even 'educated people' lapse into it on convenient occasions, or when they are genuinely moved. To ban it from our schools is, therefore, a psychological outrage. A distinctive speech cannot be so retained in the intimate social life, in the thinking of a people without an accompanying subterranean continuance of all manner of distinctive mental states and potentialities. The inhibition of these is all the worse when, as in Scotland today, they are denied their natural pabulum – when, for example, as so often happens, an appeal to Scottish sentiment is applauded by those who, owing to the way in which our educational system has been organized, have little or no knowledge of our separate history and culture, and have been taught to take it for granted that Scotland's future is wholly identified with England's, and that economic and social expediency are best served by discarding the shibboleths of 'a distinction without a difference'. It is upon these camouflaged or hidden forces, however – many of them unconscious – that the ultimate direction, if it has

any, of 'Scotland – a Nation', must depend. Only so can
Scotland, as such, re-enter the mainstream of European arts and
affairs.

Albyn, or Scotland and the Future

12   Edwin Muir, The Irrelevance of Scottish Nationalism (1935)

Though Scotland has not been a nation for some time, it has
possessed a distinctly marked style of life; and that is now falling
to pieces, for there is no visible and effective power to hold it
together. . .

It was. . .to make way against this internal ailment that the
Scottish Nationalist movement came into existence. To some
people the very name of Nationalism is hateful; it is over-
weening and dangerous in a great nation, and niggling in a small
one; trying either to set up a world empire, or to establish a
provincial caucus. No doubt Nationalism is the symptom of a
morbid state, since it springs either from inflated pride, as it did
in England's Jingo days, or from a sense of oppression, or from
a mixture of both, as in present-day Germany. When it springs
from pride it is a general danger; but when it is caused by a local
injustice it loses its virulence once the injustice is removed. The
unfortunate thing for Scotland is that it is not an obviously
oppressed nation, as Ireland was, but only a visibly depressed
one searching for the source of its depression. Glencoe and
Culloden are things of the distant past, useful perhaps for a
peroration or the refrain of a song, but with no bearing on the
present state of things, since everybody can see the English and
the Scots living side by side in peace. . .

I do not believe that Scotland will ever become a nation by the
adoption of Nationalism. . . The nationalist argument is
perfectly reasonable as far as it goes. The remedy which
Nationalists prescribe for the ills of Scotland is self-government.
There is, to anyone who knows the state of Scotland, no serious
argument against it. The National Party of Scotland does not
wish to cast loose from England; all that it claims is that in
domestic matters Scotland should rule itself. This policy is so
moderate that bills embodying it have repeatedly passed a first
reading in the House of Commons. The great majority of
Scottish Members of Parliament for many years have been in

favour of it. Yet in spite of that nothing has been done; partly no doubt because Scotland is such a distance from Westminster. What stands in the way of Home Rule for Scotland is simply apathy, the apathy of England, but chiefly the apathy of Scotland. Consequently the Scottish Nationalist movement at its present stage is mainly a movement to rouse Scotland from its indifference, an attempt to quicken national life and bring about an internal regeneration. There are faint signs that it is beginning to succeed, but its success is slow, and the great mass of the population are still sunk in indifference. They are quick to resent any insult to Scotland, but do not see the necessity of taking any action to stop their country's decline, for, being already half denationalised, they are almost unconscious of the danger. . .

One can see that self-government for Scotland is a desirable ideal, but like all Utopian ideals it takes no account of history, past or present; indeed, it takes less account of present than of past history. That being the case, where is the force that will drive the people of Scotland to proclaim themselves a nation? In the heads of a few people, mainly middle-class, with an admixture of the intelligentsia, who see that Scotland a nation is a desirable aim. But meanwhile the people themselves, like the people of every industrial country of Europe, are being driven by the logic of necessity to a quite different end, the most convenient term for which is Socialism. Who in such circum-stances can take Scottish Nationalism seriously, or even wish that it should enjoy a brief triumph, when processes so much more serious and profound are at work in the whole of society?

Scottish Journey

13   Thomas E. Ellis, Welsh Disestablishment (1892)

We ask for Disestablishment not alone as an act of political justice, but also in the interests of the religious life and social peace of Wales. The representatives of rural England here today, need not be told how the Establishment embitters and impover-ishes the life of your villages. You know its baneful influences. But in Wales, every one of these influences is accentuated, and so exercised as to affect most prejudicially the life of the people. . .

It is a real, bitter wrong. Tried by every democratic test, the Establishment in Wales is as indefensible as Dublin Castle. The Church Congress next week is going to talk about the Church Revival in Wales. But the soul of Wales has left the Episcopalian Establishment. It is a revived spirit of ascendency and privilege which galvanises its frame today.

With all its phenomenal activity, under threat of Disestablishment, the Church is still a small minority in almost every parish in Wales. It is anti-national in its sympathies. It strains the exercise of its legal and social privileges so insidiously here and so wantonly there, as to create constant heartburning and irritation. Nay, more, its continued maintenance as an Establishment is a degradation. The darkest days in the long and chequered annals of Wales were those when, after her subjugation, her fathers and her sons had to build strong castles along our border and our coast-line to harbour her baronial oppressors. To forfeit the rule and freedom of the land, for which generations had struggled and bled, was a bitter national sorrow for Wales. It was a galling degradation to have to apply the toil and skill and energy which should have been the mainstay of the freedom of their fatherland to the erection of fortresses for their subjugators. Welsh nationality has outlived Castle oppression. But an equally degrading yoke remains. The people of Wales have, during the last two centuries, in spite of the neglect and hostility of their nominal rulers, built up religious organisations of their own, dotted the hills and dales and countrysides with places of worship, purified the moral atmosphere and quickened the intellectual life. Yet, the first fruits of its land and toil and thrift are filched from it by law, to build and maintain castles for Episcopalianism, the creed of a class, – and Toryism, – the gospel of privilege. To the continuance of this degradation, Wales has determined once and for ever, that she will not submit.

Notes of a Speech delivered at Newcastle upon Tyne

14 Saunders Lewis, The Welsh Language and Nation (1937)

The fact that we set fire to the buildings and building materials at the Penrhos Bombing Range is not in dispute. We ourselves were the first to give the Authorities warning of the fire, and we proclaimed to them our responsibility. Yet we hold the conviction that our action was in no wise criminal, and that it was an act forced upon us, that it was done in obedience to conscience and to the moral law, and that the responsibility for any loss due to our act is the responsibility of the English Government.

We are professional men who hold positions of trust, of honour, and of security. I must speak now with reluctance for myself. I profess the literature of Wales in the University College of Wales at Swansea. That is my professional duty. It is also my pride and delight. Welsh literature is one of the great literatures of Europe. It is the direct heir in the British Isles of the literary discipline of classical Greece and Rome. And it is a living, growing literature, and draws its sustenance from a living language and a traditional social life. It was my sense of the inestimable value of this tremendous heirloom of the Welsh Nation that first led me from purely literary work to public affairs, and to the establishment of the Welsh Nationalist Party. It was the terrible knowledge that the English Government's Bombing Range, once it were established in Llyn, would endanger and in all likelihood destroy an essential focus of this Welsh culture, the most aristocratic spiritual heritage of Wales, that made me think my own career, the security even of my family, things that must be sacrificed in order to prevent so appalling a calamity. For in the University lecture rooms I have not professed a dead literature of antiquarian interest. I have professed the living literature of this Nation. So that this literature has claims on me as a man as well as a teacher. I hold that my action at Penrhos aerodrome on September 8th saves the honour of the University of Wales, for the language and literature of Wales are the very raison d'etre of this University. . .

In an English pamphlet stating the case against the Bombing School in Llyn, Professor Daniel has expressed with pregnant brevity the heart-felt fear of all thoughtful Welshmen. He says:

It is the plain historical fact that, from the fifth century on, Llyn has been Welsh of the Welsh, and that so long as Llyn remained unanglicised, Welsh life and culture were secure. If once the forces of Anglicisation are securely established behind as well as in front of the mountains of Snowdonia, the day when Welsh language and culture will be crushed between the iron jaws of these pincers cannot be long delayed. For Wales, the preservation of the Llyn Peninsula from this Anglicisation is a matter of life and death.

That, we are convinced, is the simple truth. So that the preservation of the harmonious continuity of the rural Welsh tradition of Llyn, unbroken for fourteen hundred years, is for us 'a matter of life and death'. I have said that my professional duty is the teaching of Welsh literature. My maternal grandfather was a minister of religion and a Welsh scholar and man of letters. He began his ministerial career in Pwllheli. He wrote the greatest Welsh prose work of the 19th century, *Cofiant John Jones Talsarn*. One of the most brilliant chapters in that book is the seventh chapter, which is a description of the religious leaders of Llyn and Eifionydd in the middle of the 19th century. It is impossible for one who has blood in his veins not to care passionately when he sees this terrible vandal bombing range in this very home of Welsh Culture. I have here in my hand an anthology of the works of the Welsh poets of Llyn, *Cynfeirdd Llyn*, 1500–1800, by Myrddin Fardd. On page 176 of this book there is a poem, a Cywydd, written in Penyberth Farmhouse in the middle of the 16th century. That house was one of the most historic in Llyn. It was a resting-place for the Welsh pilgrims of the Isle of Saints, Ynys Enlli, in the Middle Ages. It had associations with Owen Glyndwr. It belonged to the story of Welsh literature. It was a thing of hallowed and secular majesty. It was taken down and utterly destroyed a week before we burnt on its fields the timbers of the vandals who destroyed it. And I claim that the people who ought to be in this dock are the people responsible for the destruction of Penyberth Farmhouse. More-over, that destruction of Penyberth House is, in the view of most competent Welsh observers, typical and symbolic. The development of the Bombing Range at Llyn into the inevitable arsenal it will become will destroy this essential home of Welsh Culture, idiom and literature. It will shatter the spiritual basis of the Welsh Nation.

'Why We Burnt the Bombing School'

15   R. S. Thomas, A Dead Nation (1968)

There are places in Wales I don't go:
Reservoirs that are the subconscious

Of a people, troubled far down
With gravestones, chapels, villages even;
The serenity of their expression
Revolts me, it is a pose
For strangers, a watercolour's appeal
To the mass, instead of the poem's
Harsher conditions. There are the hills,
Too; gardens gone under the scum
Of the forests; and the smashed faces
Of the farms with the stone trickle
Of their tears down the hills' side.

Where can I go, then, from the smell
Of decay, from the putrefying of a dead
Nation? I have walked the shore
For an hour and seen the English
Scavenging among the remains
Of our culture, covering the sand
Like the tide and, with the roughness
Of the tide, elbowing our language
Into the grave that we have dug for it.

'Reservoirs'

B.   Empire and Race

For more than three hundred years Britain was the centre of a vast
overseas Empire. At the time of its greatest territorial extent, just
after the First World War, Britain had some form of control of about
a quarter of the Earth's land surface, from New Zealand and
Australia, through the Indian sub-continent and South, East and
West Africa, to the West Indies. This anthology being concerned
with government and society in Britain itself, the complex external
history of the Empire lies beyond its scope. But the Empire has had
an enormous impact on British society. Much of the wealth that
enabled Britain to produce the first Industrial Revolution came from
imperial commerce, including the slave trade. And in the wake of the
movement of goods and material wealth has gone the movement of
people. There have been black people in Britain since Roman times,
but their numbers have increased dramatically since the Second
World War. After the war, immigration from the West Indies and the
Indian sub-continent was officially encouraged to fulfil the need for

labour in Britain. (All these West Indians and Asians were British citizens, since under the 1948 Nationality Act United Kingdom citizenship was granted to citizens of Britain's colonies and former colonies.) By 1990 the 'ethnic minorities' (many of them second-generation residents of Britain) made up about 4.8 per cent of Britain's population. But already by the 1960s there was pressure on governments to restrict immigration, partly as a result of prejudice and hostility against these newcomers. Race had become an issue in British politics.

Underpinning both the slave trade and the later idea of Britain's 'Imperial mission' was a belief in the innate inferiority of non-white peoples. John Locke (see IV:2 above), generally considered one of the founding fathers of Western liberal thought, defended Negro slavery and himself had an investment in the Royal African Company. In the eighteenth century, David Hume (VII:16), one of the most advanced thinkers of his day and a leading figure of the 'Scottish Enlightenment', confidently expressed his belief in the intellectual inferiority of Negroes. Thirty-six years after Hume wrote that, a former slave, Olaudah Equiano, published his *Life* (VII:17), a vivid account of his capture as a child in West Africa, his experience of the horrific 'Middle Passage' to the West Indies, and his subsequent adventures which took him eventually to England. Personal testimony such as Equiano's revealed the full barbarity of slavery and played an important part in the campaign that eventually led to the abolition of the slave trade (1808) and of slavery in British colonies (1833). But racialism did not come to an end with the abolition of slavery. Indeed, in the late nineteenth century, with the renewed expansion of Empire (the period 1870–1914 is often referred to as the 'Age of Empire' or 'Age of Imperialism'), racial attitudes hardened and intensified. One of the best-known expressions of the imperialist ethos is Rudyard Kipling's 'The White Man's Burden' (VII:18), written in 1899, in which he urges the United States of America to emulate Britain by taking on an imperialist role as guardians of 'new-caught, sullen peoples/Half devil and half child'.

But the legacy of Imperial racial attitudes is only one element in an understanding of 'race relations' in Britain. There is also the testimony of the immigrants and their descendants. Among those who came from the West Indies to Britain in the 1950s was a remarkable generation of writers, including V. S. Naipaul, George Lamming and Sam Selvon. *In the Castle of My Skin*, George Lamming's autobiographical novel about growing up in colonial Barbados, includes a comic, snail's-eye view of the Empire at work (VII:19), while Sam

Selvon's *The Lonely Londoners* (VII:20) is a picaresque evocation of the lives of West Indians newly arrived in Britain. More recently, and in a soberer vein, Adewale Maja-Pearce's autobiographical essay, *How Many Miles to Babylon?* (VII:21), warns against subsuming complex questions of culture and class in simple dichotomies of black and white.

Finally, a short poem by Grace Nichols (VII:22) reminds us that questions of race are as much as anything else questions of language. English is a world language. Indeed, one can no longer speak (if one ever could) of one 'standard' English. There are many 'Englishes' (American English, West Indian English, Indian English, African English, etc.). Similarly, as writers from every part of the former British Empire come to increasing prominence in Britain, it becomes harder to demarcate a purely 'British' (still more, 'English') literature. If Britain's political and economic future is coming to be seen more and more in a European context, its cultural identity and direction continue to be influenced by the history of Empire.

16   David Hume, Eighteenth-century Racism (1748)

I am apt to suspect the Negroes to be naturally inferior to the Whites. There scarcely ever was a civilized nation of that complexion, nor even any individual, eminent either in action or speculation. No ingenious manufactures amongst them, no arts, no sciences. On the other hand, the most rude and barbarous of the Whites, such as the ancient Germans, the present Tartars, have still something eminent about them, in their valour, form of government, or some other particular. Such a uniform and constant difference could not happen, in so many countries and ages, if nature had not made an original distinction between these breeds of men. Not to mention our colonies, there are Negro slaves dispersed all over Europe, of whom none ever discovered any symptoms of ingenuity, though low people, without education, will start up amongst us, and distinguish themselves in every profession. In Jamaica, indeed, they talk of one Negro as a man of parts and learning; but it is likely he is admired for slender accomplishments, like a parrot who speaks a few words plainly.

'Of National Characters', in *Essays, Moral, Political and Literary*

17 Olaudah Equiano, A Slave's Experience (1789)

Are there not causes enough to which the apparent inferiority of
an African may be ascribed, without limiting the goodness of
God, and supposing he forbore to stamp understanding on
certainly his own image, because 'carved in ebony'. Might it not
naturally be ascribed to their situation? When they come among
Europeans, they are ignorant of their language, religion, manners, and customs. Are any pains taken to teach them these? Are
they treated as men? Does not slavery itself depress the mind,
and extinguish all its fire and every noble sentiment? But, above
all, what advantages do not a refined people possess over those
who are rude and uncultivated. Let the polished and haughty
European recollect that his ancestors were once, like the Africans, uncivilised, and even barbarous. Did Nature make *them*
inferior to their sons? and should *they too* have been made slaves?
Every rational mind answers, no. Let such reflections as these
melt the pride of their superiority into sympathy for the wants
and miseries of their sable brethren, and compel them to
acknowledge, that understanding is not confined to feature or
colour. If, when they look round the world, they feel exul-
tation, let it be tempered with benevolence to others, and
gratitude to God, 'who hath made of one blood all nations of
men for to dwell on all the face of the earth; and whose wisdom
is not our wisdom, neither are our ways his ways.'*. . .

The first object which saluted my eyes when I arrived on the
coast was the sea, and a slave ship, which was then riding at
anchor, and waiting for its cargo. These filled me with astonishment, which was soon converted into terror when I was carried
on board. I was immediately handled and tossed up to see if I
were sound by some of the crew; and I was now persuaded that
I had gotten into a world of bad spirits, and that they were
going to kill me. Their complexions too differing so much from
ours, their long hair, and the language they spoke, (which was
very different from any I had ever heard) united to confirm me
in this belief. Indeed such were the horrors of my views and
fears at the moment, that, if ten thousand worlds had been my
own, I would have freely parted with them all to have
exchanged my condition with that of the meanest slave in my

*[Acts 17: 26]

own country. When I looked round the ship too and saw a large furnace or copper boiling, and a multitude of black people of every description chained together, every one of their countenances expressing dejection and sorrow, I no longer doubted of my fate; and, quite overpowered with horror and anguish, I fell motionless on the deck and fainted. When I recovered a little I found some black people about me, who I believe were some of those who brought me on board, and had been receiving their pay; they talked to me in order to cheer me, but all in vain. I asked them if we were not to be eaten by those white men with horrible looks, red faces, and loose hair. They told me I was not; and one of the crew brought me a small portion of spirituous liquor in a wine glass; but, being afraid of him, I would not take it out of his hand. One of the blacks therefore took it from him and gave it to me, and I took a little down my palate, which, instead of reviving me, as they thought it would, threw me into the greatest consternation at the strange feeling it produced, having never tasted any such liquor before. Soon after this the blacks who brought me on board went off, and left me abandoned to despair. I now saw myself deprived of all chance of returning to my native country, or even the least glimpse of hope of gaining the shore, which I now considered as friendly; and I even wished for my former slavery in preference to my present situation, which was filled with horrors of every kind, still heightened by my ignorance of what I was to undergo. . . .

We were not many days in the merchant's custody before we were sold after their usual manner, which is this:– On a signal given, (as the beat of a drum) the buyers rush at once into the yard where the slaves are confined, and make a choice of that parcel they like best. The noise and clamour with which this is attended, and the eagerness visible in the countenances of the buyers, serve not a little to increase the apprehensions of the terrified Africans, who may well be supposed to consider them as the ministers of that destruction to which they think themselves devoted. In this manner, without scruple, are relations and friends separated, most of them never to see each other again. I remember in the vessel in which I was brought over, in the men's apartment, there were several brothers, who, in the sale, were sold in different lots; and it was very moving on this occasion to see and hear their cries at parting. O, ye nominal Christians! might not an African ask you, learned you this from your God, who says unto you, Do unto all men as you would men should do unto you? Is it not enough that we are torn from our country and friends to toil for your luxury and lust of gain? Must every tender feeling be likewise sacrificed to your avarice? Are the dearest friends and relations, now rendered more dear by their separation from their kindred, still to be parted from each other, and thus prevented from cheering the gloom of slavery with the small comfort of being together and mingling their sufferings and sorrows? Why are parents to lose their children, brothers their sisters, or husbands their wives? Surely this is a new refinement in cruelty, which, while it has no advantage to atone for it, thus aggravates distress, and adds fresh horrors even to the wretchedness of slavery.

The Life of Olaudah Equiano

18 Rudyard Kipling, The White Man's Burden (1899)

Take up the White Man's burden –
    Send forth the best ye breed –
Go bind your sons to exile
    To serve your captives' need;
To wait in heavy harness
    On fluttered folk and wild –
Your new-caught, sullen peoples,
    Half devil and half child.

Take up the White Man's burden –
    In patience to abide,
To veil the threat of terror
    And check the show of pride;
By open speech and simple,
    An hundred times made plain,
To seek another's profit,
    And work another's gain.

Take up the White Man's burden –
    The savage wars of peace –
Fill full the mouth of Famine
    And bid the sickness cease;
And when your goal is nearest
    The end for others sought,
Watch Sloth and heathen Folly
    Bring all your hope to nought.

Take up the White Man's burden –
  No tawdry rule of kings,
But toil of serf and sweeper –
  The tale of common things.
The ports ye shall not enter,
  The roads ye shall not tread,
Go make them with your living,
  And mark them with your dead!

Take up the White Man's burden –
  And reap his old reward:
The blame of those ye better,
  The hate of those ye guard –
The cry of hosts ye humour
  (Ah, slowly!) toward the light: –
'Why brought ye us from bondage,
  'Our loved Egyptian night?'

Take up the White Man's burden –
  Ye dare not stoop to less –
Nor call too loud on Freedom
  To cloak your weariness;
By all ye cry or whisper,
  By all ye leave or do,
The silent, sullen peoples
  Shall weigh your Gods and you.

Take up the White Man's burden –
  Have done with childish days –
The lightly proffered laurel,
  The easy, ungrudged praise.
Comes now, to search your manhood
  Through all the thankless years,
Cold-edged with dear-bought wisdom,
  The judgement of your peers!

'The White Man's Burden'

19 George Lamming, The British Empire (1953)

A car drove slowly through the school yard flying a flag on its
bonnet and then there was only the sound of the wind in the

trees. The inspector stepped from the car, and before he had found his feet one of the teachers had bellowed the order. With incredible precision every squad saluted, and there was silence but for the sound of the wind in the trees, and the silence moving gradually from squad to squad broke forth into an earnest, pleading resonance:

God save our gracious King,
Long live our noble King,
God save the King.

At the order of the teachers the boys dropped the salute. They stood at attention, and when the second order was given relaxed. The head teacher led the inspector to a raised platform in the middle of the school yard. The inspector wore a white suit with a red, white and blue badge on the lapel of the jacket. He smiled all the time, while the head teacher grinned jovially as if he and the inspector were part of a secret the others were to guess. The inspector stood at the centre of the platform and all eyes were fastened on him. He looked round in all directions and then spoke. 'My dear boys and teachers, we are met once again to pay our respects to the memory of a great queen. She was your queen and my queen and yours no less then mine. We're all subjects and partakers in the great design, the British Empire, and your loyalty to the Empire can be seen in the splendid performance which your school decorations and the discipline of these squads represent. We are living, my dear boys, in difficult times. We wait with the greatest anxiety the news of what is happening on the other side of the world. Those of you who read the papers may have read of the war in Abyssinia. You may have seen pictures of the King of Ethiopia, and the bigger boys may have wondered what it's all about. The British Empire, you must remember, has always worked for the peace of the world. This was the job assigned it by God, and if the Empire at any time has failed to bring about that peace it was due to events and causes beyond its control. But, remember, my dear boys, whatever happens in any part of this world, whatever happens to you here in this island of Barbados, the pride and treasure of the Empire, we are always on the side of peace. You are with us, and we with you. And together we shall always walk in the will of God. Let me say how impressed I am with the decorations. I hope I shall start no jealousy among the schools in the island under my control if I say that such a display as I see here could not have been bettered by the lads at home.'

The boys and teachers applauded and his voice was lost in the noise. The inspector waited till the shouting died down and concluded: 'Barbados is truly Little England!' He stepped from the platform and the applause was renewed with greater energy. The head teacher came forward and shook the inspector's hand gratefully, then he stepped on to the platform beaming with delight and yelled: 'Three cheers for the school. Hip, pip, pip. . . Hurararahhahrah. Hippiippip. . . Hurrahh- haarararah. . . Hip pip pip. . . Hurrrrrrraaaahh. Hippiippip. . . Hurrahhhaararah. . .'

The boys came to attention, and the teachers' voices were raised in a confusion of orders to the squads. They spoke at the same time, but the orders were different, and the movements of the squads taken on the whole were contradictory. When Class 6 was receiving the order to stand at ease, Class 5 was receiving the order to march. The inspector and the head teacher looked on from the platform and smiled at the innocent rivalry. After the orders were given and the lines were dressed to the teachers' satisfaction, the boys marched squad after squad after squad in circles round the platform. In the final circle they marched at the salute, and the inspector returned the salute and watched them march in single file into the school. The parade had come to an end.

In the Castle of My Skin

20 Samuel Selvon, The Immigrant's Experience (1956)

'All right mister London,' Galahad say, 'you been here for a long time, what you would advice me as a newcomer to do?'

'I would advice you to hustle a passage back home to Trinidad today,' Moses say, 'but I know you would never want to do that. So what I will tell you is this: take it easy. It had a time when I was first here, when it only had a few West Indians in London, and things used to go good enough. These days, spades all over the place, and every shipload is big news, and the English people don't like the boys coming to England to work and live.'

'Why is that?' Galahad ask.

'Well, as far as I could figure, they frighten that we get job in front of them, though that does never happen. The other thing is that they just don't like black people, and don't ask me why, because that is a question that bigger brains than mine trying to find out from way back.'

'Things as bad over here as in America?' Galahad ask.

'That is a point the boys always debating,' Moses say. 'Some say yes, and some say no. The thing is, in America they don't like you, and they tell you so straight, so that you know how you stand. Over here is the old English diplomacy: "thank you sir," and "how do you do" and that sort of thing. In America you see a sign telling you to keep off, but over here you don't see any, but when you go in the hotel or the restaurant they will politely tell you to haul – or else give you the cold treatment.'

'I know fellars like you,' Galahad say in turn. 'You all live in a place for some time and think you know all about it, and when any green fellars turn up you try to frighten them. If things bad like that how come you still holding on in Brit'n?'

'You don't believe, eh?' Moses say. 'Listen, I will give you the name of a place. It call Ipswich. There it have a restaurant run by a Pole call the Rendezvous Restaurant. Go there and see if they will serve you. And you know the hurtful part of it? The Pole who have that restaurant, he ain't have no more right in this country than we. In fact, we is British subjects and he is only a foreigner, we have more right than any people from the damn continent to live and work in this country, and enjoy what this country have, because is we who bleed to make this country prosperous.'

The Lonely Londoners

21   Adewale Maja-Pearce, Cultural Chauvinism (1990)

My most poignant memory of the year I lived with my grandparents was coming home from school on a winter's evening – the sharp, acrid smell of smoke on the air; a smell full of associations which still has the power to take me back to that house in Streatham – and telling them that I had been called a 'wog' in the playground. It was a measure of my hurt that I overrode my natural pride and blurted this out; and I knew, even as I spoke, that my grandparents couldn't say anything useful, just as I knew that by presenting it in this way I was only distressing them. Children almost always understand more than adults, who have themselves forgotten much of what they knew when they were children; but if I understood that it would have been better to keep silent, I was only a child after all and unable to exercise that level of emotional control.

My grandfather, a gentle and sensitive man, looked downcast as he pulled on his pipe and gazed at the coal fire that he was forever poking and prodding and complaining at, as though it was a mischievous spirit that had been sent to try him; my grandmother, more combative and more assertive, attempted to hide her own hurt by what she imagined was sound advice: 'Remember, dear, next time they call you that, just tell them the word means "gentleman".' Of course I had no intention of saying anything of the kind, but I promised her I would and I loved her for suggesting such a hopelessly inadequate response. I wonder whether they thought that was the end of the matter. At any rate I never mentioned it again and neither did they. . .

Is Britain a racist society? Do the institutions of the State, those expressions of the popular will – the schools, the police, the House of Commons – discriminate against people on the basis of colour and only colour? The short answer is, I don't know; and nor, probably, does anyone else. . . To put the question so crudely is problematical because it may only serve to hide a deeper complexity. I suspect that in so far as the British can be called racist – to the extent that they identify skin colour with inherent difference – they do so out of what might better be called cultural chauvinism.

All cultures are profoundly chauvinistic. It is their single most important defining characteristic, what they are as cultures. In Nigeria, for instance, a Yoruba parent will not take kindly to their child marrying someone from the Hausa north because the Hausas are different: they speak a different language, they wear different clothes, they have different customs. The Yoruba word for the Igbos in the east translates as 'a race of cannibals'. If the Hausas and the Igbos were a different colour we would doubtless call the Yoruba response racist, which it clearly isn't.

Colour, in fact, may only be the convenient shorthand for a much larger concept; and its very obviousness, the ease with which we can identify an immediate visual difference with a profounder difference of what it means to belong to a particular society, may for that reason be misleading. People will always dissemble where they can. This isn't necessarily because human beings are mendacious by nature, though they are that, but because they don't themselves know what they think, and will simplify every time.

How Many Miles to Babylon?

22   Grace Nichols, The Many 'Englishes' (1984)

I have crossed an ocean
I have lost my tongue
from the root of the old one
a new one has sprung.

'Epilogue', *The Fat Black Woman's Poems*

VIII
Democracy and the Economy

Economic issues dominate modern electoral politics. Other questions – foreign affairs, welfare, education, immigration, nationality and so on – may sporadically take the electoral stage, but elections are generally decided by electors' judgements of which party is most likely to secure economic prosperity, perhaps for the whole society, perhaps only for the individual voter. To say this is not necessarily to indulge in the often heard lamentations on the 'materialism' of modern society. For, even if voters believe that the saving of their immortal souls, or the quality of their social experience, or their moral probity or the fulfilment of their creative potential are more important than material prosperity, they might also believe that those nobler objectives are beyond the reach or should be beyond the ambition of politicians, whilst the attainment of prosperity is within the power and therefore within the range of responsibility of government. So government and opposition parties are judged on how well they have managed or would manage the economy, even if they claim that governments have little or only indirect influence on economic well-being.

These controversial questions of how far and in what ways a government can act beneficially in the economic sphere – how far and how it can maintain prosperity or achieve economic growth – have been central to political debate over the last two centuries, most particularly in Britain which was the first to experience an industrial revolution and was in the vanguard of the development of economics as a system of ideas. This chapter will look briefly at the emergence of the connected ideas of commercial society and the market, will examine the expectations and fears that have been expressed about the possible economic results of democratization and will illustrate the continuing controversies over the relationship between the state and the economy.

A.   Society, Economy, Market

To ask questions like, 'How far can and should the state seek to control and fashion the economy or civil society?' is to posit a contrast between a 'natural' socio-economic order and an 'artificial', wilfully constructed political order. We have seen in Chapter IV that Locke implies such a contrast in his account of the emergence of an ordered society, in particular of a money economy, in the state of nature, that is, before the creation of political authority by the social contract. Here, as elsewhere, Tom Paine restated and expanded Lockean ideas in a radical direction (VIII:1). Like Locke, he makes the distinction between society and government in defence of revolution, in his case the American War of Independence; even if formal government breaks down completely in a rebellion, order is still maintained through the persistence of a coherent society, as American experience showed. Paine traces two courses for this ordered society – innate, altruistic feelings of social affection and the need for individuals to enter into mutual relations to satisfy their own wants and interests.

In making this last point, Paine was perhaps following Adam Smith more than Locke. For it was Adam Smith and his followers, together with the Physiocrats in France, who developed the related concepts of commercial society and the market. Smith pursued the two themes in his *Wealth of Nations*. He posed a hypothetical history in which societies passed through successive stages related to their primary modes of production. This history culminated in the commercial society characteristic of advanced systems of his own day. Commercial society was the product of increased division of labour and the consequent expansion of the exchange economy, or the market. Economics, or the science of exchanges as some followers of Smith termed it, became primarily the study of the market and of the laws governing it. The market was a self-adjusting mechanism whose operation achieved general social goods without these being aimed at by any of the actors in the market. All needed the services and the products of others. They could not rely on the altruism of other people to procure those goods, so they had to rely on mutual exchanges, barter or purchase, to get what they wanted. Despite the fact that, within any market, the actions of individuals were purely self-interested, the general interest was nevertheless served by market processes, which ensured that production was geared precisely to consumption and that productive resources were efficiently allocated to different areas of production.

The rise of the concept of the market economy, together with the actual expansion of that economy consequent upon the industrial revolution, brought to the forefront of political debate the question of the relationship between the state and the economy. This large question covered a number of more particular issues. What was the relationship between the distribution of power within the state and the distribution of property? How far does the political and constitutional system determine the kind of economic policies and objectives the state will pursue? How far and in what ways should the state intervene in the economy?

Differing answers to these questions, and particularly the last, have set much of the political agenda over the last two centuries. In the nineteenth century and, it could be argued, in the late twentieth century, the answers given by Adam Smith and his successors, the classical political economists, were highly influential in the agenda-setting. Smith's answer was that a 'system of natural liberty' should prevail (VIII:2). Within the constraints of laws of justice, all should be free to pursue their own interest as they saw fit, in competition with others. State intervention in economic activity should therefore be limited. Nevertheless Smith attributed crucial economic functions to the state; the provision of justice, that is to say, for instance, security of property and contracts; the provision for public goods which could not be supplied through the market; action to prevent monopolies and other business conspiracies in restraint of trade. Implicit in Smith's argument is that the establishment of his 'system of natural liberty' required an underlying constitutional order in which government is limited, law-governed and non-arbitrary, in other words very like the constitutional order of Britain in Smith's own time, within which the rapid economic growth of the industrial revolution was being achieved.

A pupil and academic successor of Adam Smith, Dugald Stewart, took up this question of the relation between constitutional structure and the pursuit of rational economic policies (VIII:3). Stewart's answer was that, whilst there might be some tendency for wise forms of government to follow just and expedient economic policies, this was not inevitable. Constitutionally admirable governments could follow bad policies, and bad government could follow admirable policies. From the point of view of the general utility, the pursuit of the right economic policies was much more important than the possession of a just constitution.

1   Thomas Paine, A Natural Economic Order (1791)

Great part of that order which reigns among mankind is not the effect of Government. It has its origin in the principles of society and the natural constitution of man. It existed prior to Government, and would exist if the formality of Government was abolished. The mutual dependence and reciprocal interest which man has upon man, and all the parts of a civilised community upon each other, create that great chain of connection which holds it together. The landholder, the farmer, the manufacturer, the merchant, the tradesman, and every occupation, prospers by the aid which each receives from the other, and from the whole. Common interest regulates their concerns, and forms their law; and the laws which common usage ordains, have a greater influence than the laws of Government. In fine, society performs for itself almost everything which is ascribed to Government.

To understand the nature and quantity of Government proper for man, it is necessary to attend to his character. As nature created him for social life, she fitted him for the station she intended. In all cases she made his natural wants greater than his individual powers. No one man is capable, without the aid of society, of supplying his own wants; and those wants, acting upon every individual, impel the whole of them into society, as naturally as gravitation acts to a centre.

But she has gone further. She has not only forced man into society by a diversity of wants which the reciprocal aid of each other can supply, but she has implanted in him a system of social affections, which, though not necessary to his existence, are essential to his happiness. There is no period in life when this love for society ceases to act. It begins and ends with our being.

If we examine with attention the composition and constitution of man, the diversity of his wants and talents in different men for reciprocally accommodating the wants of each other, his propensity to society, and consequently to preserve the advantages resulting from it, we shall easily discover that a great part of what is called Government is mere imposition.

Government is no farther necessary than to supply the few cases to which society and civilisation are not conveniently competent; and instances are not wanting to show, that everything which Government can usefully add thereto, has been performed by the common consent of society, without Government.

The Rights of Man

2 Adam Smith, The System of Natural Liberty (1791)

It is thus that every system which endeavours, either, by extraordinary encouragements, to draw towards a particular species of industry a greater share of the capital of the society than what would naturally go to it; or, by extraordinary restraints, to force from a particular species of industry some share of the capital which would otherwise be employed in it; is in reality subversive of the great purpose which it means to promote. It retards, instead of accelerating, the progress of the society towards real wealth and greatness; and diminishes, instead of increasing, the real value of the annual produce of its land and labour.

All systems either of preference or of restraint, therefore, being thus completely taken away, the obvious and simple system of natural liberty establishes itself of its own accord. Every man, as long as he does not violate the laws of justice, is left perfectly free to pursue his own interest his own way, and to bring both his industry and capital into competition with those of any other man, or order of men. The sovereign is completely discharged from a duty, in the attempting to perform which he must always be exposed to innumerable delusions, and for the proper performance of which no human wisdom or knowledge could ever be sufficient; the duty of superintending the industry of private people, and of directing it towards the employments most suitable to the interest of the society. According to the system of natural liberty, the sovereign has only three duties to attend to; three duties of great importance, indeed, but plain and intelligible to common understandings: first, the duty of protecting the society from the violence and invasion of other independent societies; secondly, the duty of protecting, as far as possible, every member of the society from the injustice or oppression of every other member of it, or the duty of establishing an exact administration of justice; and, thirdly, the duty of erecting and maintaining certain public works and certain public institutions, which it can never be for the interest of any individual, or small number of individuals, to erect and maintain; because the profit could never repay the expence to any individual or small number of individuals, though it may frequently do much more than repay it to a great society.

The proper performance of those several duties of the sovereign necessarily supposes a certain expence; and this expence again necessarily requires a certain revenue to support it.

An Inquiry into the Nature and Causes of the Wealth of Nations

3 Dugald Stewart, Forms of Government and Political Economy (1809–10)

It is on the particular system of Political Economy which is established in any country, that the happiness of the people *immediately* depends; and it is from the *remote* tendency that wise forms of Government have to produce wise systems of Political Economy, that the utility of the former in a great measure arises. The one, indeed, leads *naturally* to the other; but it does not lead to it *necessarily*; for it is extremely possible that inexpedient laws may, in consequence of ignorance and prejudice, be sanctioned for ages by a Government excellent in its constitution, and just in its administration; while the evils threatened by a Government fundamentally bad, may, to a great degree, be corrected by an enlightened system of internal policy. . .

In farther illustration of this fundamental principle, it may be remarked, that there are two very different points of view in which *Laws* may be considered; *first*, with respect to their *origin*; and, *secondly*, with respect to their *tendency*. If they are equitable in *both* respects, that is, if they arise from a just constitution of Government, and if they are favourable to general happiness, they possess every *possible* recommendation; but if they are to want the one recommendation or the other, the former (it ought always to be recollected) is of trifling moment in comparison of the latter. Unfortunately, however, for the world, the contrary idea has very generally prevailed; and has led men to direct their efforts much more to improve the Theory of Government, than to ascertain the just principles of *Political Economy*. . .

Happiness is, in truth, the only object of legislation which is of *intrinsic* value; and what is called *Political Liberty*, is only one of the means of obtaining this end. With the advantage of good laws, a people, although not possessed of political power, may yet enjoy a great degree of happiness; and, on the contrary, where laws are unjust and inexpedient, the political power of the people, so far from furnishing any compensation for their misery, is likely to oppose an insurmountable obstacle to improvement, by employing the despotism of numbers in support of principles of which the multitude are incompetent to judge.

Lectures on Political Economy

B. ECONOMIC CONSEQUENCES OF DEMOCRACY

Stewart's view that constitutional forms were largely irrelevant to economic policy was not shared by many of his contemporaries. As we have seen in Chapter III, the movement for parliamentary reform changed its character in the early nineteenth century, and earlier constitutional objectives were displaced by economic objectives. For moderate Whig reformers, reforms which made the Commons more representative of the rising industrial society would bring greater governmental sensitivity to the truths of political economy. Spokesmen for lower classes, more subject to economic distress, were more extreme in their hopes and expectations. William Cobbett, for whom the one test of political improvement was the welfare of ordinary people, in 1831 expressed unlimited hopes of the result of the Whig reform measures (VIII:4). Inevitably disillusionment followed. Six years after the Reform Act, the Working Men's Association expressed its profound disappointment, but maintained the view that alleviation of distress could follow only from electoral reform and that only a democratic political system would act for the welfare of the people at large (VIII:5).

These wide expectations of democracy were balanced by wide fears of the economic consequences of democracy. One constant fear during the nineteenth century was that extension of the franchise would lead to attacks upon property and attempts by the poor majority to despoil the rich minority. The charge was put by Macaulay in his critique of James Mill's *Essay on Government* (VIII:6). He argued that, on Mill's own utilitarian assumptions, including the assumption that individuals inevitably seek to maximize their own interests, the poor would use their power in a democracy to overturn the existing unequal distribution of wealth. The utilitarian reply to this claim was that undermining the security of property was not in the real, long-term interests of the poor majority, as the political economists could clearly demonstrate, and therefore the poor would refrain from the pursuit of equality. However, this was to assume (unrealistically, as Macaulay thought) that the poor would pursue their long-term rather than their immediate interests. In anticipation of Keynes's observation that, in the long run, we are all dead, Macaulay urged that the 'long-term interest' must include the interest of others, that is to say succeeding generations.

Macaulay's argument had the wider implication that a democracy is incapable of following rational, long-term economic policies. This has been an often-repeated charge. Dugald Stewart had already deemed it unlikely that a democracy would follow the truths of political economy (VIII:7). In recent years, Samuel Brittan has expressed a similar scepticism about the capacity of a democracy to manage an economy (VIII:8). Within a competitive party system, in which the prime purpose of parties is to win elections, parties will compete in the economic promises they offer to different groups in the electorate. The consequent pressure on public expenditure, together with electoral disincentives to raise taxation or interest rates, creates a political stimulus to inflation. The answer given to these problems of democracy, by Brittan and others, is that there should be less democracy, at least in the sense that economic decision-making should be taken out of the hands of politicians subject to electoral temptations and assigned to independent agencies or to supposedly impartial mechanisms such as the market.

How far have these hopes and fears been shown by time to be well-founded? The growth of the welfare state since the achievement of universal adult male suffrage at the end of the nineteenth century is perhaps some indication that the hope that democracy would further the welfare of the people at large was not without foundation. Of course, there are still political arguments about the adequacy of levels of welfare provision and about the most efficient methods of provision; but political parties are agreed at least on the need to have a welfare safety net to protect the most needy and deprived. The fear that democracy would lead to attacks on individual property rights have proven to be less well-founded. Public ownership has not been an attraction electorally; and the distribution of wealth has remained highly unequal, despite some attempts at redistributive tax systems.

The charge that it is difficult for democracies to follow rational economic policies is still made but the charge is ambiguous so long as there is disagreement on what the correct mode of economic analysis is, as well as disagreement on what priorities should be given to various economic ends – full employment, low inflation, economic growth, greater equality and so on.

4   William Cobbett, Hopes of Parliamentary Reform (1831)

It may be asked, Will a reform of the Parliament give the labouring man a cow or a pig; will it put bread and cheese into his satchell instead of infernal cold potatoes; will it give him a bottle of beer to carry to the field instead of making him lie down upon his belly to drink out of the brook; will it put upon his back a Sunday coat and send him to church, instead of leaving him to stand lounging about shivering with an unshaven face and a carcass half covered with a ragged smock-frock, with a filthy cotton shirt beneath it as yellow as a kite's foot? Will parliamentary reform put an end to the harnessing of men and women by a hired overseer to draw carts like beasts of burden; will it put an end to the practice of putting up labourers to auction like negroes in Carolina or Jamaica; will it put an end to the system which caused the honest labourer to be fed worse than the felons in the jails; will it put an end to the system which caused almost the whole of the young women to incur the indelible disgrace of being on the point of being mothers before they were married, owing to that degrading poverty which prevented the fathers themselves from obtaining the means of paying the parson and the clerk: will parliamentary reform put an end to the foul, the beastly, the nasty practice of separating men from their wives by force, and committing to the hired overseer the bestial superintendence of their persons day and night; will parliamentary reform put an end to this which was amongst the basest acts which the Roman tyrants committed towards their slaves? The enemies of reform jeeringly ask us, whether reform would do these things for us; and I answer distinctly that IT WOULD DO THEM ALL!

Cobbett's Weekly Political Register, 1 April 1831

5   William Lovett, Political Rights and Popular Welfare (1837)

Fellow Countrymen, – It is now nearly six years since the Reform Bill became a part of the laws of our country. To carry that measure, despite the daring advocates of corruption, the co-operation of the millions was sought for, and cheerfully and honestly given. They threw their hearts into the contest, and would have risked their lives to obtain that which they were led to believe would give *to all* the blessings of LIBERTY. Alas! their hopes were excited by promises which have not been kept, and their expectations of freedom have been bitterly disappointed in seeing the men, whom they had assisted to power, spurning their petition with contempt, and binding them down by still more slavish enactments. . .

But the people have learnt a profitable lesson from experience, and will not again be stimulated to contend for any measure which excludes them from its advantages. They now perceive that most of our oppressive laws and institutions, and the consequent ignorance and wretchedness to which we are exposed, *can be traced to one common source* – EXCLUSIVE LEGISLATION; and they therefore have their minds intently fixed *on the destruction of this great and pernicious monopoly*; being satisfied that, while the power of law-making is confined *to the few*, the exclusive interests *of the few* will be secured at the expense of the many.

Seeing this, it will be well for their cause if honest Reformers throw their fears and scruples aside, and generously repose confidence in those who have no exclusive interests to protect, unjust privileges to secure, or monopolies to retain: but whose interest is in the peace and harmony of society, and in having a parliament selected from *the wise and good of every class*, devising the most efficient means for advancing the happiness of all.

But it has been urged, as a plea to keep up exclusive legislation, that the people are *too ignorant* to be trusted with the elective franchise. Are Englishmen less enlightened than Americans? – and has the exercise of their political liberty proved them not to have deserved it? – Nay, in our own country, are the unrepresented *as a body* more ignorant than the present possessors of the franchise? – Can they possibly return more enemies to liberty, more self-interested legislators than are returned by the present constituency to Parliament? The ignor-

ance of which they complain is the offspring of exclusive
legislation, for the exclusive few from time immemorial have
ever been intent in blocking up every avenue to knowledge.
POLITICAL RIGHTS necessarily stimulate men to enquiry –
give self-respect – lead them to know their duties as citizens –
and, under a wise government, would be made the best
corrective of vicious and intemperate habits.

Fellow countrymen, – with these facts and convictions
strongly impressed upon us, we have from the commencement
of our Association diligently sought to impress on our fellow-
men the necessity of contending for political power as the most
certain means of redressing all their wrongs. We have shown in
the addresses and publications we have put forth the utter
hopelessness of their ever obtaining justice from the House of
Commons as it is now constituted.

Life and Struggles

6   Lord Macaulay, Democracy and the Security of Property (1829)

Is it desirable that all males arrived at years of discretion should
vote for representatives, or should a pecuniary qualification be
required? Mr Mill's opinion is, that the lower the qualification
the better; and that the best system is that in which there is none
at all. . .

The first remark which we have to make on this argument is,
that, by Mr Mill's own account, even a government in which
every human being should vote would still be defective. For,
under a system of universal suffrage, the majority of the
representatives make the law. The whole people may vote,
therefore, but only the majority govern. So that, by Mr Mill's
own confession, the most perfect system of government con-
ceivable, is one in which the interest of the ruling body to
oppress, though not great, is something.

But is Mr Mill in the right, when he says that such an interest
could not be very great? We think not. If, indeed, every man in
the community possessed an equal share of what Mr Mill calls
the objects of desire, the majority would probably abstain from
plundering the minority. A large minority would offer a
vigorous resistance; and the property of a small minority would

not repay the other members of the community for the trouble
of dividing it. But it happens that in all civilized communities
there is a small minority of rich men, and a great majority of
poor men. If there were a thousand men with ten pounds
a-piece, it would not be worthwhile for nine hundred and
ninety of them to rob ten, and it would be a bold attempt for six
hundred of them to rob four hundred. But if ten of them had a
hundred thousand pounds a-piece, the case would be very
different. There would then be much to be got, and nothing to
be feared.

'That one human being will desire to render the person and
property of another subservient to his pleasures, notwithstanding the pain or loss of pleasure which it may occasion to that
other individual, is,' according to Mr Mill, 'the foundation of
government.' That the property of the rich minority can be
made subservient to the pleasures of the poor majority, will
scarcely be denied. But Mr Mill proposes to give the poor
majority power over the rich minority. Is it possible to doubt to
what, on his own principles, such an arrangement must lead?

It may perhaps be said that, in the long run, it is for the
interest of the people that property should be secure, and that
therefore they will respect it. We answer thus:– It cannot be
pretended that it is not for the immediate interest of the people
to plunder the rich. Therefore, even if it were quite certain that,
in the long run, the people would, as a body, lose by doing so, it
would not necessarily follow that the fear of remote ill consequences would overcome the desire of immediate acquisitions.
Every individual might flatter himself that the punishment
would not fall on him. . .

But we are rather inclined to think that it would, on the
whole, be for the interest of the majority to plunder the rich. If
so, the Utilitarians will say, that the rich *ought* to be plundered.
We deny the inference. . . We have to notice one most important distinction which Mr Mill has altogether overlooked.
Throughout his Essay, he confounds the community with the
species. He talks of the greatest happiness of the greatest
number: but when we examine his reasonings, we find that he
thinks only of the greatest number of a single generation. . .

Even if we were to grant that he had found out the form of
government which is best for the majority of the people now
living on the face of the earth, we might still without inconsistency maintain that form of government to be pernicious to

mankind. It would still be incumbent on Mr Mill to prove that the interest of every generation is identical with the interest of all succeeding generations.

'On Mill's Essay on Government', *Edinburgh Review*

7 Dugald Stewart, Democracy and Economic Policy (1855)

The happiness of mankind depends *immediately*, not on the *form of government*, but on the particular system of *law and policy* which that form introduces; and. . .the advantage which one form of government possesses over another, arises chiefly from the facility it affords to the introduction of such legislative improvements as the general interests of the community recommend. Now, I do not think that in the present state of the world, Democratic constitutions in any form which it is possible to give them, are favourable to the establishment of those systematic and enlightened principles of Political Economy which are subservient to the progressive happiness and improvement of mankind. Under every form of government, (whatever it may be), provided its general spirit be favourable to liberty, and allows an unrestrained freedom of discussion, these enlightened views of Political Economy will gradually and slowly prevail in proportion to the progress of reason and the diffusion of knowledge. And they will command the general assent of mankind soonest in those countries where a strong executive power and a vigilant police allow men to prosecute calmly and dispassionately those important but difficult studies, which lead to the melioration of the human race.

Lectures on Political Economy

8 Samuel Brittan, Can Democracy Manage an Economy? (1977)

To understand the political threat posed by short-term temptations of money creation and excessive deficit spending, it is helpful to turn to the analysis of democracy of one of Keynes's contemporaries, the Austrian–American economist Joseph Schumpeter (see his *Capitalism, Socialism and Democracy*). One is not surprised to find that the two thinkers had very little understanding of each other.

Schumpeter's analysis starts with the truism that democracy in a large country cannot be – as the literal-minded see it – the rule of all the people by all the people. . .

A more realistic definition of democracy, which would include the essential characteristics of many of the systems of government in the Western hemisphere, was provided by Schumpeter. He conceived of democratic representatives as akin to other economic agents: they deal in votes as steelmen deal in steel or oilmen in oil. The democratic character of their behaviour results from the competition between different politicians and parties for votes. To gain or to regain power, they must offer policies or, more characteristically, promise results that will attract votes away from other potential governments. To this extent, the views of at least part of the electorate will influence the way in which the country is governed.

The electors are assumed to act according to their own self-interest. . .

The commercial market place is characterised by the *individual* pursuit of self-interest. This is unlikely to cause irresistible demands for more than the economy can provide. Individuals in their own lives are subject to budget constraints; they cannot spend more than they can earn or borrow.

The political market place is characterised by the pursuit of self-interest by large groups, where these personal budget constraints are absent. Electors can rather more easily demand an increased slice of the cake without any agreement on the part of those who are supposed to have the thinner slices. The costs of the handouts, whether met through taxation or inflation, will not necessarily accrue to the groups who benefit from them. In each individual case, whether a subsidy is paid to council-house dwellers, cheese eaters or car makers, there is a strong incentive for the interest group to press its demands as forcefully as possible without any real discipline on the sum total of interest-group demands.

Even with fixed rules on public finance, the process will induce a bias toward public expenditure. Nevertheless, because taxpayers or borrowers have votes, an increase in public expenditure which requires an increase in taxation or high

interest rates is likely to be somewhat less attractive to a
government than an increase which can be financed effectively
by printing money. With traditional rules such as the balanced-
budget principle, or gold-standard limits on money creation,
the bias towards government overspending is likely to have
some limits on it by opposition from taxpayers.

If, on the other hand, the government is permitted to boost
aggregate demand by extra expenditure without extra taxes or
higher interest rates, its trade-off is different. One alternative is
to lose votes by failing to offer an interest group as much as
other parties offer. The other is to join the competitive bidding
and offer as much.

If the effects of printing money on inflation were immediate,
the government might have some qualms about substituting,
say, temporary job-preservation for stable prices. But, as the
inflationary effects are delayed, the government is presented
with a choice between a certain benefit in increased electoral
support in the short run and the uncertain cost of some very
unpleasant choices between a slump and runaway inflation in
some years' time. It is not surprising that governments, conscious of Keynes's view of long-run mortality, accept the
inflationary alternative.

In short, therefore, there are two reasons why governments
are liable to overstimulate demand, or attempt to promote
unsustainably high employment: the benefits are short-run,
while the costs are long-run; and the benefits are specific and
easily attributable to the government, while the costs are general
and less easily attributed to any single cause.

'Can Democracy Manage an Economy?'

C.   The State and the Economy

It is to disagreements on the correct mode of economic analysis and
the proper objectives of economic policy that we now turn. For most
of the nineteenth century, thinking on economic policy was dominated by so-called *laissez-faire* ideas. These were a restatement,
perhaps an exaggeration, of Smith's 'system of natural liberty'.
Government should maintain civil order, protect the person and
property of its subjects and help in the enforcement of contracts;
within these constraints, men should be free to compete with each
other and also to co-operate with each other on whatever terms were

mutually agreed. This view was to remain the conventional wisdom until late in the century, but in practice *laissez-faire* principles were breached from early in the century. Two instances stand out – the legal regulation of the employment of children and women, and the legal allowance of the organization of labour combinations, trade unions. In both areas, legal interventions constituted, and indeed were by some opposed as, violations of the freedom of individual contract. By the turn of the century, a radical Liberal such as L. T. Hobhouse could present a defence of such intervention and an extensive critique of the *laissez-faire* position on the grounds of the extension of individual liberty (VIII:9).

The most thorough challenge to *laissez-faire* thought came, however, from socialist movements and thinkers; or more particularly from a form of socialism which has been termed state socialism, for which neither economic efficiency nor economic justice could be attained without considerable state ownership of industry and an extensive system of central economic planning. Such a wholesale rejection of *laissez-faire* beliefs was to be embraced most ardently in the twentieth century by the communist regimes of the Soviet Union, China and Eastern Europe; but it has had its perhaps more restrained admirers in this country. In the constitution of the Labour Party, adopted in 1918 more than a decade after its formation, the party committed itself, in the famous – or notorious – clause 4, to the common ownership of the means of production (VIII:10). At the same time, a programme of action was drafted by a committee under Sidney Webb (who was later, with his wife Beatrice, to be a strong apologist for the Soviet experiment) which committed the party to a programme of nationalization of the commanding heights of the economy (plus alcohol) and the continuation and extension of wartime controls on industry (VIII:11). Whilst the state socialist tendency was never wholly dominant in the Labour Party, it nevertheless provided at least until the 1950s general guidelines for party policy.

Even before this limited commitment by Labour to state socialism, there had been reactions against it amongst radicals. L. T. Hobhouse who, as we have seen, condemned as a liberal the *laissez-faire* liberals, was nevertheless adamant that the true liberal could never be reconciled to state socialism (VIII:12). He foresaw the possibility of a liberal socialism, which would aim at egalitarian objectives within a democratic and free-market frame, but he opposed any such liberal socialism to 'mechanical socialism' (Marxism) or 'official socialism' (Fabian socialism of the Webb variety). In 1926, John Maynard

Keynes took much the same position as Hobhouse, even-handedly combining rejection of central tenets of *laissez-faire* thought with a critique of state socialism (VIII:13). But Keynes does not rule out state direction in the economic sphere; here he outlines those areas – currency and credit, investment, population – which he then thought should be on the state's agenda. The most important Keynesian contribution to the debate on the state and the economy was however to be the idea of demand management as a political means of countering business cycles and in particular of achieving full employment.

Hobhouse and Keynes were Liberals. The revisionist socialist Anthony Crosland moved close to their position in the mid-1950s (VIII:14). His book, *The Future of Socialism*, was in many ways an attempt to persuade the Labour Party to abandon the state socialist tradition. He attacked the detailed central planning mechanism of the Soviet Union and argued that public ownership was no guarantee of achieving such socialist ends as economic equality or a classless society; equally, he argued, such ends might be furthered in a privately owned economy. He sought to maintain his socialist credentials by appealing to an alternative tradition, that of the search for social equality.

Margaret Thatcher's views have often been seen as a reversion to *laissez-faire* thinking. Certainly her faith in the efficiency of the market, her suspicion of government intervention and her wish to roll back the frontiers of the state (at least in the economic sphere) seem to bring her close to Adam Smith's 'system of natural liberty'. But in her lecture on these themes in 1979 shortly after her first election victory, moral evangelism tends to drown out economic argument (VIII:15). A moral rather than an economic individualism is preached and the promised economic prosperity seems as much a reward for moral rectitude as a product of rational economic policies.

Are there any positions on the proper relationship of the state and the economy which are incompatible with a democratic system? It might seem that a developed state socialism would require such a centralization of power and direction of individual behaviour as to make democratic practices difficult if not impossible. On the other side, however, if democratic accountability must inevitably disrupt market operations, or if the introduction by government of free-market structures will raise violent opposition from groups in the population, then some dilution if not the abandonment of democracy might be necessary to the creation or maintenance of a free-market system. Perhaps the truth is that the prophet and the expert will always have a problem with democracy. A person who believes that he (or she) is in possession of an absolute truth, either scientific or moral, cannot embrace democracy with conviction unless he believes that the *demos* will reciprocally embrace and act on that truth. As Dicey pointed out, this assumption, often made by reformers, is illusory since it is impossible to predict *a priori* what a democratic majority might prefer or demand (VIII:16).

9   L. T. Hobhouse, Laissez-faire and Individual Liberty (1911)

In place of the system of unfettered agreements between individual and individual which the school of Cobden contemplated, the industrial system which has actually grown up and is in process of further development rests on conditions prescribed by the State, and within the limits of those conditions is very largely governed by collective arrangements between associations of employers and employed. . .

This development is sometimes held to have involved the decay and death of the older Liberalism. It is true that in the beginning factory legislation enjoyed a large measure of Conservative support. It was at that stage in accordance with the best traditions of paternal rule, and it commended itself to the religious convictions of men of whom Lord Shaftesbury was the typical example. It is true, also, that it was bitterly opposed by Cobden and Bright. On the other hand, Radicals like J. Cam Hobhouse took a leading part in the earlier legislation, and Whig Governments passed the very important Acts of 1833 and 1847. The cleavage of opinion, in fact, cut across the ordinary divisions of party. What is more to the purpose is that, as experience ripened, the implications of the new legislation became clearer, and men came to see that by industrial control they were not destroying liberty but confirming it. A new and more concrete conception of liberty arose and many old presuppositions were challenged.

Let us look for a moment at these presuppositions. We have seen that the theory of *laissez-faire* assumed that the State would hold the ring. That is to say, it would suppress force and fraud, keep property safe, and aid men in enforcing contracts. On these conditions, it was maintained, men should be absolutely free to compete with one another, so that their best energies

should be called forth, so that each should feel himself responsible for the guidance of his own life, and exert his manhood to
the utmost. But why, it might be asked, on these conditions,
just these and no others? Why should the State ensure protection
of person and property? The time was when the strong man
armed kept his goods, and incidentally his neighbour's goods
too if he could get hold of them. Why should the State intervene
to do for a man that which his ancestor did for himself? Why
should a man who has been soundly beaten in physical fight go
to a public authority for redress? How much more manly to
fight his own battle! Was it not a kind of pauperization to make
men secure in person and property through no efforts of their
own, by the agency of a state machinery operating over their
heads? Would not a really consistent individualism abolish this
machinery? 'But,' the advocate of *laissez-faire* may reply, 'the
use of force is criminal, and the State must suppress crime.' So
men held in the nineteenth century. But there was an earlier
time when they did not take this view, but left it to individuals
and their kinsfolk to revenge their own injuries by their own
might. Was not this a time of more unrestricted individual
liberty? Yet the nineteenth century regarded it, and justly, as an
age of barbarism. What, we may ask in our turn, is the essence
of crime? May we not say that any intentional injury to another
may be legitimately punished by a public authority, and may we
not say that to impose twelve hours' daily labour on a child was
to inflict a greater injury than the theft of a purse for which a
century ago a man might be hanged? On what principle, then, is
the line drawn, so as to specify certain injuries which the State
may prohibit and to mark off others which it must leave
untouched? Well, it may be said, *volenti non fit injuria*. No
wrong is done to a man by a bargain to which he is a willing
party. That may be, though there are doubtful cases. But in the
field that has been in question the contention is that one party is
not willing. The bargain is a forced bargain. The weaker man
consents as one slipping over a precipice might consent to give
all his fortune to one who will throw him a rope on no other
terms. This is not true consent. True consent is free consent,
and full freedom of consent implies equality on the part of both
parties to the bargain. Just as government first secured the
elements of freedom for all when it prevented the physically
stronger man from slaying, beating, despoiling his neighbours,
so it secures a larger measure of freedom for all by every

restriction which it imposes with a view to preventing one man from making use of any of his advantages to the disadvantage of others.

Liberalism

10   Common Ownership of the Means of Production (1917)

Party Objects

National

a)   To organise and maintain in Parliament and in the country a Political Labour Party, and to ensure the establishment of a Local Labour Party in every County Constituency and every Parliamentary Borough, with suitable divisional organisation in the separate constituencies of Divided Boroughs.

b)   To co-operate with the Parliamentary Committee of the Trades Union Congress, or other Kindred Organisations, in joint political or other action in harmony with the Party Constitution and Standing Orders.

c)   To give effect as far as may be practicable to the principles from time to time approved by the Party Conference.

d)   To secure for the producers by hand or by brain the full fruits of their industry, and the most equitable distribution thereof that may be possible, upon the basis of the common ownership of the means of production and the best obtainable system of popular administration and control of each industry or service.

e)   Generally to promote the Political, Social, and Economic Emancipation of the People, and more particularly of those who depend directly upon their own exertions by hand or by brain for the means of life.

The Constitution of the Labour Party

11 Sidney Webb, Nationalisation (1918)

The Labour Party stands not merely for the principle of the Common Ownership of the nation's land, to be applied as suitable opportunities occur, but also, specifically, for the immediate Nationalisation of Railways, Mines and the production of Electrical Power. We hold that the very foundation of any successful reorganisation of British Industry must necessarily be found in the provision of the utmost facilities for transport and communication, the production of power at the cheapest possible rate and the most economical supply of both electrical energy and coal to every corner of the kingdom. Hence the Labour Party stands, unhesitatingly, for the National Ownership and Administration of the Railways and Canals, and their union, along with Harbours and Roads, and the Posts and Telegraphs – not to say also the great lines of steamers which could at once be owned, if not immediately directly managed in detail, by the Government – in a united national service of Communication and Transport. . .

But the sphere of immediate Nationalisation is not restricted to these great industries. We shall never succeed in putting the gigantic system of Health Insurance on a proper footing, or secure a clear field for the beneficent work of the Friendly Societies, or gain a free hand for the necessary development of the urgently called for Ministry of Health and the Local Public Health Service, until the nation expropriates the profit-making Industrial Insurance Companies, which now so tyrannously exploit the people with their wasteful house-to-house Industrial Life Assurance. . .

In quite another sphere the Labour Party sees the key to Temperance Reform in taking the entire manufacture and retailing of alcoholic drink out of the hands of those who find profit in promoting the utmost possible consumption. . .

Meanwhile, however, we ought not to throw away the valuable experience now gained by the Government in its assumption of the importation of wheat, wool, metals, and other commodities, and in its control of the shipping, woollen, leather, clothing, boot and shoe, milling, baking, butchering, and other industries. The Labour Party holds that, whatever may have been the shortcomings of this Government importation and control, it has demonstrably prevented a lot of 'profiteering.' Nor can it end immediately on the Declaration of

Peace. The people will be extremely foolish if they ever allow their indispensable industries to slip back into the unfettered control of private capitalists.

Labour and the New Social Order

12 L. T. Hobhouse, Liberal Socialism (1911)

There are two forms of Socialism with which Liberalism has nothing to do. These I will call the mechanical and the official. Mechanical Socialism is founded on a false interpretation of history. It attributes the phenomena of social life and development to the sole operation of the economic factor, whereas the beginning of sound sociology is to conceive society as a whole in which all the parts interact. The economic factor, to take a single point, is at least as much the effect as it is the cause of scientific invention. There would be no world-wide system of telegraphy if there was no need of world-wide intercommunication. But there would be no electric telegraph at all but for the scientific interest which determined the experiments of Gauss and Weber. Mechanical Socialism, further, is founded on a false economic analysis which attributes all value to labour, denying, confounding or distorting the distinct functions of the direction of enterprise, the unavoidable payment for the use of capital, the productivity of nature, and the very complex social forces which, by determining the movements of demand and supply actually fix the rates at which goods exchange with one another. Politically, mechanical Socialism supposes a class war, resting on a clear-cut distinction of classes which does not exist. Far from tending to clear and simple lines of cleavage, modern society exhibits a more and more complex interweaving of interests, and it is impossible for a modern revolutionist to assail 'property' in the interest of 'labour' without finding that half the 'labour' to which he appeals has a direct or indirect interest in 'property'. As to the future, mechanical Socialism conceives a logically developed system of the control of industry by government. Of this all that need be said is that the construction of Utopias is not a sound method of social science; that this particular Utopia makes insufficient provision for liberty, movement, and growth; and that in order to bring his ideals into the region of practical discussion, what the Socialist needs is to formulate not a system to be substituted as a whole for our present arrangements but a principle to guide statesmanship in the practical work of reforming what is amiss and developing what is good in the actual fabric of industry. . .

Official Socialism is a creed of different brand. Beginning with a contempt for ideals of liberty based on a confusion between liberty and competition, it proceeds to a measure of contempt for average humanity in general. It conceives mankind as in the mass a helpless and feeble race, which it is its duty to treat kindly. True kindness, of course, must be combined with firmness, and the life of the average man must be organized for his own good. He need not know that he is being organized. The socialistic organization will work in the background, and there will be wheels within wheels, or rather wires pulling wires. Ostensibly there will be a class of the elect, an aristocracy of character and intellect which will fill the civil services and do the practical work of administration. Behind these will be committees of union and progress who will direct operations, and behind the committees again one or more master minds from whom will emanate the ideas that are to direct the world. The play of democratic government will go on for a time, but the idea of a common will that should actually undertake the organization of social life is held the most childish of illusions. The master minds can for the moment work more easily through democratic forms, because they are here, and to destroy them would cause an upheaval. But the essence of government lies in the method of capture. The ostensible leaders of democracy are ignorant creatures who can with a little management be set to walk in the way in which they should go, and whom the crowd will follow like sheep. The art of governing consists in making men do what you wish without knowing what they are doing, to lead them on without showing them whither until it is too late for them to retrace their steps. Socialism so conceived has in essentials nothing to do with democracy or with liberty. It is a scheme of the organization of life by the superior person, who will decide for each man how he should work, how he should live, and indeed, with the aid of the Eugenist, whether he should live at all or whether he has any business to be born. At any rate, if he ought not to have been born – if, that is, he comes of a stock whose qualities are not approved – the Samurai will take care that he does not perpetuate his race.

Now the average Liberal might have more sympathy with this view of life if he did not feel that for his part he is just a very ordinary man. He is quite sure that he cannot manage the lives of other people for them. He finds it enough to manage his own. But with the leave of the Superior he would rather do this in his own way than in the way of another, whose way may be much wiser but is not his. . .

If, then, there be such a thing as a Liberal Socialism – and whether there be is still a subject for inquiry – it must clearly fulfil two conditions. In the first place, it must be democratic. It must come from below, not from above. Or rather, it must emerge from the efforts of society as a whole to secure a fuller measure of justice, and a better organization of mutual aid. It must engage the efforts and respond to the genuine desires not of a handful of superior beings, but of great masses of men. And, secondly, and for that very reason, it must make its account with the human individual. It must give the average man free play in the personal life for which he really cares. It must be founded on liberty, and must make not for the suppression but for the development of personality.

Liberalism

13　John Maynard Keynes, Against Laissez-faire and State Socialism (1926)

Let us clear from the ground the metaphysical or general principles upon which, from time to time, *laissez-faire* has been founded. It is *not* true that individuals possess a prescriptive 'natural liberty' in their economic activities. There is *no* 'compact' conferring perpetual rights on those who Have or on those who Acquire. The world is *not* so governed from above that private and social interest always coincide. It is *not* so managed here below that in practice they coincide. It is *not* a correct deduction from the principles of economics that enlightened self-interest always operates in the public interest. Nor is it true that self-interest generally *is* enlightened; more often individuals acting separately to promote their own ends are too ignorant or too weak to attain even these. Experience does *not* show that individuals, when they make up a social unit, are always less clear-sighted than when they act separately. . .

I criticise doctrinaire State Socialism, not because it seeks to engage men's altruistic impulses in the service of society, or because it departs from *laissez-faire*, or because it takes away from man's natural liberty to make a million, or because it has courage for bold experiments. All these things I applaud. I criticise it because it misses the significance of what is actually happening; because it is, in fact, little better than a dusty survival of a plan to meet the problems of fifty years ago, based on a misunderstanding of what someone said a hundred years ago. Nineteenth-century State Socialism sprang from Bentham, free competition, etc., and is in some respects a clearer, in some respects a more muddled version of just the same philosophy as underlies nineteenth-century individualism. Both equally laid all their stress on freedom, the one negatively to avoid limitations on existing freedom, the other positively to destroy natural or acquired monopolies. They are different reactions to the same intellectual atmosphere.

I come next to a criterion of *Agenda* which is particularly relevant to what it is urgent and desirable to do in the near future. We must aim at separating those services which are *technically social* from those which are *technically individual*. The most important *Agenda* of the State relate not to those activities which private individuals are already fulfilling, but to those functions which fall outside the sphere of the individual, to those decisions which are made by *no one* if the State does not make them. The important thing for government is not to do things which individuals are doing already, and to do them a little better or a little worse; but to do those things which at present are not done at all.

It is not within the scope of my purpose on this occasion to develop practical policies. I limit myself, therefore, to naming some instances of what I mean from amongst those problems about which I happen to have thought most.

Many of the greatest economic evils of our time are the fruits of risk, uncertainty, and ignorance. It is because particular individuals, fortunate in situation or in abilities, are able to take advantage of uncertainty, and ignorance, and also because for the same reason big business is often a lottery, that great inequalities of wealth come about; and these same factors are also the cause of the unemployment of labour, or the disappointment of reasonable business expectations, and of the impairment of efficiency and production. Yet the cure lies outside the operations of individuals; it may even be to the interest of individuals to aggravate the disease. I believe that the cure for these things is partly to be sought in the deliberate control of the currency and of credit by a central institution, and partly in the collection and dissemination on a great scale of data relating to the business situation, including the full publicity, by law if necessary, of all business facts which it is useful to know. These measures would involve society in exercising directive intelligence through some appropriate organ of action over many of the inner intricacies of private business, yet it would leave private initiative and enterprise unhindered. Even if these measures prove insufficient, nevertheless, they will furnish us with better knowledge than we have now for taking the next step.

My second example relates to savings and investment. I believe that some coordinated act of intelligent judgement is required as to the scale on which it is desirable that the community as a whole should save, the scale on which these savings should go abroad in the form of foreign investments, and whether the present organisation of the investment market distributes savings along the most nationally productive channels. I do not think that these matters should be left entirely to the chances of private judgement and private profits, as they are at present.

My third example concerns population. The time has already come when each country needs a considered national policy about what size of population, whether larger or smaller than at present or the same, is most expedient. And having settled this policy, we must take steps to carry it into operation. The time may arrive a little later when the community as a whole must pay attention to the innate quality as well as to the mere numbers of its future members.

'The End of Laissez-faire'

14 C. A. R. Crosland, Socialism and State Ownership (1956)

Since private ownership has little to do with the loss of control by the workers, and indeed is not itself the main source of control even where it still survives, it seems unlikely that the pattern of ownership will uniquely determine anything. Let us test this view against each of those basic characteristics of a society which have, historically, been of most concern to socialists.

First, political freedom and parliamentary democracy. Recent history demonstrates that these may (though of course they need not) exist in a largely privately-owned economy, and not in a collectivist one. Presumably no one would deny that they were present in Britain, and absent in Soviet Russia.

Secondly, class stratification. . .may be either more or less marked in a collectivist than in a privately-owned economy. The once-popular equation of state ownership and the classless society rested either on a tautological proof (that is, class was defined in terms solely of the presence or absence of private ownership, from which it followed that if there were no private ownership, there could be no classes), or on the assumption that when the state expropriated industry, no one class would control the state. But there was no logical reason why this should be true. Most people would judge that in Russia it is not, and that a distinct ruling-class exists, its power resting on control of the state machine. . .

Thirdly, the degree of 'exploitation' – that is, the extent to which the workers, instead of being paid and consuming the whole value of what they produce, surrender some part in the form of 'surplus value' – again does not depend uniquely on ownership. It is determined primarily by the fiscal policy of the government, and by managerial decisions about the disposal of profits. . .

Fourthly, the distribution of personal income is not uniquely determined by the pattern of ownership. It depends on the share of wages in the national income, the taxation policy of the government, and the behaviour of relative prices; and these in turn depend on many different factors such as the level of employment, the degree of competition, the strength of the Trade Unions, and above all the political complexion of the government. . . The same is true of the distribution of capital. This is determined by the structure of inheritance taxes, and the possibilities of accumulation during lifetime. . .

Fifthly, the degree of government planning does not depend exclusively on ownership. Post-war experience has shown that private industry can be subjected to a close degree of government control, while nationalised industries may behave in a rather independent fashion, and prove not altogether easy to plan. . .

Lastly, the status of the worker may be either better or worse in a collectivist than in a privately-owned economy. So far as real income is concerned, this depends partly on the share of wages in the national income, but in the long run mainly on the rate of growth of the economy; and there is no definite evidence that this must be higher in a collectivist society. So far as status at work is concerned, the Marxist criticism of 'proletarianisation', in the direct sense that most employees work for wages in mass factory units, is of course as easily levelled at Soviet Russia as at the United States but what really matters is the degree to which management is autocratic or democratic, the extent of joint consultation and participation, and the freedom of the worker to strike or leave his job. In all these respects the Soviet worker is more proletarianised than the British worker. . .

Now it is true that the planned full-employment welfare state, which has been the outcome of the first successful spell of Labour government, is a society of exceptional merit and quality by historical standards, and by comparison with pre-war capitalism. It would have seemed a paradise to many early socialist pioneers. Poverty and insecurity are in process of disappearing. Living standards are rising rapidly; the fear of unemployment is steadily weakening; and the ordinary young worker has hopes for the future which would never have entered his father's head. There is much less social injustice; the economy works efficiently; and the electorate, as the Labour Party discovered at the last election, is in no mood for large-scale change, and certainly not for the complete overthrow of the present system. Many liberal-minded people, who were instinctively 'socialist' in the 1930s as a humanitarian protest against poverty and unemployment, have now concluded that 'Keynes-plus-modified-capitalism-plus-Welfare State' works perfectly well; and they would be content to see the Labour Party become (if the Tories do not filch the role) essentially a Party for the defence of the present position, with occasional minor reforms thrown in to sweeten the temper of the local activists.

Yet this is not socialism. True, it is not pure capitalism either; and it does fulfil some part of the traditional socialist aspirations, and to this extent has socialist features. Yet it could clearly be a great deal more socialist than it is – not, as people sometimes think, because it now has only 25% public ownership and is not fully planned down to the minutest detail, any more than Soviet society is more socialist because it has 100% public ownership and complete state planning: but simply because the traditional socialist ideals could be more fully realised than they are. To put the matter simply, we have won many important advances; but since we could still have more social equality, a more classless society, and less avoidable social distress, we cannot be described as a socialist country.

The Future of Socialism

15 Margaret Thatcher, The Welfare State and Individual Responsibility (lecture delivered in 1979)

Theorists of Socialism, like Laski, Tawney and their followers, motivated by a genuine desire for social justice, elevated the State as an instrument of social regeneration. Simultaneously, Keynes and later various schools of neo-Keynesian economists, exalted the role of Government and humbled the role of the individual in their pursuit of economic stability and prosperity. . .

The desire to bring about a society which promotes greater human fulfilment is not the monopoly of any one political party. I acknowledge, readily, the sincerity and generosity of some Socialists. However, I believe that the Socialist approach is based upon a moral confusion which in practice is profoundly damaging. The moral fallacy of Socialism is to suppose that conscience can be collectivized. One sees this fallacy most plainly in Marxist theory. Marxists are quite unable to say why a proletarian revolution, a hate-filled and violent act of expropriation, should be morally cleansing and lead to a better society. Their failure in theory has been heavily and tragically underlined by the reality of life in twentieth-century Marxist States.

But the gentler proponents of Socialism, who stop short of subscribing to the full Marxist view of history, are equally unconvincing in their view of human nature. Experience has shown the practical failure of two fundamental Socialist arguments: that nationalization is justified because it makes economic power accountable to the people whose lives it affects; and that State planning can point to better ways forward than can be charted by free enterprise. The Socialists had grossly expanded State intervention in the economy. They were going so far as to claim that the State should have monopoly rights in the provision of health and education.

It is certainly the duty of Government to do all it can to ensure that effective succour is given to those in need, and this is a Conservative principle as much as a Socialist one. Where Conservatives part company from Socialists is in the degree of confidence which we can place in the exclusive capacity of a Welfare State to relieve suffering and promote well-being. Charity is a personal quality – the supreme moral quality, according to St Paul – and public compassion, State philanthropy and institutionalized charity can never be enough. There is no adequate substitute for genuine caring for one another on the part of families, friends and neighbours.

I think that this proposition would be widely accepted. And yet the collectivist ethos has made individuals excessively prone to rely on the State to provide for the well-being of their neighbours and indeed of themselves. There cannot be a welfare system in any satisfactory sense which tends, in this way, to break down personal responsibility and the sense of responsibility to family, neighbourhood and community. The balance has moved too far towards collectivism. In recent years, it has been quite widely held to be morally wrong for the individual to choose to make his own provision for the education of his children or the health of his family.

Yet if the State usurps or denies the right of the individual to make, where he is able to do so, the important decisions in his life and to provide the essentials for himself and his family, then he is demeaned and diminished as a moral being. We need, therefore, to achieve a better balance between the spheres of public and private activity. . .

The extent of our decline compared with other countries may show up most clearly in economic statistics. But that does not mean that the remedy lies only in economics. The economics will come right if the spirit and the determination is there. The mission of this Government is much more than the promotion of economic progress. It is to renew the spirit and the solidarity of the nation. To ensure that these assertions lead to action, we need to inspire a new national mood, as much as to carry through legislation.

At the heart of a new mood in the nation must be a recovery of our self-confidence and our self-respect. Nothing is beyond us. Decline is not inevitable. But nor is progress a law of nature. The ground gained by one generation may be lost by the next.

The foundation of this new confidence has to be individual responsibility. If people come to believe that the State, or their employer, or their union, owe them a living, and that, in turn, the world owes Britain a living, we shall have no confidence and no future. It must be quite clear that the responsibility is on each of us to make the full use of our talents and to care for our families. It must be clear, too, that we have a responsibility to our country to make Britain respected and successful in the world. The economic counterpart of these personal and national responsibilities is the working of the market economy in a free society. I am sure that there is wide acceptance in Britain, going far beyond the supporters of our party, that production and distribution in our economy is best operated through free competition.

The Revival of Britain

16 A. V. Dicey, The Unpredictability of Democratic Demands (1905)

Let us now see how far the advance of democracy is likely to affect laws which have not a constitutional character, or, in other words, which do not tell upon the distribution of sovereign power.

In respect of the influence of democracy on such laws, we can draw with some confidence one probable conclusion. We may with high probability assume that no law will be carried, or at any rate that no law will long remain in force, which is opposed to the wish of the people, or, in other words, to the sentiment prevailing among the distinct majority of the citizens of a given country. It is, however, absolutely impossible from the advance of democracy to draw, with regard to laws which do not touch the balance of political power, anything more than this merely negative inference. The impossibility arises from the patent fact that, though in a democratic country the laws which will be passed, or at any rate will be put into effect, must be the laws which the people like, it is absolutely impossible to predict on any *a priori* ground what are the laws which the people of a country will at any given time wish to be passed or put in force.

The reason why the truth of a conclusion which is hardly disputable is not universally admitted, is to be found in a singular illusion which affects alike the friends and the opponents of democratic change. Democracy is a comparatively new form of government. Reformers, or revolutionists, who have attempted to achieve definite changes, e.g. the disestablishment of the Church, the abolition of primogeniture, the creation of peasant proprietorship, or, it may be, the regulation of public labour by the State for the advantage of artisans and labourers, stand in a position like that of men who look for immense blessing to the country from the accession to the throne of a new monarch; they tacitly or openly assume that the new sovereign – in this case the democracy – will carry out the ideas of beneficent legislation and good government entertained by the reformers who have placed the sovereign in power. . .

Nor have the opponents of democratic innovation been free from a delusion strictly analogous to the error which has falsified the forecasts of democrats. Tories or Conservatives, who looked with terror and aversion on democratic progress, have for the most part assumed that the sovereign people would of necessity support legislation which is hateful to every man of conservative instincts. During the debates on the great Reform Bill the attacks made upon it by Tory zealots teemed with anticipations of iniquitous legislation. Men who hated revolution could not believe that democrats might be conservatives. At the bottom, in short, of all speculations about the effects of the advance of democracy, constantly lies the assumption that there exists such a thing as specially democratic legislation which every democracy is certain to favour. Yet there never was an assumption more clearly at variance with the teaching of history.

Law and Public Opinion in England

IX
A Democratic Culture?

Democracy is more than just a system of government. It is also an ideal, an appeal to our common humanity. It is an assertion of (to quote the famous slogan of the French Revolution) 'liberty, equality and fraternity'. The aim of this chapter is to illustrate how various British writers have reflected on this wider, philosophical aspect of democracy.

Democracy contains an implicit appeal to the notion of the 'common man', to a natural equality of worth that takes precedence over hierarchies of rank and wealth. British writers have been variously attracted and repelled by this idea, and this chapter gives examples of the views of both 'democrats' and 'anti-democrats' (or, at least, those who have anxieties about democracy in this wide sense). The first section considers the question 'Does Britain have a democratic culture?' by looking for evidence of a democratic 'spirit' or attitude of mind both in literature and in society at large. The second section examines the relationship between democracy and culture from a different perspective, by considering the argument that the 'masses' constitute a threat to the very existence of culture.

A.   THE DEMOCRATIC SPIRIT

There is not the same tradition in British literature of celebrating 'democracy' as a broad, almost aesthetic idea that there is, for example, in America. (Two of the extracts in this section – those by Edward Carpenter and D. H. Lawrence – are influenced in different ways by the American poet Walt Whitman, while a third – '1st September 1939' by W. H. Auden – was written in the United States and has a particular American flavour). It is perhaps significant that all the writers who celebrate the deeper meaning of democracy in this section (William Blake, Percy Bysshe Shelley, Edward Carpenter,

D. H. Lawrence and W. H. Auden) were in different ways radicals, at odds with the literary, political and intellectual establishments of their day.

At first sight it would seem odd to include William Blake as a 'democrat'. Although he supported the ideals of the French Revolution (until 1800), he was certainly not primarily an advocate of any political system – indeed, it was against all 'systems' that his thought and art were directed. He was as opposed to the rationalism and materialism of the Enlightenment as he was to religion. His art was built on a transcendent belief in the power of the human imagination and on a burning desire for its liberation from the constraints (the 'mind-forg'd manacles') imposed on it by society. (Blake became a totemic figure for radicals of the 1960s.) In his poem 'London' (IX:1) from the *Songs of Innocence and Experience*, he swiftly traces the workings of this oppression on the inhabitants of the city, from the young chimney-sweep forced to clean the soot from a church ('Black'ning' refers not just to the physical soot, but also to accretions of religious dogma), to the young prostitute whose existence pollutes marriage and kills the new-born infant with venereal disease. (Like Carpenter and Lawrence, Blake believed in sexual liberation, in the liberation of sexual feeling from the false moralism – and hence hypocrisy – that had been imposed on it.)

Whereas Blake was one of the most complex and sometimes baffling figures in English literature, Shelley, a 'Romantic' poet of a younger generation, was a rebel of a much more easily comprehensible kind. His long poem *The Mask of Anarchy* (IX:2) – written in protest at the 'Peterloo Massacre' of 1819, when a peaceful political reform demonstration in Manchester was attacked by the army, and eleven demonstrators were killed – is one of the most famous assertions of political radicalism in English literature. Shelley is often anthologized and has an assured place in the canon, but Edward Carpenter is an all-but-forgotten figure nowadays, though his book-length poem *Towards Democracy* (IX:3) went through several editions in the 1890s and 1900s. Perhaps the most famous lines of Blake's come at the beginning of his poem 'Auguries of Innocence': 'To see the World in a Grain of Sand/And a Heaven in a Wild Flower,/Hold Infinity in the palm of your hand/And Eternity in an hour'. In these lines we can perhaps see the seed of what might be called a 'democratic aesthetic', an aesthetic that was to be exhaustively worked out in Carpenter's vast poem. Its main feature is an attention to the wonder of the mundane, of that which many artists pass over

in favour of the illustrious or sublime. This is stated explicitly in the
first excerpt from *Towards Democracy* given here, while the second
presents an expansive, panoptic vision of England that consciously
echoes Whitman's vistas of the American continent in *Leaves of
Grass*.

Even more so than with William Blake, it may appear strange to
include D. H. Lawrence in a collection of 'democrats'. Indeed, he has
often been charged with fascism. His essay 'Democracy' (IX:4),
though framed as an attack on Whitman, suggests that charge is
simplistic. He criticizes Whitman (whether justly or not is another
matter) for reducing Democracy to an abstract ideal that measures all
things by a single, mechanical rule of 'equality'. In place of that,
Lawrence asserts the irreducible vitality of all individuals – and,
indeed, of all living creatures. This movement away from the abstract
towards the particular and towards the extraordinariness of the
ordinary again reminds us of Blake.

In W. H. Auden's '1st September 1939' (IX:5), the movement is
one away from the political ideologies of fascism and communism
that had brought Europe to the brink of war, and towards the other
ordinary citizens sitting in the New York bar. The movement is not
towards 'solidarity' with them (since what 'each woman and each
man/Craves' is 'Not universal love/But to be loved alone') or
towards the 'Collective Man' represented by the skyscrapers, but
rather towards an appreciation of the 'Ironic points of light' that flash
between individuals.

It was suggested at the beginning of this section that there are
comparatively few celebrations of democracy as an ideal in British
literature. This may partly be a function of that general British
empiricism and suspicion of abstract ideas that was discussed in the
Introduction. One should perhaps also see a democratic spirit at work
in those writers who have pointed out or satirized the lack of
democratic spirit in British society as a whole. It is a truism of British
social life that it lacks a 'democratic culture'. Indeed, the petty
intricacies of class and snobbery have formed a major theme of
British literature since the eighteenth century. From the vast range of
material that could illustrate this, we have chosen passages from
Charles Dickens's *Bleak House* (IX:6) – on the aristocrat Sir Leicester
Deadlock's problems with poor relations – and, on a less humorous
note, from George Orwell's *Road to Wigan Pier* (IX:7).

1 William Blake, London (1789)

I wander thro' each charter'd street,
Near where the charter'd Thames does flow,
And mark in every face I meet
Marks of weakness, marks of woe.

In every cry of every Man,
In every Infant's cry of fear,
In every voice, in every ban,
The mind-forg'd manacles I hear.

How the Chimney-sweeper's cry
Every black'ning Church appalls;
And the hapless Soldier's sigh
Runs in blood down Palace walls.

But most thro' midnight streets I hear
How the youthful Harlot's curse
Blasts the new born Infant's tear,
And blights with plagues the Marriage hearse.

'London'

2 Percy Bysshe Shelley, Let a Great Assembly Be (1819)

'Let a great Assembly be
Of the fearless and the free
On some spot of English ground
Where the plains stretch wide around.

'Let the blue sky overhead,
The green earth on which ye tread,
All that must eternal be
Witness the solemnity.

'From the corners uttermost
Of the bounds of English coast;
From every hut, village, and town
Where those who live and suffer moan
For others' misery or their own,

'From the workhouse and the prison
Where pale as corpses newly risen,
Women, children, young and old,
Groan for pain, and weep for cold –

'From the haunts of daily life
Where is waged the daily strife
With common wants and common cares
Which sows the human heart with tares –

'Lastly from the palaces
Where the murmur of distress
Echoes, like the distant sound
Of a wind alive around

'Those prison halls of wealth and fashion,
Where some few feel such compassion
For those who groan, and toil, and wail
As must make their brethren pale –

'Ye who suffer woes untold,
Or to feel, or to behold
Your lost country bought and sold
With a price of blood and gold –

'Let a vast assembly be,
And with great solemnity
Declare with measured words that ye
Are, as God made ye, free –

'Be your strong and simple words
Keen to wound as sharpened swords,
And wide as targes let them be,
With their shade to cover ye.

'Let tyrants pour around
With a quick and startling sound,
Like the loosening of a sea,
Troops of armed emblazonry.

'Let the charged artillery drive
Till the dead air seems alive
With the clash of clanging wheels,
And the tramp of horses' heels.

'Let the fixèd bayonet
Gleam with sharp desire to wet
Its bright point in English blood
Looking keen as one for food.

'Let the horsemen's scimitars
Wheel and flash, like sphereless stars
Thirsting to eclipse their burning
In a sea of death and mourning.

'Stand ye calm and resolute,
Like a forest close and mute,
With folded arms and looks which are
Weapons of an unvanquished war,

'And let Panic, who outspeeds
The career of armèd steeds
Pass, a disregarded shade
Through your phalanx undismayed.

'Let the laws of your own land,
Good or ill, between ye stand
Hand to hand, and foot to foot,
Arbiters of the dispute,

'The old laws of England–they
Whose reverend heads with age are gray,
Children of a wiser day;
And whose solemn voice must be
Thine own echo–Liberty!

'On those who first should violate
Such sacred heralds in their state
Rest the blood that must ensue,
And it will not rest on you.

'And if then the tyrants dare
Let them ride among you there,
Slash, and stab, and maim, and hew, –
What they like, that let them do.

'With folded arms and steady eyes,
And little fear, and less surprise,
Look upon them as they slay
Till their rage has died away.

'Then they will return with shame
To the place from which they came,
And the blood thus shed will speak
In hot blushes on their cheek.

'Every woman in the land
Will point at them as they stand –
They will hardly dare to greet
Their acquaintance in the street.

'And the bold, true warriors
Who have hugged Danger in wars
Will turn to those who would be free,
Ashamed of such base company.

'And that slaughter to the Nation
Shall steam up like inspiration,
Eloquent, oracular;
A volcano heard afar.

'And these words shall then become
Like Oppression's thundered doom
Ringing through each heart and brain,
Heard again – again – again –

'Rise like Lions after slumber
In unvanquishable number –
Shake your chains to earth like dew
Which in sleep had fallen on you –
Ye are many – they are few.'

'The Mask of Anarchy'

3   Edward Carpenter, Towards Democracy (1883)

Far around and beyond whatever is exceptional and illustrious
in human life stretches that which is average and unperceived;
   All distinctions, all attainments, all signal beauty, skill, wit,
and whatever a man can exhibit in himself, swim and are lost in
that great ocean.
   The subtle learning of the learned, the beauty of the excep-

tionally beautiful, the wit of the witty, the fine manners and customs of the courtly – all these things proceed immediately out of the common and undistinguished people and those who stand in direct contact with Nature, and return into them again.

The course of all is the same; they are tossed up thinner and thinner, into mere spray at last – like a wave from the breast of the Ocean – and fall back again.

You try to set yourself apart from the vulgar. It is in vain. In that instant vulgarity attaches itself to you.

If it did not, you would cease to exist.

England spreads like a map below me. I see the mud-flats of the Wash striped with water at low tide, the embankments grown with mugwort and sea-asters, and Boston Stump and King's Lynn, and the squaresail brigs in the offing.

Beachy Head stands up beautiful, with white walls and pinnacles, from its slopes of yellow poppy and bugloss; the sea below creeps with a grey fog, the vessels pass and are folded out of sight within it. I hear their foghorns sounding.

Flamborough Head stands up, dividing the waves. Up its steep gullies the fishermen haul their boats; in its caves the waters make perpetual music.

I see the rockbound coast of Anglesey with projecting ribs of wrecks; the hills of Wicklow are faintly outlined across the water. I ascend the mountains of Wales; the tarns and streams lie silver below me, the valleys are dark. Moel Siabod stands up beautiful, and Trifan and Cader Idris in the morning air.

I descend the Wye, and pass through the ancient streets of Monmouth and of Bristol.

I ascend the high points of the Cotswolds, and look out over the rich vale of Gloucester to the Malvern hills, and see the old city clustering round its Church, and the broad waters of the Severn, and the distant towers of Berkeley Castle.

The river-streams run on below me. The broad deep-bosomed Trent through rich meadows full of cattle, under tall shady trees runs on. I trace it to its birthplace in the hills. I see the Derbyshire Derwent darting in trout-haunted shallows over its stones. I taste and bathe in the clear brown moor-fed water.

I see the sweet-breathed cottage homes and homesteads dotted for miles and miles and miles. It comes near to them. I enter the wheelwright's cottage by the angle of the river. The door stands open against the water, and catches its changing syllables all day long; roses twine, and the smell of the woodyard comes in wafts.

The Castle rock of Nottingham stands up bold over the Trent valley, the tall flagstaff waves its flag, the old market-place is full of town and country folk. The river goes on broadening seaward. I see where it runs beneath the great iron swing-bridges of railroads, there are canals connecting with it, and the sails of the canal-boats gliding on a level with the meadows.

The great sad colorless flood of the Humber stretches before me, the low-lying banks, the fog, the solitary vessels, the brackish marshes and the water-birds; Hull stretches with its docks, vessels are unlading – bags of shell-fish, cargoes of oranges, timber, fish; I see the flat lands beyond Hull, and the enormous flights of pewits.

The Thames runs down – with the sound of many voices. I hear the sound of the saw-mills and flour-mills of the Cots-wolds, I can see racing boats and hear the shouts of partisans, villages bask in the sun below me; Sonning and Maidenhead; anglers and artists are hid in nooks among tall willow-herbs; I glide with tub and outrigger past flower-gardens, meadows, parks; parties of laughing girls handle the oars and tiller ropes; Teddington, Twickenham, Richmond, Brentford glide past; I hear the songs, I hear Elizabethan echoes; I come within sound of the roar of London.

I see the woodland and rocky banks of the Tavy and the Tamar, and of the arrowy Dart. The Yorkshire Ouse winds sluggish below me; afar off I catch the Sussex Ouse and the Arun, breaking seaward through their gaps in the Downs; I look down from the Cheshire moors upon the Dee.

In their pride the beautiful cities of England stand up before me; from the midst of her antique elms and lilac and laburnum haunted gardens the grey gateways and towers of Cambridge stand up; ivy-grown Warwick peeps out of thick foliage; I see Canterbury and Winchester and Chester, and Worcester proud by her river-side, and the ancient castles – York and Lancaster looking out seaward, and Carlisle; I see the glistening of carriage wheels and the sumptuous shine of miles of sea frontage at Brighton and Hastings and Scarborough; Clifton climbs to her heights over the Avon; the ruins of Whitby Abbey are crusted with spray.

I hear the ring of hammers in the ship-yards of Chatham and

Portsmouth and Keyham, and look down upon wildernesses of masts and dock-basins. I see the observatory at Greenwich and catch the pulses of star-taken time spreading in waves over the land. I see the delicate spider-web of the telegraphs, and the rush of the traffic of the great main lines, North, West, and South. I see the solid flow of business men northward across London Bridge in the morning, and the ebb at evening. I see the eternal systole and diastole of exports and imports through the United Kingdom, and the armies of those who assist in the processes of secretion and assimilation – and the great markets.

I explore the palaces of dukes – the parks and picture galleries – Chatsworth, Hardwicke, Arundel; and the numberless old Abbeys. I walk through the tall-windowed hospitals and asylums of the great cities and hear chants caught up and wandering from ward to ward.

I see all over the land the beautiful centuries-grown villages and farmhouses nestling down among their trees; the dear old lanes and footpaths and the great clean highways connecting; the fields, every one to the people known by its own name, and hedgerows and little straggling copses, and village greens; I see the great sweeps of country, the rich wealds of Sussex and Kent, the orchards and deep lanes of Devon, the willow-haunted flats of Huntingdon, Cambridge and South Lincolnshire; Sherwood Forest and the New Forest, and the light pastures of the North and South Downs; the South and Midland and Eastern agricultural districts, the wild moorlands of the North and West, and the intermediate districts of coal and iron.

The oval-shaped manufacturing heart of England lies below me; at night the clouds flicker in the lurid glare; I hear the sob and gasp of pumps and the solid beat of steam and tilt-hammers; I see streams of pale lilac and saffron-tinted fire. I see the swarthy Vulcan-reeking towns, the belching chimneys, the slums, the liquor-shops, chapels, dancing saloons, running grounds, and blameless remote villa residences.

I see the huge warehouses of Manchester, the many-storied mills, the machinery, the great bale-laden drays, the magnificent horses; I walk through the Liverpool Exchange; the brokers stand in knots; the greetings; the frock-coats, the rosebuds; the handling and comparing of cotton samples.

Leeds lies below me; I hear the great bell; I see the rush along Boar Lane and Briggate. I enter the hot machine shops, smelling of oil and wooldust. I see Sheffield among her hills, and the white dashing of her many water-wheels, and the sulphurous black cloud going up to heaven in her midst.

Newcastle I recognise, and her lofty bridge; and I look out over the river gates of the Mersey.

I see a great land poised as in a dream – waiting for the word by which it may live again.

I see the stretched sleeping figure – waiting for the kiss and the re-awakening.

I hear the bells pealing, and the crash of hammers, and see beautiful parks spread – as in toy show.

I see a great land waiting for its own people to come and take possession of it.

Towards Democracy

4   D. H. Lawrence, A Democracy of Single Selves (*c.*1917)

The true identity. . . is the identity of the living self. If we look for God, let us look in the bush where he sings. That is, in living creatures. Every living creature is single in itself, a *ne plus ultra* of creative reality, *fons et origo* of creative manifestation. Why go further? Why begin to abstract and generalize and include? There you have it. Every single living creature is a single creative unit, a unique, incommutable self. Primarily, in its own spontaneous reality, it knows no law. It is a law unto itself. Secondarily, in its material reality, it submits to all the laws of the material universe. But the primal, spontaneous self in any creature has ascendance, truly, over the material laws of the universe; it uses these laws and converts them in the mystery of creation.

This then is the true identity: the inscrutable, single self, the little unfathomable well-head that bubbles forth into being and doing. We cannot analyse it. We can only know it is there. It is not by any means a Logos. It precedes any knowing. It is the fountain-head of everything: the quick of the self.

Not people melted into a oneness: that is not the new Democracy. But people released into their single, starry identity, each one distinct and incommutable. This will never be an ideal; for of the living self you cannot make an idea, just as you have not been able to turn the individual 'soul' into an idea. Both are impossible to idealize. An idea is an abstraction from reality, a generalization. And you can't generalize the incommutable. . .

Since every individual is, in his first reality, a single, incommutable soul, not to be calculated or defined in terms of any other soul, there can be no establishing of a mathematical ratio. We cannot say that all men are equal. We cannot say A = B. Nor can we say that men are unequal. We may not declare that A = B + C.

Where each thing is unique in itself, there can be no comparison made. One man is neither equal nor unequal to another man. When I stand in the presence of another man, and I am my own pure self, am I aware of the presence of an equal, or of an inferior, or of a superior? I am not. When I stand with another man, who is himself, and when I am truly myself, then I am only aware of a Presence, and of the strange reality of Otherness. There is me, and there is *another being*. That is the first part of the reality. There is no comparing or estimating. There is only this strange recognition of *present otherness*. I may be glad, angry, or sad, because of the presence of the other. But still no comparison enters in. Comparison enters only when one of us departs from his own integral being and enters the material-mechanical world. Then equality and inequality starts at once.

So, we know the first great purpose of Democracy: that each man shall be spontaneously himself – each man himself, each woman herself, without any question of equality or inequality entering in at all; and that no man shall try to determine the being of any other man, or of any other woman.

'Democracy'

5 W. H. Auden, 1st September 1939

I sit in one of the dives
On Fifty-second Street
Uncertain and afraid
As the clever hopes expire
Of a low dishonest decade:
Waves of anger and fear
Circulate over the bright
And darkened lands of the earth,
Obsessing our private lives;

The unmentionable odour of death
Offends the September night.

Accurate scholarship can
Unearth the whole offence
From Luther until now
That has driven a culture mad,
Find what occurred at Linz,
What huge imago made
A psychopathic god:
I and the public know
What all schoolchildren learn,
Those to whom evil is done
Do evil in return.

Exiled Thucydides knew
All that a speech can say
About Democracy,
And what dictators do,
The elderly rubbish they talk
To an apathetic grave;
Analysed all in his book,
The enlightenment driven away,
The habit-forming pain,
Mismanagement and grief:
We must suffer them all again.

Into this neutral air
Where blind skyscrapers use
Their full height to proclaim
The strength of Collective Man,
Each language pours its vain
Competitive excuse:
But who can live for long
In an euphoric dream;
Out of the mirror they stare,
Imperialism's face
And the international wrong.

Faces along the bar
Cling to their average day:
The lights must never go out,
The music must always play,
All the conventions conspire

To make this fort assume
The furniture of home;
Lest we should see where we are,
Lost in a haunted wood,
Children afraid of the night
Who have never been happy or good.

The windiest militant trash
Important Persons shout
Is not so crude as our wish:
What mad Nijinsky wrote
About Diaghilev
Is true of the normal heart;
For the error bred in the bone
Of each woman and each man
Craves what it cannot have,
Not universal love
But to be loved alone.

From the conservative dark
Into the ethical life
The dense commuters come,
Repeating their morning vow;
'I *will* be true to the wife,
I'll concentrate more on my work,'
And helpless governors wake
To resume their compulsory game:
Who can release them now,
Who can reach the deaf,
Who can speak for the dumb?

Defenceless under the night
Our world in stupor lies;
Yet, dotted everywhere,
Ironic points of light
Flash out wherever the Just
Exchange their messages:
May I, composed like them
Or Eros and of dust,
Beleaguered by the same
Negation and despair,
Show an affirming flame.

'1st September 1939'

6 Charles Dickens, Poor Relations (1853)

It is a melancholy truth that even great men have their poor relations. Indeed great men have often more than their fair share of poor relations; inasmuch as very red blood of the superior quality, like inferior blood unlawfully shed, *will* cry aloud, and *will* be heard. Sir Leicester's cousins, in the remotest degree, are so many Murders, in the respect that they 'will out'. Among whom there are cousins who are so poor, that one might almost dare to think it would have been the happier for them never to have been plated links upon the Dedlock chain of gold, but to have been made of common iron at first, and done base service.

Service, however (with a few limited reservations; genteel but not profitable), they may not do, being of the Dedlock dignity. So they visit their richer cousins, and get into debt when they can, and live but shabbily when they can't, and find – the women no husbands, and the men no wives – and ride in borrowed carriages, and sit at feasts that are never of their own making, and so go through high life. The rich family sum has been divided by so many figures, and they are the something over that nobody knows what to do with.

Everybody on Sir Leicester Dedlock's side of the question, and of his way of thinking, would appear to be his cousin more or less. From my Lord Boodle, through the Duke of Foodle, down to Noodle, Sir Leicester, like a glorious spider, stretches his threads of relationship. But while he is stately in the cousinship of the Everybodys, he is a kind and generous man, according to his dignified way, in the cousinship of the Nobodys; and at the present time, in despite of the damp, he stays out the visit of several such cousins at Chesney Wold, with the constancy of a martyr.

Bleak House

7 George Orwell, Snobbery (1937)

The real bourgeoisie, those in the £2,000 a year class and over, have their money as a thick layer of padding between themselves and the class they plunder; in so far as they are aware of the Lower Orders at all they are aware of them as employees, servants and tradesmen. But it is quite different for the poor devils lower down who are struggling to live genteel lives on what are virtually working-class incomes. These last are forced into close and, in a sense, intimate contact with the working class, and I suspect it is from them that the traditional upper-class attitude towards 'common' people is derived.

And what is this attitude? An attitude of sniggering superiority punctuated by bursts of vicious hatred. Look at any number of *Punch* during the past thirty years. You will find it everywhere taken for granted that a working-class person, as such, is a figure of fun, except at odd moments when he shows signs of being too prosperous, whereupon he ceases to be a figure of fun and becomes a demon. It is no use wasting breath in denouncing this attitude. It is better to consider how it has arisen, and to do that one has got to realise what the working classes look like to those who live among them but have different habits and traditions.

A shabby-genteel family is in much the same position as a family of 'poor whites' living in a street where everyone else is a Negro. In such circumstance you have got to cling to your gentility because it is the only thing you have; and meanwhile you are hated for your stuck-up-ness and for the accent and manners which stamp you as one of the boss class. I was very young, not much more than six, when I first became aware of class-distinctions. Before that age my chief heroes had generally been working-class people, because they always seemed to do such interesting things, such as being fishermen and blacksmiths and bricklayers. I remember the farm hands on a farm in Cornwall who used to let me ride on the drill when they were sowing turnips and would sometimes catch the ewes and milk them to give me a drink; and the workmen building the new house next door, who let me play with the wet mortar and from whom I first learned the word 'b. . . .'; and the plumber up the road with whose children I used to go out bird-nesting. But it was not long before I was forbidden to play with the plumber's children; they were 'common' and I was told to keep away from them. This was snobbish, if you like, but it was also necessary, for middle-class people cannot afford to let their children grow up with vulgar accents. So, very early, the working class ceased to be a race of friendly and wonderful beings and became a race of enemies. We realised that they hated us, but we could never understand why, and naturally we set it down to pure, vicious malignity. To me in my early boyhood, to nearly all children of

families like mine 'common' people seemed almost sub-human.
They had coarse faces, hideous accents and gross manners, they
hated everyone who was not like themselves, and if they got
half a chance they would insult you in brutal ways. That was
our view of them, and though it was false it was understandable. For one must remember that before the war there was
much more *overt* class-hatred in England than there is now. In
those days you were quite likely to be insulted simply for
looking like a member of the upper classes; nowadays, on the
other hand, you are more likely to be fawned upon. Anyone
over thirty can remember the time when it was impossible for a
well-dressed person to walk through a slum street without
being hooted at. Whole quarters of big towns were considered
unsafe because of 'hooligans' (now almost an extinct type), and
the London gutter-boy everywhere, with his loud voice and
lack of intellectual scruples, could make life a misery for people
who considered it beneath their dignity to answer back. A
recurrent terror of my holidays, when I was a small boy, was
the gangs of 'cads' who were liable to set upon you five or ten to
one. In term time, on the other hand, it was we who were in the
majority and the 'cads' who were oppressed; I remember a
couple of savage mass-battles in the cold winter of 1916–17.
And this tradition of open hostility between upper and lower
class had apparently been the same for at least a century past. A
typical joke in *Punch* in the 'sixties is a picture of a small,
nervous looking gentleman riding through a slum street and a
crowd of street-boys closing in on him with shouts of ''Ere
comes a swell! Let's frighten 'is 'oss!' Just fancy the street-boys
trying to frighten his horse now! They would be much likelier
to hang round him in vague hopes of a tip. During the past
dozen years the English working class have grown servile with a
rather horrifying rapidity. It was bound to happen, for the
frightful weapon of unemployment has cowed them. Before the
war their economic position was comparatively strong, for
though there was no dole to fall back upon, there was not much
unemployment, and the power of the boss class was not so
obvious as it is now. A man did not see ruin staring him in the
face every time he cheeked a 'toff', and naturally he did cheek a
'toff' whenever it seemed safe to do so. G. J. Renier, in his book
on Oscar Wilde, points out that the strange, obscene bursts of
popular fury which followed the Wilde trial were essentially
social in character. The London mob had caught a member of

the upper classes on the hop, and they took care to keep him hopping. All this was natural and even proper. If you treat people as the English working class have been treated during the past two centuries, you must expect them to resent it. On the other hand the children of shabby-genteel families could not be blamed if they grew up with a hatred of the working class, typified for them by prowling gangs of 'cads'.

But there was another and more serious difficulty. Here you come to the real secret of class distinctions in the West – the real reason why a European of bourgeois up-bringing, even when he calls himself a Communist, cannot without a hard effort think of a working man as his equal. It is summed up in four frightful words which people nowadays are chary of uttering, but which were bandied about quite freely in my childhood. The words were: *The lower classes smell*.

That was what we were taught – *the lower classes smell*. And here, obviously, you are at an impassable barrier. For no feeling of like or dislike is quite so fundamental as a *physical* feeling. Race hatred, religious hatred, differences of education, of temperament, of intellect, even differences of moral code, can be got over; but physical repulsion cannot. You can have an affection for a murderer or a sodomite, but you cannot have an affection for a man whose breath stinks – habitually stinks, I mean. However well you may wish him, however much you may admire his mind and character, if his breath stinks he is horrible and in your heart of hearts you will hate him. It may not greatly matter if the average middle-class person is brought up to believe that the working classes are ignorant, lazy, drunken, boorish and dishonest; it is when he is brought up to believe that they are dirty that the harm is done.

The Road to Wigan Pier

B. Culture and the Masses

In the previous section we considered 'democracy' as an ideal or aesthetic, and as an attitude of mind whose opposite is snobbery. Another (closely related) meaning that British writers have given to the term 'democracy' is to use it to describe a broad process of social change since the Industrial Revolution, encompassing not just political reform but such things as the diffusion of education, the growth of the popular press and other media of mass communication (TV, radio, etc.), and the general commercialization represented by, for example, advertising. This wider meaning of 'democracy' has often been encapsulated in the phrase 'mass society'.

Throughout the nineteenth and twentieth centuries there has been a vigorous debate about the relationship between culture and this 'mass society'. Does 'high art' ('serious' literature, 'classical' music, etc.) depend for its survival on the guardianship of a minority? Is it inevitably tainted or 'vulgarized' once it is appropriated by 'the masses'? Or, conversely, is this fear based on a restrictive, elitist definition of 'culture'? In this section we consider a range of responses to these questions.

William Wordsworth's 'Preface' to his *Lyrical Ballads* (1800) (IX:8) is one of the most famous artistic manifestos in English literature. Wordsworth allies his imagination to the 'common life', and attacks those who would see poetry merely as a sign of aristocratic refinement. This democratic credo (clearly related to the democratic 'aesthetic' discussed above) is echoed later in the century, when the eponymous hero of Charles Kingsley's novel *Alton Locke* (IX:9) reflects on his self-education. One should not underestimate the radical intent of what Wordsworth was saying in the context of his time, but it is also significant that the particular 'common life' to which he is referring is rustic and backward-looking. It is not the common life of the new urban populations that as Wordsworth was writing were being drawn from the countryside to work in the factories of Britain's towns and cities.

In this sense, Wordsworth's call for poetry to concern itself with 'the common life' lies somewhat outside the debate about culture and 'the masses'. It was only later in the century, with the extensions of the franchise and the social changes mentioned above, that the debate became prominent. We have already seen (III:14) the concern expressed by George Eliot that the purely 'mechanical' reforms of the franchise should be accompanied by a deeper, moral reform. *Felix Holt*, though it deals with the First Reform Bill of 1832, was written in the context of the agitation surrounding the passing of the Second Reform Bill in 1867. Matthew Arnold's influential book *Culture and Anarchy* (IX:10), written at about the same time, echoes much of the concern and even language of George Eliot, particularly in the use of the word 'mechanical'. 'Culture' is a word that has its origins in biology, and one rhetorical device much used in this debate has been to contrast the 'mechanical' (industrialism, commercialism, liberal constitutionalism) with the 'organic' (culture, tradition, deference).

(This linguistic theme is explored in Raymond Williams (see below), *Culture and Society 1780–1950*.) Arnold sees culture as a calming influence, emanating 'sweetness and light' from above the battlefield of 'Barbarians, Philistines and Populace' (his terms for the aristocracy and middle and working classes). Culture is, in fact, our last protection against anarchy. One could not imagine a view of art further removed from Blake's explosive, liberationist vision of the human imagination.

In terms of the politics of his day, Matthew Arnold might be described as a 'conservative liberal'. Wyndham Lewis (IX:11), who associated himself with the political Right, and even with fascism, is much more forthright and deliberately shocking in the way he denounces what he sees as the homogeneity fostered by 'mass society'. T. S. Eliot (IX:12) expresses the same anxiety, but detects a possible solution in a segregated hierarchy of cultures. This, he argues, is the only way of maintaining 'true democracy'.

Raymond Williams's essay 'Culture is Ordinary' (IX:13), written in 1958, introduces some important distinctions into the debate. First, he distinguishes between two senses of 'culture' – a whole way of life and a specialized creation of 'Art'. Both senses are vital, he argues, and they are interdependent. Second, he distinguishes between the diffusion of education and commercial popular culture. And third, he distinguishes between the crass character of much popular culture and the character of the people at whom it is directed.

In the final extract, contemporary poet Tony Harrison (IX:14) welds together, in a single finely wrought sonnet, 'high art' and the inarticulate, literature and common aspiration.

8 William Wordsworth, From Common Life (1800)

The principal object. . .proposed in these Poems was to choose incidents and situations from common life, and to relate or describe them, throughout, as far as was possible in a selection of language really used by men, and, at the same time, to throw over them a certain colouring of imagination, whereby ordinary things should be presented to the mind in an unusual aspect; and, further, and above all, to make these incidents and situations interesting by tracing in them, truly though not ostentatiously, the primary laws of our nature: chiefly, as far as regards the manner in which we associate ideas in a state of excitement. Humble and rustic life was generally chosen, because, in that condition, the essential passions of the heart find a better soil in which they can attain their maturity, are less under restraint, and speak a plainer and more emphatic language; because in that condition of life our elementary feelings coexist in a state of greater simplicity, and, consequently, may be more accurately contemplated, and more forcibly communicated; because the manners of rural life germinate from those elementary feelings, and, from the necessary character of rural occupations, are more easily comprehended, and are more durable; and, lastly, because in that condition the passions of men are incorporated with the beautiful and permanent forms of nature. The language, too, of these men has been adopted (purified indeed from what appear to be its real defects, from all lasting and rational causes of dislike or disgust) because such men hourly communicate with the best objects from which the best part of language is originally derived; and because, from their rank in society and the sameness and narrow circle of their intercourse, being less under the influence of social vanity, they convey their feelings and notions in simple and unelaborated expressions. Accordingly, such a language, arising out of repeated experience and regular feelings, is a more permanent, and a far more philosophical language, than that which is frequently substituted for it by Poets, who think that they are conferring honour upon themselves and their art, in proportion as they separate themselves from the sympathies of men, and indulge in arbitrary and capricious habits of expression, in order to furnish food for fickle tastes, and fickle appetites, of their own creation.

'Preface', *Lyrical Ballads*

9   Charles Kingsley, Democratic Art (1850)

Then, in a happy day, I fell on Alfred Tennyson's poetry, and found there, astonished and delighted, the embodiment of thoughts about the earth around me which I had concealed, because I fancied them peculiar to myself. Why is it that the latest poet has generally the greatest influence over the minds of the young? Surely not for the mere charm of novelty? The reason is that he, living amid the same hopes, the same temptations, the same sphere of observation as they, gives utterance and outward form to the very questions which, vague and wordless, have been exercising their hearts. And what endeared Tennyson especially to me, the working man, was, as I afterwards discovered, the altogether democratic tendency of his poems. True, all great poets are by their office democrats; seers of man only as man; singers of the joys, the sorrows, the aspirations common to all humanity; but in Alfred Tennyson there is an element especially democratic, truly levelling; not his political opinions, about which I know nothing, and care less, but his handling of the trivial everyday sights and sounds of nature. Brought up, as I understand, in a part of England which possesses not much of the picturesque, and nothing of that which the vulgar call sublime, he has learnt to see that in all nature, in the hedgerow and the sandbank, as well as in the alp peak and the ocean waste, is a world of true sublimity − a minute infinite − an ever fertile garden of poetic images, the roots of which are in the unfathomable and the eternal, as truly as any phenomenon which astonishes and awes the eye. The descriptions of the desolate pools and creeks where the dying swan floated, the hint of the silvery marsh mosses by Mariana's moat, came to me like revelations. I always knew there was something beautiful, wonderful, sublime, in those flowery dykes of Battersea Fields; in the long gravelly sweeps of that lone tidal shore; and here was a man who had put them into words for me! This is what I call democratic art − the revelation of the poetry which lies in common things. And surely all the age is tending in that direction: in Landseer and his dogs − in Fielding and his downs, with a host of noble fellow-artists − and in all authors who have really seized the nation's mind, from Crabbe and Burns and Wordsworth to Hood and Dickens, the great tide sets ever onward, outward, towards that which is common to the many, not that which is exclusive to the few.

Alton Locke, Tailor and Poet − An Autobiography

10 Matthew Arnold, Sweetness and Light (1869)

The idea of perfection as an *inward* condition of the mind and spirit is at variance with the mechanical and material civilisation in esteem with us, and nowhere, as I have said, so much in esteem as with us. The idea of perfection as a *general* expansion of the human family is at variance with our strong individualism, our hatred of all limits to the unrestrained swing of the individual's personality, our maxim of 'every man for himself'. Above all, the idea of perfection as a *harmonious* expansion of human nature is at variance with our want of flexibility, with our inaptitude for seeing more than one side of a thing, with our intense energetic absorption in the particular pursuit we happen to be following. So culture has a rough task to achieve in this country. . .

Culture looks beyond machinery, culture hates hatred; culture has one great passion, the passion for sweetness and light. It has one even yet greater! – the passion for making them *prevail*. It is not satisfied till we *all* come to a perfect man; it knows that the sweetness and light of the few must be imperfect until the raw and unkindled masses of humanity are touched with sweetness and light. . . Only it must be *real* thought and *real* beauty; *real* sweetness and *real* light. Plenty of people will try to give the masses, as they call them, an intellectual food prepared and adapted in the way they think proper for the actual condition of the masses. The ordinary popular literature is an example of this way of working on the masses. Plenty of people will try to indoctrinate the masses with the set of ideas and judgments constituting the creed of their own profession or party. Our religious and political organisations give an example of this way of working on the masses. I condemn neither way; but culture works differently. It does not try to teach down to the level of inferior classes; it does not try to win them for this or that sect of its own, with ready-made judgments and watchwords. It seeks to do away with classes; . . .the men of culture are the true apostles of equality. . .

For a long time, as I have said, the strong feudal habits of subordination and deference continued to tell upon the working class. The modern spirit has now almost entirely dissolved those habits, and the anarchical tendency of our worship of freedom in and for itself, of our superstitious faith, as I say, in machinery, is becoming very manifest. More and more, because of this our blind faith in machinery, because of our want of light to enable us to look beyond machinery to the end for which machinery is valuable, this and that man, and this and that body of men, all over the country, are beginning to assert and put in practice an Englishman's right to do what he likes; his right to march where he likes, meet where he likes, enter where he likes, hoot as he likes, threaten as he likes, smash as he likes. All this, I say, tends to anarchy. . .

Now, if culture, which simply means trying to perfect oneself, and one's mind as part of oneself, brings us light, and if light shows us that there is nothing so very blessed in merely doing as one likes, that the worship of the mere freedom to do as one likes is worship of machinery, that the really blessed thing is to like what right reason ordains, and to follow her authority, then we have got a practical benefit out of culture. We have got a much wanted principle, a principle of authority, to counteract the tendency to anarchy which seems to be threatening us. . .

In our political system everybody is comforted. Our guides and governors who have to be elected by the influence of the Barbarians, and who depend on their favour, sing the praises of the Barbarians, and say all the smooth things that can be said of them. With Mr Tennyson, they celebrate 'the great broad-shouldered genial Englishman', with his 'sense of duty', his 'reverence for the laws' and his 'patient force', who saves us from the 'revolts, republics, revolutions, most no graver than a schoolboy's barring out', which upset other and less broad-shouldered nations. Our guides who are chosen by the Philistines and who have to look to their favour, tell the Philistines how 'all the world knows that the great middle class of this country supplies the mind, the will, and the power requisite for all the great and good things that have to be done', and congratulate them on their 'earnest good sense, which penetrates through sophisms, ignores commonplaces, and gives to conventional illusions their true value'. Our guides who look to the favour of the Populace, tell them that 'theirs are the brightest powers of sympathy, and the readiest powers of action. . .'

So the voice which makes a permanent impression on each of our classes is the voice of its friends, and this is from the nature of things, as I have said, a comforting voice. The Barbarians remain in the belief that the great broad-shouldered genial Englishman may be well satisfied with himself; the Philistines remain in the belief that the great middle-class of this country, with its earnest common-sense penetrating through sophisms and ignoring commonplaces, may be well satisfied with itself; the Populace, that the working man with his bright powers of sympathy and ready powers of action, may be well satisfied with himself. What hope, at this rate, of extinguishing the taste of the bathos implanted by nature itself in the soul of man, or of inculcating the belief that excellence dwells among high and steep rocks, and can only be reached by those who sweat blood to reach her?

Culture and Anarchy. An Essay in Political and Social Criticism

11   Wyndham Lewis, The Mass Mind (1925)

The associational habit in its present development is the result of mass production. It is fostered in the interests of economy in our overcrowded world, and people are encouraged to get as quickly as possible into the category that offers the nearest approach to what they require or what they can hope for, and there remain. The mass mind is required to gravitate to a standard size to receive the standard idea. The alternative is to go naked: the days of made-to-order and made-to-measure are past. The standardization of women's dress, which is effected by the absolutist machinery of fashion, is the type of all the other compulsions tending to a greater and greater uniformity and standardization. There a colour – 'nigger-brown', for instance – is imposed. The great syndic of the manufacturers, dressmakers, etc., agree on 'nigger-brown', and so the world flowers universally in 'nigger-brown' for a season, with perhaps a steak of mushroom-pink exuviae from the last season. In the interest of great-scale industry and mass production the smaller the margin of diversity the better. The nearer the fashion is to a uniform the bigger the returns, the fewer dresses unsold – for where there is little difference in cut, colour, and fancy there is the less temptation to be individualistically fussy. When there is so little essential difference between one costume and another, the difference is so slight it is not worth holding out about.

The closer and closer enregimentation of women, with the rhythmic seasonal changes of sex-uniform, is effected without difficulty by simple fiats of fashion. The overpowering instinct for conformity, and the horror of antiquation or of the eccentric, sees to the rest. In all this vast smooth-running process you see the image of a political state in which no legislation, police, or any physical compulsion would be required: in which everything would be effected by public opinion, snobbery, and the magic of *fashion*. We have, historically, in the hebrew state, a type of non-executive state such as might be arrived at on those lines. The legislature, of the greek city-state sort, did not exist; of all coercive administrative machinery, only the judiciary was required. God did the rest, or rather the teachings of *righteousness*, the anxious fanatical conscience of the citizen, and a great system of ritual. That is an example of moral rule, or rule by opinion, as opposed to rule by physical force: of much more effective *interior*, mental, domination, in place of a less intelligent *exterior* form of government. Theocratic and theurgic forms of government are the highest form of democracy – a kind of super-democracy, in fact.

'The Art of Being Ruled'

12   T. S. Eliot, A Hierarchy of Cultures (1948)

What is important is a structure of society in which there will be, from 'top' to 'bottom', a continuous gradation of cultural levels: it is important to remember that we should not consider the upper levels as possessing more culture than the lower, but as representing a more conscious culture and a greater specialisation of culture. I incline to believe that no true democracy can maintain itself unless it contains these different levels of culture. The levels of culture may also be seen as levels of power, to the extent that a smaller group at a higher level will have equal power with a larger group at a lower level; for it may be argued that complete equality means universal irresponsibility; and in such a society as I envisage, each individual would inherit greater or less responsibility towards the commonwealth, according to the position in society which he inherited – each class would have somewhat different responsibilities. A democracy in which everybody had an equal responsibility in everything would be oppressive for the conscientious and licentious for the rest. . .

In a society so graded as to have several levels of culture, and several levels of power and authority, the politician might at least be restrained, in his use of language, by his respect for the judgement, and fear of the ridicule, of a smaller and more critical public, among which was maintained some standard of prose style. . .

Error creeps in again and again through our tendency to think of culture as group culture exclusively, the culture of the 'cultured' classes and elites. We then proceed to think of the humbler part of society as having culture only in so far as it participates in this superior and more conscious culture. To treat the 'uneducated' mass of the population as we might treat some innocent tribe of savages to whom we are impelled to deliver the true faith, is to encourage them to neglect or despise that culture which they should possess and from which the more conscious part of culture draws vitality; and to aim to make everyone share in the appreciation of the fruits of the more conscious part of culture is to adulterate and cheapen what you give. For it is an essential condition of the preservation of the quality of the culture of the minority, that it should continue to be a minority culture. . . A 'mass-culture' will always be a substitute-culture, and sooner or later the deception will become apparent to the more intelligent of those upon whom this culture has been palmed off. . .

There is no doubt that in our headlong rush to educate everybody, we are lowering our standards, and more and more abandoning the study of those subjects by which the essentials of our culture — of that part of it which is transmissible by education — are transmitted; destroying our ancient edifices to make ready the ground upon which the barbarian nomads of the future will encamp in their mechanised caravans.

Notes Towards the Definition of Culture

13   Raymond Williams, Culture is Ordinary (1958)

Culture is ordinary: that is the first fact. Every human society has its own shape, its own purposes, its own meanings. Every human society expresses these, in institutions, and in arts and learning. The making of a society is the finding of common meanings and directions, and its growth is an active debate and amendment under the pressures of experience, contact, and discovery, writing themselves into the land. The growing society is there, yet it is also made and remade in every individual mind. The making of a mind is, first, the slow learning of shapes, purposes, and meanings, so that work, observation and communication are possible. Then, second, but equal in importance, is the testing of these in experience, the making of new observations, comparisons, and meanings. A culture has two aspects: the known meanings and directions, which its members are trained to; the new observations and meanings, which are offered and tested. These are the ordinary processes of human societies and human minds, and we see through them the nature of a culture: that it is always both traditional and creative; that it is both the most ordinary common meanings and the finest individual meanings. We use the word culture in these two senses: to mean a whole way of life – the common meanings; to mean the arts and learning – the special processes of discovery and creative effort. Some writers reserve the word for one or other of these senses; I insist on both, and on the significance of their conjunction. The questions I ask about our culture are questions about our general and common purposes, yet also questions about deep personal meanings. Culture is ordinary, in every society and in every mind. . .

At home we were glad of the Industrial Revolution, and of its consequent social and political changes. True, we lived in a very beautiful farming valley, and the valleys beyond the limestone we could all see were ugly. But there was one gift that was overriding, one gift which at any price we would take, the gift of power that is everything to men who have worked with their hands. It was slow in coming to us, in all its effects, but steam power, the petrol engine, electricity, these and their host of products in commodities and services, we took as quickly as we could get them, and were glad. I have seen all these things being used, and I have seen the things they replaced. I will not listen with patience to any acid listing of them – you know the sneer you can get into plumbing, baby Austins, aspirin, contraceptives, canned food. But I say to these Pharisees: dirty water, an early bucket, a four-mile walk each way to work, headaches, broken women, hunger and monotony of diet. The working people, in town and country alike, will not listen (and I support them) to any account of our society which supposes that these things are not progress: not just mechanical, external progress either, but a real service of life. . .

I don't believe that the ordinary people in fact resemble the normal description of the masses, low and trivial in taste and habit. I put it another way: that there are in fact no masses, but only ways of seeing people as masses. With the coming of industrialism, much of the old social organization broke down and it became a matter of difficult personal experience that we were constantly seeing people we did not know, and it was tempting to mass them, as 'the others', in our minds. Again, people were physically massed, in the industrial towns, and a new class structure (the names of our social classes, and the world 'class' itself in this sense, date only from the Industrial Revolution) was practically imposed. The improvement in communications, in particular the development of new forms of multiple transmission of news and entertainment, created unbridgeable divisions between transmitter and audience, which again led to the audience being interpreted as an unknown mass. Masses became a new word for mob: the others, the unknown, the unwashed, the crowd beyond one. As a way of knowing other people, this formula is obviously ridiculous, but, in the new conditions, it seemed an effective formula – the only one possible. Certainly it was the formula that was used by those whose money gave them access to the new communication techniques; the lowness of taste and habit, which human beings assign very easily to other human beings, was assumed, as a bridge. . .

I deny, and can prove my denial, that popular education and commercial culture are cause and effect. I have shown elsewhere that the myth of 1870 – the Education Act which is said to have produced, as its children grew up, a new cheap and nasty press – is indeed myth. There was more than enough literacy, long before 1870, to support a cheap press, and in fact there were cheap and really bad newspapers selling in great quantities before the 1870 Act was heard of. The bad new commercial culture came out of the social chaos of industrialism, and out of the success, in this chaos, of the 'masses' formula, not out of popular education. . .

It is easy to assemble, from print and cinema and television, a terrifying and fantastic congress of cheap feelings and moronic arguments. It is easy to go on from this and assume this deeply degrading version of the actual lives of our contemporaries. Yet do we find this confirmed, when we meet people? This is where 'masses' comes in again, of course: the people *we* meet aren't

vulgar, but God, think of Bootle and Surbiton and Aston! I
haven't lived in any of those places; have you? But a few weeks
ago I was in a house with a commercial traveller, a lorry driver,
a bricklayer, a shopgirl, a fitter, a signalman, a nylon operative,
a domestic help (perhaps, dear, she is your very own treasure). I
hate describing people like this, for in fact they were my family
and family friends. Now they read, they watch, this work we
are talking about; some of them quite critically, others with a
good deal of pleasure. Very well, I read different things, watch
different entertainments, and I am quite sure why they are
better. But could I sit down in that house and make this
equation we are offered? Not, you understand, that shame was
stopping me; I've learned, thank you, how to behave. But
talking to my family, to my friends, talking, as we were, about
our own lives, about people, about feelings, could I in fact find
this lack of quality we are discussing? I'll be honest – I looked;
my training has done that for me. I can only say that I found as
much natural fineness of feeling, as much quick discrimination,
as much clear grasp of ideas within the range of experience as I
have found anywhere. . .

Nothing has done more to sour the democratic idea, among
its natural supporters, and to drive them back into an angry self-
exile, than the plain, overwhelming cultural issues: the apparent
division of our culture into, on the one hand, a remote and self-
gracious sophistication, on the other hand, a doped mass. So
who then believes in democracy? The answer is really quite
simple: the millions in England who still haven't got it, where
they work and feel. There, as always, is the transforming
energy, and the business of the socialist intellectual is what it
always was: to attack the clamps on that energy – in industrial
relations, public administration, education, for a start; and to
work in his own field on ways in which that energy, as released,
can be concentrated and fertile. The technical means are difficult
enough, but the biggest difficulty is in accepting, deep in our
minds, the values on which they depend: that the ordinary
people should govern; that culture and education are ordinary;
that there are no masses to save, to capture, or to direct, but
rather this crowded people in the course of an extraordinary
rapid and confusing expansion of their lives. A writer's job is
with individual meanings, and with making these meanings
common. I find these meanings in the expansion, there along
the journey where the necessary changes are writing themselves

into the land, and where the language changes but the voice is the same.

'Culture is Ordinary'

14 Tony Harrison, On Not Being Milton (1978)

for Sergio Vieira & Armando Guebuza (Frelimo)

Read and committed to the flames, I call
these sixteen lines that go back to my roots
my *Cahier d'un retour au pays natal*,
my growing black enough to fit my boots.

The stutter of the scold out of the branks
of condescension, class and counter-class
thickens with glottals to a lumpen mass
of Ludding morphemes closing up their ranks.
Each swung cast-iron Enoch★ of Leeds stress
clangs a forged music on the frames of Art,
the looms of owned language smashed apart!

Three cheers for mute ingloriousness!

Articulation is the tongue-tied's fighting.
In the silence round all poetry we quote
Tidd the Cato Street conspirator who wrote:

Sir, I Ham a Very Bad Hand at Righting.

'On Not Being Milton'

Note: An 'Enoch' is an iron sledge-hammer used by the Luddites to smash the frames which were also made by the same Enoch Taylor of Marsden. The cry was: 'Enoch made them, Enoch shall break them!'

Bibliography of Sources

Sources of each extract are arranged in alphabetical order by author, or in the case of documents, by title. References to chapter and extract number appear at the end of each entry. All details refer to editions used for the purpose of this anthology. Unless otherwise stated, the place of publication is London.

Lord Acton, *Essays on Freedom and Power* (Thames and Hudson, 1956), pp. 158–60, 168 (VII:2); *Lectures on Modern History* (1906), pp. 12–13 (I:7).

Shabbir Akhtar, *Be Careful with Muhammed! The Salman Rushdie Affair* (Bellew Press, 1989), pp. 6–7 (VI:13).

Matthew Arnold, *Culture and Anarchy. An Essay in Political and Social Criticism* (John Murray, 1920), pp. 10, 31–43, 75–6 (IX:10).

W. H. Auden, '1st September 1939', in *Collected Shorter Poems 1930–44* (Faber and Faber, 1950), pp. 74–6 (IX:5).

Francis Bacon, 'Of Faction', in *Essays* (Oxford: The World's Classics, 1958) (V:3).

Walter Bagehot, *The English Constitution*, ed. R. H. S. Crossman (C. A. Watts, 1964), pp. 60–9 (II:8); pp. 3–39, 51–3 (II:11).

Hilaire Belloc, 'On a General Election', in *Oxford Book of Twentieth Century Verse* (Oxford University Press, 1973), p. 105 (V:2).

Jeremy Bentham, *The Handbook of Political Fallacies* (New York: Harper, 1962), pp. 155–6 (I:14); pp. 249–50 (V:5).

Isaiah Berlin, 'Two Concepts of Liberty', in *Four Essays on Liberty* (Oxford University Press, 1969), pp. 123–44 (VI:2).

Aneurin Bevan, *In Place of Fear* (MacGibbon and Kee, 1961), p. 35 (III:23).

Bill of Rights, 1689 in *Great Britain: The Lion at Home*, ed. Joel H. Wiener (New York: 1983), vol. I, p. 156 (VI:5).

William Blackstone, *Commentaries on the Laws of England* (1765), vol. I, pp. 49–51 (II:6); vol. I, p. 156 (II:7).

William Blake, 'London', in *The Complete Writings of William Blake*, ed. Geoffrey Keynes (Oxford University Press, 1979), p. 216 (IX:1).

V. Bogdanor, *What Is Proportional Representation?* (Oxford: Martin Robertson), pp. 153–5 (V:14).

Lord Bolingbroke, *The Idea of a Patriot King* (Oxford: Clarendon Press, 1917), pp. 48–9 (I:13); pp. 57–8 (II:9); pp. 92–3 (V:4).

Howard Brenton and David Hare, *Pravda. A Fleet Street Comedy* (Methuen, 1985), pp. 63–5 (VI:19).

Samuel Brittan, 'Can Democracy Manage an Economy', in *The End of the Keynesian Era, Essays on the Disintegration of the Keynesian Political Economy*, ed. Robert Skidelsky (Macmillan, 1977), pp. 44–6 (VIII:8).

James Bryce *The American Commonwealth* (1888), pp. 71–2 (II:15).

Edmund Burke, *Appeal from the New to the Old Whigs*, in *Works* (1854), vol. I, p. 524 (III:4); *A Letter to Sir Hercules Langrishe, MP*, in *Works* (1854), vol. I, p. 557 (III:18); *Reflections on the Revolution in France*, in *Works* (1854), vol. I, pp. 393–4 (I:10); pp. 403–4 (IV:7); pp. 416–17 (IV:5); p. 414 (Introduction:1); *Speech at the Conclusion of the Poll*, in *Works* (1854), vol. I, p. 180 (III:19); *Speech to the Electors of Bristol*, in *Works* (1854), vol. I, pp. 179–80 (II:14); *Thoughts on the Cause of the Present Discontents*, in *Works*, vol. I (1854), pp. 140–51 (V:8).

Edward Carpenter, *Towards Democracy* (George Allen & Co., 1913), pp. 41, 55–8 (IX:3).

Lord Robert Cecil, in *The Law and Working of the Constitution*, ed. W. C. Costin and J. Steven Watson, (A. & C. Black, 1964), vol. II, pp. 222–3 (II:10).

Charles, I., in *The Stuart Constitution: Documents and Commentary* ed. J. P. Kenyon (Cambridge University Press, 1966), pp. 21–3 (II:5).

Charter 88 (1988) (I:18).

William Cobbett, *Cobbett's Weekly Political Register, LXXII*, pp. 4–5 (VIII:4).

Henry Cockburn, *Memorials of his Time*, (Edinburgh: Adam and Charles Black, 1856), pp. 80–1, 99–103 (VII:9).

S. T. Coleridge, *On the Constitution of the Church and State* (Routledge, 1976) pp. 18–19 (I:4).

Bernard Crick, 'An Englishman Considers His Passport' in *The Irish Review* (1988), pp. 1–7 (VII:1); and subsequently in *Political Thoughts and Polemics* (Edinburgh University Press, 1990).

C. A. R. Crosland, *The Future of Socialism* (Jonathan Cape, 1980), pp. 38–40, 79 (VIII:14).

R. H. S. Crossman, *The Crossman Diaries: Selections from the Diaries of a Cabinet Minister, 1964–1970*, ed. Anthony Howard (Hamish Hamilton, 1979), pp. 246–7 (I:15); pp. 85–6 (II:12); pp. 323–5 (VI:12); *Planning for Freedom* (Hamish Hamilton, 1965), pp. 3–4 (Introduction:2); and introduction to Walter Bagehot, *The English Constitution* (C. A. Watts, 1964), pp. 3–39, 51–3 (II:11).

Declaration of Arbroath, in W. C. Dickinson, E. Donaldson and Isobel A. Milne, *A Source Book of Scottish History*, vol. I (Edinburgh: Thomas Nelson, 1952), p. 133 (VII:8).

A. V. Dicey, *The Law of the Constitution* (1908), pp. 3–6 (I:1); pp. 22–3 (I:2); *Introduction to the Study of the Law of the Constitution* (1885), pp. 183–93 (VI:6); *Law and Public Opinion in England* (1905), pp. 54–7 (VIII:16).

Charles Dickens, *Bleak House* (Oxford University Press, 1948), pp. 389–90 (IX:6); *The Pickwick Papers* (Penguin, 1972), pp. 237–41 (V:10).

Benjamin Disraeli, *Coningsby* (Longmans, Green & Co., New Collected Edition) pp. 36–8 (III:3).

John Dryden, *Absalom and Achitophel*, in *Poetical Works* (Macmillan, 1934) pp. 112–13 (IV:3).

George Eliot, *Felix Holt* (Penguin, 1972), pp. 123–8 (III:14); pp. 609–11 (IV:12).

T. S. Eliot, *Notes Towards the Definition of Culture* (Faber and Faber, 1948) pp. 48, 87, 106–8 (IX:12).

Thomas E. Ellis, *Speeches and Addresses* (Wrexham: Hughes and Son, 1912), pp. 197–201 (VII:13).

Olaudah Equiano, *The Life of Olaudah Equiano*, ed. Paul Edwards, (Harlow: Longman, 1989), pp. 14–28 (VII:17).

K. D. Ewing and C. A. Gearty, *Freedom Under Thatcher: Civil Liberties in Modern Britain* (Oxford: Clarendon Press, 1990), p. 163 (VI:7); pp. 262–71 (VI:8).

E. M. Forster, *Two Cheers for Democracy* (Edward Arnold, 1951), p. 79 (VI:3).

Sir John Fortescue, *On The Governance of England*, ed. Charles Plummer (Oxford: 1885), p. 109 (II:1).

W. E. Gladstone, *Gladstone's Speeches*, ed. A. T. Bassett (1916), pp. 401–25 (III:5).

Lord Hailsham, *The Dilemma of Democracy* (Collins, 1978), pp. 151–3 (III:9); *Elective Dictatorship* (BBC Publications, 1976), pp. 7–9 (II:13), pp. 14–15 (I:5).

James Harrington, *A System of Politics*, in *The Political Writings of James Harrington* (New York: Liberal Arts Press, 1955), pp. 6–7 (III:11).

Tony Harrison, 'On Not Being Milton', *Selected Poems* (Penguin, 1984), p. 112 (IX:14).

Seamus Heaney, *Preoccupations. Selected Prose 1968–78* (Faber and Faber, 1980), pp. 30–3 (VII:6).

John Hewitt, 'Once Alien Here', in *The Collected Poems of John Hewitt*, ed. Frank Ormsby (Belfast: Blackstaff Press, 1991), p. 20 (VII:7).

Thomas Hobbes, *Leviathan* (Everyman, 1973), pp. 63–5, 87–90 (IV:1).

L. T. Hobhouse, *Liberalism* (Oxford University Press, 1964), pp. 48–50 (VIII:9); pp. 88–91 (VIII:12).

David Hume, *Essays, Moral, Political and Literary*, ed. T. H. Green and T. H. Grose (1875), 2 vols, vol. I, pp. 443–53 (IV:4); p. 252 (VII:16).

Independent Labour Party, Programme of (V:13).

Sir Robert Inglis, 3 Hansard II 1108–9 (III:17).

James VI and I, *Werkes* (1616), pp. 529–31 (II:3).

Sir David Lindsay Keir, *The Constitutional History of Modern Britain since 1485* (A. & C. Black, 1964), pp. 1–2 (I:8).

John Maynard Keynes, 'The End of Laissez-faire', in *The Collected Writings of John Maynard Keynes*, vol. IX, pp. 287–8, 290–2 (VIII:13).

Charles Kingsley, *Alton Locke, Tailor and Poet – An Autobiography* (1850), pp. 74–5 (IX:9).

Rudyard Kipling, 'The White Man's Burden', in *A Choice of Kipling's Verse*, ed. T. S. Eliot (Faber and Faber, 1941), pp. 136–7 (VII:18).

Labour Party, the Constitution of, 1917 (VIII:10).

Labour Party, Programme of the Independent (V:13).

George Lamming, *In the Castle of My Skin* (Longman, 1979), pp. 37–9 (VII:19).

D. H. Lawrence, 'Democracy', in *Phoenix. The Posthumous Papers of D. H. Lawrence* (Heinemann, 1936), pp. 708–9, 715–16 (IX:4).

Levellers, 'The True Levellers' Standard Advanced', in *Puritanism and Liberty*, ed. A. S. P. Woodhouse (Dent, 1974), p. 383 (I:12).

Saunders Lewis, 'Why We Burnt the Bombing School', in *British Pamphleteers*, ed. A. J. P. Taylor and Reginald Reynolds, vol. II (Allan Wingate, 1951), pp. 289–92 (VII:14).

Wyndham Lewis, *The Art of Being Ruled*, in *The Essential Wyndham Lewis. An Introduction to his Work*, ed. Julian Symons (André Deutsch, 1989), pp. 85–6 (IX:11).

Lord Lindsay, *The Essentials of Democracy* (Oxford University Press, 1929), pp. 36–8 (VI:11).

Lord Liverpool, *Parliamentary History*, vol. XXX (Hansard, 1817), pp. 810–11 (III:15).

John Locke, *Two Treatises on Government*, ed. Peter Laslett (Cambridge University Press, 1964), pp. 287–94, 341–3, 365–6, 372–3 (IV:2); pp. 368–9 (III:10).

William Lovett, *Life and Struggles* (1920), vol. I, pp. 103–4 (III:21); pp. 118–20 (VIII:5); vol. II, pp. 440–2 (IV:15).

Lord Macaulay, *Miscellaneous Writings and Speeches* (Longmans, Green, 1905), pp. 175–7 (VIII:6); p. 487 (III:13).

Hugh MacDiarmid (C. M. Grieve), *Albyn, or Scotland and the Future* (Kegan Paul, 1927), pp. 48–51 (VII:11).

John Maclean, 'All Hail, the Scottish Workers' Republic!', in *In the Rapids of Revolution. Essays, Articles and Letters 1902–23*, ed. N. Milton (Allison and Busby, 1978), pp. 217–18 (VII:10).

Magna Carta, ed. Michael Borrie (British Museum Publications, 1976), pp. 30–41 (VI:4).

Sir Henry Maine, *Popular Government* (1885), pp. 98–101 (V:6).

Adewale Maja-Pearce, *How Many Miles to Babylon? An essay* (Heinemann, 1990), pp. 62–6 (VII:21).

James Mill, *Essay on Government*, in J. Lively and J. Rees, *Utilitarian Logic and Politics* (Oxford University Press, 1978), pp. 84–5 (III:20).

John Stuart Mill, *Utilitarianism, Liberty and Representative Government* (Everyman, 1910), pp. 67–8 (VI:1); pp. 192–5 (IV:13); pp. 208–9 (IV:11).

Harriet Taylor Mill, *On the Enfranchisement of Women* (Virago, 1983), pp. 6, 13–14, 23–25 (IV:17).

John Milton, *Areopagitica*, in *The Portable Milton*, ed. Douglas Bush (New York, 1955), pp. 155–6 (VI:10).

John Morley, in *Parliamentary Debates, House of Lords 5th Series*, vol. VIII, pp. 700–1 (II:16).

Ferdinand Mount, *The British Constitution Now: Recovery or Decline?* (Heinemann, 1992), p. 16 (I:9); pp. 191–3 (VI:9).

Edwin Muir, *Scottish Journey* (Heinemann, 1935), pp. 25–30, 232 (VII:12).

Grace Nichols, *The Fat Black Woman's Poems* (Virago, 1984), p. 64 (VII:22).

T. H. B. Oldfield, *The Representative History of Great Britain and Ireland* (1816), Preface, vol. I, pp. xi–xvi (I:11).

George Orwell, *Animal Farm* (Penguin, 1951), pp. 28, 42–8 (VI:20); *The Road to Wigan Pier* (Penguin, 1939), pp. 116–19 (IX:7).

M. Ostrogorski, *Democracy and the Organisation of Political Parties* (London, 1902), pp. 3–5 (V:12).

Thomas Paine, *The Rights of Man* (Everyman, 1915), pp. 12–16 (IV:6); pp. 42–5 (IV:8); pp. 48–9 (I:3); pp. 59–60 (III:6); pp. 157–8 (VIII:1).

Christabel Pankhurst, *Unshackled. The Story of How We Won the Vote* (Hutchinson, 1987), pp. 46–9 (IV:19); p. 57 (III:22).

Parliament Act, 1 & 2 Geo. V, c.13 (III:8).

Parliamentary Proceedings, Parl. Hist., x, 800, 13 April 1738 (VI:15); Parl. Deb., N. S. (Hansard), XV, Col. 132 April 1826 (V:9).

People's Charter, in *The Nineteenth Century Constitution*, ed. H. Hanham, (Cambridge University Press, 1969), p. 270 (IV:9).

Petition of Right, in *Constitutional Documents of the Puritan Revolution* ed. S. R. Gardiner (1906), pp. 66–70 (II:4).

R. v. Ponting, in *Criminal Law Review* (1985), pp. 318–21 (I:16).

Enoch Powell, *A Nation or No Nation?* (Batsford, 1978), pp. 134–6 (I:17).

Proclamation of the Irish Republic, in Roy Foster, *Modern Ireland* (Penguin, 1988), pp. 597–8 (VII:5).

Putney Debates, The in *Puritanism and Liberty*, ed. A. S. P. Woodhouse (Dent, 1974), pp. 53–6 (IV:10).

Salman Rushdie, *Imaginary Homelands – Essays and Criticism 1981–91* (Granta Books, 1991), pp. 394–5 (VI:14).

Lord John Russell, *An Essay on the History of the English Government and Constitution* (1821), pp. 182–3 (III:16).

Lord Scarman, *Why Britain Needs a Written Constitution* (Charter 88 Trust, 1992) (I:6).

Samuel Selvon, *The Lonely Londoners* (Harlow: Longmans, 1985), pp. 39–40 (VII:20).

William Shakespeare, *Henry V*, I.ii., pp. 184–210 (III:2); *Troilus and Cressida*, I., pp. 85–136 (III:1).

Percy Bysshe Shelley, 'The Mask of Anarchy', in *The Complete Poetical Works of Shelley* (Oxford: Clarendon Press, 1904), pp. 372–6 (IX:2).

Samuel Smiles, *Self-Help* (John Murray, 1886), pp. 1–3 (IV:14).

Adam Smith, *Lectures on Jurisprudence* (Oxford University Press, 1978), pp. 401–5 (III:12); *An Inquiry into the Nature and Causes of the Wealth of Nations*, ed. E. Cannan, (1925), vol. II, pp. 184–5 (VIII:2).

Sir Thomas Smith, *De Republica Anglorum*, ed. L. Alston (Cambridge: 1906), pp. 48–9 (II:2).

Robert Southey, *Letters from England by Don Manual Alvarez Espriella, translated from the Spanish*, vol. III (London: Longman, Hurst Rees and Orme, 1807), pp. 54–6 (VI:16); pp. 121–4 (III:7).

Dugald Stewart, *Lectures on Political Economy*, in *Collected Works of Dugald Stewart*, ed. Sir William Hamilton (1855), vol. VIII, pp. 21–3 (VIII:3); vol. IX, p. 376 (VIII:7).

John Strachey, *The Theory and Practice of Socialism* (Gollancz, 1936), pp. 158–60 (V:7).

Jonathan Swift, *Gulliver's Travels* (Oxford University Press, 1976), pp. 38–40 (V:1); *The Drapier's Letters*, in *The Prose Works of Jonathan Swift*, ed. Herbert Davis, (Oxford: Blackwell, 1941), vol. X, pp. 61–3 (VII:3).

Margaret Thatcher, *The Revival of Britain* (Aurum Press, 1989), pp. 85–9 (VIII:15); pp. 198–9 (III:24).

R. S. Thomas, 'Reservoirs', in *Selected Poems 1946–68* (Newcastle upon Tyne: Bloodaxe Books, 1986), p. 105 (VII:15).

E. P. Thompson, *Writing by Candlelight* (Merlin, 1980), pp. 2–3 (VI:18).

Wolfe Tone, 'Declaration and Resolutions of the Society of United Irishmen of Belfast', in *Political Works of Theobald Wolfe Tone*, (Washington, 1826), pp. 367–8 (VII:4).

Anthony Trollope, *Phineas Finn* (Oxford University Press, 1982), pp. 4–7 (V:11).

'The True Levellers' Standard Advanced', in *Puritanism and Liberty*, ed. A. S. P. Woodhouse (Dent, 1974), pp. 383 (I:12).

Douglas Wass, *Government and the Governed*, BBC Reith Lectures (Routledge & Kegan Paul, 1984), pp. 107–9 (II:17).

Sidney Webb, *Labour and the New Social Order* (Labour Party, 1918) (VIII:11).

Rebecca West, *The Young Rebecca. Writings of Rebecca West 1911–17*, ed. Jane Marcus (Macmillan, 1982) pp. 99–101 (IV:18).

Raymond Williams, 'Culture is Ordinary', in *Resources of Hope* (Verso, 1989), pp. 4, 10–12, 17–18 (IX:13).

Humbert Wolfe, 'The British Journalist', in *Oxford Book of Twentieth Century Verse* (Oxford University Press, 1973), p. 201 (VI:17).

Mary Wollstonecraft, *A Vindication of the Rights of Woman* (1891), pp. 34–5 (IV:16).

William Wordsworth, 'Preface', *Lyrical Ballads*, in *Wordsworth's Literary Criticism*, ed. Nowell C. Smith (Oxford University Press, 1925), pp. 13–15 (IX:8).

Biographical Notes

John Emerich Edward Dahlberg Acton (1834–1902), First Baron, was Regius Professor of Modern History at Cambridge and initiated the twelve-volume *Cambridge Modern History*.

Dr Shabbir Akhtar has worked as a Community Relations Officer in Bradford and is a member of the Bradford Council of Mosques.

Matthew Arnold (1822–88) was Inspector of Schools from 1851 to 1886 and wrote extensively on education. His poetry, nearly all of which was written before the age of forty-five includes 'The Scholar Gypsy' (1853) and 'Dover Beach' (1867). Towards the end of his life he also gained a considerable reputation as a literary critic.

W. H. Auden (1907–73) established his reputation with his first book of poetry, published in 1930. During the thirties, he was at the centre of a famous group of left-wing *literati* that included Louis MacNeice, Cecil Day-Lewis and Stephen Spender. In 1939 he emigrated to America, becoming an American citizen in 1944. In 1956 he was elected Professor of Poetry at Oxford.

Francis Bacon (1561–1626) was educated at Cambridge and entered Parliament in 1584. Appointed Solicitor-General in 1607, he rose to become Lord Chancellor in 1618. In 1621 he was charged with bribery and imprisoned in the Tower of London. On his release he retired from politics and devoted himself to literary work. As a philosopher, he sought to provide a basis for the new 'natural sciences'.

Walter Bagehot (1826–77) was from 1860 editor of *The Economist*. In addition to *The English Constitution* (1867), his most famous book, he published *Lombard Street* (1873), which scrutinized the financial world of his day.

Hilaire Belloc (1870–1953), born of a French father and English mother, wrote some 150 books (essays, poetry, fiction, travel and history). He was elected as a Liberal Member of Parliament in 1906, but gave up party politics in disgust in 1910.

Jeremy Bentham (1748–1832). A child prodigy, Bentham entered Queen's College Oxford, at the age of twelve and then studied law. By the age of forty he had published two major works on utilitarianism, *A Fragment on Government* (1776) and *Introduction to the Principles of Morals and Legislation* (1789), which argued that legislation should be guided by the 'utility principle' ('the greatest happiness of the greatest number'). In 1792 he was made an honorary citizen of the French Republic. In addition to political theory and jurisprudence, he wrote extensively on economics and penal and social reform. At his own request, his preserved body was displayed after his death at the college he founded, University College London, where it can be seen to this day.

Sir Isaiah Berlin (1909–) is a political philosopher and historian. His best-known works, apart from the essay quoted here, include *Vico and Herder* (1976), *Russian Thinkers* (1978) and a biography of Karl Marx.

Aneurin Bevan (1897–1960) followed his father in becoming a mine worker at the age of thirteen. He led the Welsh miners in the 1926 strike and was elected to Parliament in 1929. As a Minister in the 1945–50 Labour government he was responsible for the creation of the National Health Service.

Bill of Rights of 1689 Charles II died in 1685 and was succeeded by his catholic brother, James II. James alienated much of the political establishment by his appointment of Catholics to high office, by his attempt to rule without Parliament and, following rebellions in 1685, by his establishment of a permanent standing army. In June 1688 James's Queen gave birth to a son and heir. This proved the breaking point, and prominent figures issued an invitation to the protestant William of Orange, husband of James's eldest daughter Mary, to invade and dethrone James. It was the last successful invasion in English history. In 1689, William called a 'Convention Parliament', which drew up the Bill of Rights in order to limit the powers of the sovereign and establish those of Parliament. As one of the most eminent historians of the period, Christopher Hill, has written: 'Henceforth Parliament was a necessary and continuous part of the constitution, in closer dependence on the electorate.'

Sir William Blackstone (1723–80) became the first Vinerian Professor of English Law at Oxford in 1758. His *Commentaries*, regularly updated, have become a standard text on English law.

William Blake (1757–1827) never went to school, but was apprenticed to an engraver. He published many of his books himself, combining text and engraved illustration in a single, extraordinary vision. The best-known works are the *Songs of Innocence* (1789), *The Marriage of Heaven and Hell* (1790–3), *Visions of the Daughters of Albion* (1793) and the *Songs of Experience* (1794). His later, 'prophetic' books increasingly used arcane symbolism and invented mythology. Regarded as at best eccentric and at worst insane during his lifetime, interest in Blake's work has grown steadily in the twentieth century.

Vernon Bogdanor is Reader in Politics in the University of Oxford.

Henry St John, 1st Viscount Bolingbroke (1678–1751) entered Parliament in 1701. In 1704 he was made Secretary of War, and in 1710 Secretary of State. He fled to France in 1715 and supported the unsuccessful Jacobite cause. In 1723 he was allowed to return to England, where he pursued a career as a historian and propagandist for the Tories against the Whig party. A noted conversationalist and orator, his friends included Jonathan Swift, Alexander Pope and Daniel Defoe.

Howard Brenton (1942–) and **David Hare** (1947–) both emerged as popular left-wing playwrights in the 1970s. *Pravda* (1985) was their second collaboration.

Samuel Brittan is Assistant Editor of the *Financial Times*.

James Bryce (1838–1922), 1st Viscount, was Regius Professor of Civil Law at Oxford, 1870–93, and entered Parliament in 1880.

Edmund Burke (1729–97) Educated at Trinity College, Dublin, Burke soon abandoned legal studies for literature, publishing in 1757 his *Philosophical Inquiry into the Origin of our Ideas on the Sublime and Beautiful* and *Vindication of Natural Society*, a parody of Bolingbroke (see above). In 1765 Burke began his political career, entering Parliament as private secretary to the Whig Marquis of Rockingham. From 1770 he published many influential pamphlets and speeches critical of the government of Lord North, especially its policies in the American colonies and its general corruption. He held office again in 1782–3 as Paymaster of the Forces and remained a prominent public figure through his writings and his involvement in the impeachment of Warren Hastings, Governor-General of the East India Company.

Edward Carpenter (1844–1929) abandoned his career in the Church in 1874 and devoted himself through his many writings and his life-style (vegetarianism, overt homosexuality, etc.) to challenging middle-class conventions and supporting a variety of progressive causes. He was an influence on, among others, E. M. Forster (see below).

Robert Cecil (1864–1954) was first elected to Parliament in 1906 as a Conservative. A keen supporter of women's suffrage he broke with the party in 1910. He was to be one of the architects of the League of Nations.

Charles I (1600–49), second son of James I, was King of England, Scotland and Ireland from 1625 to 1649. Following constitutional and religious conflicts, Charles dissolved Parliament in 1629 and for the next eleven years attempted to rule without it. Financial problems and conflicts with the Scottish Presbyterians forced him to recall it in 1640, and Parliament successfully impeached his two principal lieutenants, the Earl of Strafford and Archbishop Laud. Early in 1642 Charles unsuccessfully tried to arrest one member of the Lords and five members of the Commons for treason, an event that marked the final and irrevocable rift with Parliament. Charles withdrew from London and raised the royal standard at Nottingham: the Civil War had begun.

Charles was captured at Newark in 1646, but escaped from the parliamentarians in 1647. In 1648 he was recaptured and taken to London, where he was tried by a special parliamentary court. He was executed in Whitehall on 30 January 1649.

Charter 88 was founded in 1988 as a pressure group advocating constitutional and electoral reform.

The People's Charter Working-class societies all over the country associated themselves with the Charter, and in 1839 a petition advocating its demands was presented to Parliament with 1,200,000 signatures. In the same year a General Convention of the Industrious Classes met in London and Birmingham, and there was an attempt at armed rebellion at Newport, Monmouthshire, in which 14 people were killed. The Chartist movement then died down until 1842, when a petition for universal male suffrage and other reforms was presented to Parliament with 3,000,000 signatures. The last great Chartist demonstration took place in 1848.

William Cobbett (1762–1835), son of a farm labourer, began his adult life as a soldier and then turned to journalism and politics. He was known particularly for his writings on economics and agriculture.

Henry Cockburn (1779–1854) was a prominent Scottish lawyer. *Memorials of his Time* (1856) contains vivid accounts of literary life in Edinburgh.

Samuel Taylor Coleridge (1772–1834) left Cambridge without taking a degree. He met William Wordsworth (see below) in 1797, beginning a long and important friendship. His philosophical and critical works show a strong German influence. The best-known of his poems include 'The Rime of the Ancient Mariner', 'Christabel' and 'Kubla Khan' (all 1797–8).

Bernard Crick (1929–) is Emeritus Professor of Politics at Birkbeck College, London and the author of a number of books, including *In Defence of Politics* and *George Orwell* (1980).

Anthony Crosland (1918–77) was a Labour Cabinet minister from 1964 to 1970 and Foreign Secretary from 1976 until his death.

Richard Crossman (1907–74) began his career as a university lecturer and journalist. He became a Labour MP in 1945 and was a Cabinet minister from 1964 to 1970. His diaries were published posthumously between 1975 and 1977.

A. V. Dicey (1835–1922) was Vinerian Professor of English Law and Fellow of All Souls, Oxford from 1882 to 1909. An ardent 'unionist' (see below), his principal works are *The Law of the Constitution* (1885) and *Law and Public Opinion in England* (1905).

Charles Dickens (1812–70) was sent to work in a factory at the age of twelve. His childhood poverty made a deep impression on his work (notably on *Oliver Twist* (1837–8)), and many of his novels address social issues of the day. *Pickwick Papers* (1836–7) was his first novel. His later novels (including *Great Expectations* (1860–1) and *Our Mutual Friend* (1864–5)), while retaining the characteristic 'Dickensian' humour, include darker elements.

Benjamin Disraeli (1804–81), a Conservative of Italian Jewish descent, was twice British Prime Minister (1868 and 1874–80). His first novel, *Vivian Grey* (1826) was published anonymously and achieved considerable success. His trilogy *Coningsby* (1844), *Sybil* (1845) and *Tancred* (1847) have been described as 'the first truly political novels in English'.

John Dryden (1631–1700). From the Restoration (1660), Dryden made his living as a professional playwright and poet. His literary self-promotion led Samuel Johnson to remark of him that 'he no longer retains shame in himself, nor supposes it in his patron'. In the 1680s he turned his talents to political satire, producing in addition to *Absalom and Achitophel* such works as *The Medall. A Satyre against Sedition* (1682). As well as poetry and plays, he wrote translations of Homer and other classics, 'adaptations' of Shakespeare, and a libretto, *King Arthur* (1691), for the most celebrated English composer of the time, Henry Purcell.

George Eliot (1819–80) was the pseudonym of Mary Ann Evans. Her first publications were translations from German, but her reputation as a novelist was established with *Adam Bede* (1859). *Felix Holt, The Radical* (1866) was not one of her most successful novels, but by the time *Middlemarch* appeared

(1871–2) she was widely recognized as the leading English novelist of her day.

T. S. Eliot (1888–1965) was born in Missouri, USA, but settled in England in 1914. His first volume of poetry, *Prufrock and Other Observations* was published in 1917, and in 1922 *The Waste Land* made a considerable impression. His other well-known longer sequence of poems is the *Four Quartets* (1943). Eliot also wrote plays (some in verse) and literary criticism.

Thomas Ellis (1859–99) was the son of a tenant farmer in North Wales. In 1886 he was elected as the Gladstonian Liberal Member of Parliament for Merioneth on a platform of Home Rule for Wales. In Parliament he campaigned vigorously for Welsh education, disestablishment and land reform.

Olaudah Equiano (*c*.1745–97), also known as 'Gustavus Vassa', was born in the interior of the eastern part of modern Nigeria. As a slave and free man, he travelled to Britain, Canada, the Arctic and the Mediterranean. Towards the end of his life he settled in London, becoming active in the Abolitionist movement and the settlement of former slaves in Sierra Leone. By his death, his *Life* had run into nine editions.

K. D. Ewing is Professor of Public Law at King's College, University of London. **C. A. Gearty** is a University Lecturer in Law, Cambridge and a Fellow of Emmanuel College, Cambridge.

E. M. Forster (1879–1970) was educated at King's College, Cambridge, with which he maintained a lifelong connection. He was in Alexandria during the First World War with the Red Cross, and later wrote two books about the city. His novels include *The Longest Journey* (1907), *Howards End* (1910), *A Room with a View* (1908), and *A Passage to India* (1924). He also wrote, with Eric Crozier, the libretto for Benjamin Britten's opera *Billy Budd*.

Sir John Fortescue (*c*.1394–*c*.1476) became Chief Justice in 1442. His works on constitutional law are notable for having been written in English as well as the more usual Latin. His most important book was *On the Governaunce of England* (*c*.1473).

C. A. Gearty, *see* **K. D. Ewing**, *above*.

William Ewart Gladstone (1809–98) was a Member of Parliament from 1832 to 1895 (except for 1846) and Prime Minister four times (1868–74; 1880–5; February–July 1886; 1892–4). He first entered politics as a Tory, holding office under Sir Robert Peel, but in 1866 succeeded Lord John Russell (see below) as leader of the Liberal Party.

Lord Hailsham (1907–) was first elected a Conservative MP in 1938. He was Lord High Chancellor from 1970 to 1974 and from 1979 to 1983.

David Hare, *see* **Brenton**, *above*

James Harrington (1611–77) was influenced in his republican views by his first-hand observations of Holland and Venice. *The Commonwealth of Oceana*, sometimes said to be a reply to Hobbes's *Leviathan* (see below), was published in 1656, and in 1659 he founded the Rota, a political discussion club. He was imprisoned for a time following the Restoration.

Tony Harrison (1937–) was born in Leeds and in addition to volumes of poetry has written extensively for the stage, including opera libretti.

Seamus Heaney (1939–) was educated at Queen's University, Belfast, where he was a lecturer from 1966 to 1972. His volumes of poetry include *North* (1975), *Field Work* (1979) and *The Haw Lantern* (1987).

John Hewitt (1907–87) was born in Belfast and educated at the Queen's University. He worked in museums and art galleries in Belfast and Coventry until his retirement in 1972.

Thomas Hobbes (1588–1679). In 1608, after graduating from Oxford, Hobbes became tutor to the eldest son of Lord Cavendish of Hardwick, Derbyshire. His connection with this family was to last to the end of his life. His first publication was a translation of Thucydides, but he soon developed an interest in science and philosophy, encouraged by travels in continental Europe in 1629–31 and 1634–7. In 1640 he fled to Paris and stayed there during the course of the Civil War, returning in 1651. After *Leviathan*, which has been described by one historian as 'among the classics of political philosophy', Hobbes published little on political matters. At the age of eighty-four he wrote an autobiography in Latin verse. He died at Hardwick.

Leonard Hobhouse (1864–1929) was the first Professor of Sociology at the University of London, 1907–29.

David Hume (1711–76) was one of the leading figures of the Scottish Enlightenment. Although he is chiefly remembered nowadays for his sceptical and empiricist philosophical works, including *A Treatise of Human Nature* (1739–40), *Philosophical Essays* (later called *An Inquiry concerning Human Understanding* (1748)) and *Dialogues concerning Natural Religion* (published 1779), he was more noted in his own country during his lifetime for his *History of England* (1754–62). In the 1780s he spent some time in Paris, associating with such figures of the French Enlightenment as Voltaire, Diderot and d'Alembert.

Sir Robert Inglis (1786–1855) was first elected to Parliament in 1824. In the *Dictionary of National Biography* he is described as 'an old fashioned tory, a strong churchman, with many prejudices and of no great ability'.

James I of England (VI of Scotland) (1566–1625), King of Scots from 1567 to 1625 and of England and Ireland from 1607 to 1625, was one of the more intellectually distinguished of British monarchs. He wrote works on the art of government and on theology, as well as poetry in Scots, Latin and English. His most famous work (though some scholars have doubted whether he was the actual author) is the *True Law of Free Monarchies*, which sets out the doctrine of the divine right of kings.

John Maynard Keynes (1883–1946), in addition to his influential academic career as an economist, played a role in government at various times. He had a long association with the Liberal Party and was a leading participant in the Bretton Woods conference (1946) from which emerged the International Monetary Fund and the International Bank.

Charles Kingsley (1819–75) was a prominent Christian Socialist and Regius Professor of Modern History at Cambridge from 1860 to 1869. Apart from *Alton Locke* (1850) he wrote historical novels (notably *Westward Ho!* (1855)) and a classic children's book, *The Water Babies* (1863).

Rudyard Kipling (1865–1936) was born in Bombay and from 1882 to 1889 worked as a journalist in India. His vast and immensely popular output included *Plain Tales from the Hills* (1888), *The Jungle Book* (1894) and *Kim* (1901) as well as several collections of verse.

George Lamming (1927–) was born in Barbados. His books include the novels *In the Castle of my Skin* (1953) and *Natives of my Person* (1972), and the autobiographical essay *The Pleasures of Exile* (1960).

D. H. Lawrence (1885–1930), the son of a miner, studied to be a teacher at Nottingham University. His large output covered novels, including *The White Peacock* (1911), the autobiographical *Sons and Lovers* (1913), *The Rainbow* (1915), *Women in Love* (1916) and *Lady Chatterley's Lover* (1928), short stories, poetry, and works of history and criticism. He was frequently in trouble with the law over sexual frankness in his novels.

Saunders Lewis (1893–1985), widely regarded as the most important Welsh literary figure of the twentieth century, was a dramatist, poet, literary historian and critic as well as a political activist. He was imprisoned for his attack on the RAF bombing school and dismissed from his post at University College, Swansea. For a while he made his living from journalism, and in 1952 was appointed to the University College, Cardiff.

Wyndham Lewis (1882–1957) was one of the most prominent advocates of the modernist movement in Britain. An artist as well as a novelist and critic, his savage satires and leanings towards fascism alienated him from the literary establishment of his day.

The Levellers emerged in 1647 as a radical republican movement within the parliamentarian New Model Army. In 1649 Lilburne and other Leveller leaders were arrested and a Leveller mutiny crushed by Lord Fairfax, commander of the New Model Army and Cromwell (see also *Putney Debates* below).

A. D. Lindsay (1879–1952), 1st Baron, was Master of Balliol College, Oxford, 1924–49. His books included *The Essentials of Democracy* (1929) and *The Modern Democratic State* (1943).

Sir David Lindsay Keir (1895–1973) was Master of Balliol College, Oxford, 1949–65.

Lord Liverpool (Robert Banks Jenkinson) (1770–1828) was Prime Minister from 1812 to 1827. The early years of his ministry were marked by a repressive, anti-revolutionary conservatism, but he moved towards a more liberal Toryism after 1822.

John Locke (1632–1704). A schoolmate of the poet John Dryden (see above) at Westminster, Locke went on to Christ Church, Oxford, where he studied medicine and became interested in politics. The course of his life changed in 1666, when he met Lord Ashley, first Earl of Shaftesbury and one of the most powerful political figures of the time. Locke became Shaftesbury's personal physician and confidant, and under his patronage held various political offices. He also began the philosophical works for which he is still celebrated, notably the *Essays on Toleration* (1667) and the *Essay on Human Understanding* (1671). In the early 1680s, Locke's patron was involved in attempts to force on Charles II the exclusion from the succession of his brother and heir apparent, the Catholic James, Duke of York. Shaftesbury died in 1683, and Locke was forced into exile in Holland. In 1689, following the Revolution, he returned to England, and for the last fifteen years of his life enjoyed a considerable intellectual reputation and political influence. His later works include the *Thoughts Concerning Education* (1694).

William Lovett (1800–77) was a self-educated cabinet-maker. In 1836 he founded the London Working Men's Association, which devised the six-point People's Charter (see above). Lovett became inadvertently involved in Chartist disturbances in Birmingham in 1839, and he was imprisoned for a year. During that time he wrote *Chartism: A New Organisation of the People*. On his release, his emphasis on moral protest rather than political organization caused him to be marginalized within the Chartist movement by other, more radical, figures.

Thomas Babington Macaulay (1800–59), First Baron, became a Member of Parliament in 1830 and made his name as an orator in the debates surrounding the 1832 Reform Bill. His best-known literary work is the *History of England* (1848–55).

Hugh MacDiarmid (Christopher Murray Grieve) (1892–1978) was one of the most important Scottish literary figures of the twentieth century. He was a founder of the National Party of Scotland in 1928, but was expelled in 1933 and joined the Communist Party in the following year. The most famous of his poems – many of which were written in Scots – is 'A Drunk Man Looks at the Thistle' (1926).

John Maclean (1879–1923) was born in Glasgow, the son of a potter. He was partly responsible for the establishment of the Scottish Labour College, and during the First World War he advocated the termination of hostilities and the downfall of capitalism. He was arrested and imprisoned four times between 1916 and 1921.

Magna Carta, the 'Great Charter', was agreed by King John at his meeting with the barons at Runnymede on 15 June 1215. It was forced on him by opposition to his disastrous foreign policy and what was seen as his arbitrary rule. *Magna Carta* consists of a preamble and sixty-three clauses.

Sir Henry Maine (1822–88) was professor of jurisprudence at Oxford, 1871–8, and of international law at Cambridge, 1887–8.

Adewale Maja-Pearce was born of a Nigerian father and Scottish mother. In addition to *How Many Miles to Babylon?* (1990), he has written a book about Nigeria, *In My Father's Country* (1987).

Harriet Taylor Mill (1807–58) married John Stuart Mill (see below) in 1851, two years after the death of her husband, though she and Mill had been intimate friends for many years. She was an important influence on Mill's thought. The essay 'On the Enfranchisement of Women', published in the *Westminster Review* in 1851 was attributed to her when Mill declared his share to have been 'little more than that of an editor and amanuensis'.

James Mill (1773–1836) was closely associated with Jeremy Bentham (see above). His most famous work was his *History of British India* (1817), as a result of which he was given an important post in the East India Company. His son was John Stuart Mill (see below).

John Stuart Mill (1806–1873). Systematically and rigorously educated by his father, James Mill (see above), John Stuart Mill had by the age of twenty become the leader of the younger 'philosophical radicals'. But in 1826, as he was later to describe in his *Autobiography*, he went through an emotional and intellectual crisis that led him to question the overbearing influence of his father and his father's friend Jeremy Bentham (see above). By the 1840s, in his *System of Logic* (1843) and *Principles of Political Economy* (1848), he was setting out an independent philosophical position. His other well-known works include *On Liberty* (1859), *Representative Government* (1861) and *Utilitarianism* (1863). From 1865 to 1868 he was a Member of Parliament, voting with the Radical party and advocating women's suffrage. His views during the later part of his life were strongly influenced by his wife, Harriet Taylor Mill (see above).

John Milton (1608–74) was by the age of twenty writing poetry in English, Latin and Italian. His early works include *L'Allegro* (1631), *Il Penseroso* (1631) and a masque, *Comus* (1637). During the Civil War Milton was a committed supporter of the Parliamentarian side, producing many pamphlets, of which the most famous is the *Areopagitica* (1644). In 1649 he became Latin Secretary to Cromwell's Council of State, a position he held till the Restoration, despite the fact that in 1653 he succumbed to blindness. His most famous work is the epic poem *Paradise Lost* (1667).

John Morley (1838–1923), 1st Viscount, was a Liberal MP and biographer. His most famous work was a four-volume study of Gladstone.

Ferdinand Mount (1939–) was a policy adviser to Margaret Thatcher and is currently editor of *The Times Literary Supplement*.

Edwin Muir (1887–1959) was born in Orkney. As well as poetry, he published four novels and an autobiography.

Grace Nichols (1950–) was born in Guyana and came to Britain in 1977. Her volumes of poetry include *i is a long memoried woman*, which won the Commonwealth Poetry Prize in 1983.

T. H. B. Oldfield was an early-nineteenth-century political thinker and historian whose monumental work was his history of representative institutions.

George Orwell (1903–50) was the pen-name of Eric Blair, who was educated at Eton and served as a colonial policeman in Burma from 1922 to 1927. His experiences in the Far East formed the basis of his first novel, *Burmese Days* (1934). Later in the thirties he fought in the Spanish Civil War and wrote a book about it, *Homage to Catalonia* (1937). In addition to a large amount of journalism and books of reportage such as *The Road to Wigan Pier* (1937), his novels include *Animal Farm* (1941) and *Nineteen Eighty-Four* (1949).

Moisei Yakovlevic Ostrogorski was a political thinker whose book *Deomcracy and the Organization of Political Parties*, originally written in French, was influential in Britain and the United States in the early years of the twentieth century.

Thomas Paine (1737–1809) became a corset-maker at the age of thirteen and went through a variety of jobs until 1774, when he emigrated to the American colonies and began a new career as a radical journalist. His *Common Sense* (1776), published after the outbreak of the American Revolution, advocated immediate independence. He was back in England for the publication of *The Rights of Man* (1791), but had to flee to France when he was indicted for treason. In Paris he took French citizenship and became a deputy in the National Convention (1792–3). He was imprisoned by Robespierre for his opposition to the execution of Louis XVI, and 1802 he returned to America. But his attacks on religion in *The Age of Reason* had alienated many of his former supporters, and he died in virtual poverty.

Christabel Pankhurst (1880–1958) was the daughter of Emmeline Pankhurst, with whom she helped to form the Women's Social and Political Union (the 'suffragettes') in 1903. The suffragettes, generally younger and more militant, were so called to distinguish them from the 'suffragists' of the National Union of Women's Suffrage Societies.

Enoch Powell (1912–) was elected as a Conservative MP in 1950 and was a Minister in the late 1950s and early 1960s. In the late 1960s and 1970s he was known for his opposition to immigration and to Britain's membership of the EEC.

The Putney Debates took place as a result of splits in the Parliamentarian side following the defeat of the Royalist forces at Naseby (June 1645) and the capture of the king (1646). In 1647 the Generals of the Parliamentarian army conducted negotiations with Charles for the establishment of a limited monarchy (the 'Heads of Proposals'). Radicals in the Army (the 'Levellers') responded by producing a rival, more democratic constitution (the 'Agreement of the People'). It was these two constitutions that were debated by the Army Council at Putney in October 1647.

Salman Rushdie (1947–) was born in Bombay and is the author of the novels *Grimus, Midnight's Children, Shame* and *The Satanic Verses*.

Lord John Russell (1792–1878) was largely responsible for drafting the 1832 Reform Bill. He went on to become Prime Minister from 1846 to 1852 and from 1865 to 1866.

Lord Scarman (1911–) was appointed to the High Court of Justice in 1961. He was a Lord Justice of Appeal from 1973 to 1977 and a Lord of Appeal from 1977 to 1986.

Samuel Selvon (1923–) was born in Trinidad. His novels include *A Brighter Sun* (1952), *The Lonely Londoners* (1956) and *Moses Ascending* (1975).

William Shakespeare (1564–1616) is widely held to be not only the greatest dramatist but also the greatest poet in the English language. He was born in Stratford-upon-Avon, and by 1592 he seems to have been established on the London literary and theatrical scene. (Few details are known about his life.) He became a leading member of the Lord Chamberlain's Men, which developed into the leading theatrical company of the day.

Percy Bysshe Shelley (1792–1822) was expelled from Oxford in 1811 for circulating a pamphlet titled *The Necessity of Atheism*. His subsequent short and colourful life has been a favourite subject of romantic biographers. In 1814 he eloped with Mary Godwin, author of *Frankenstein* and daughter of William Godwin and Mary Wollstonecraft (see below), and much of the last years of his life was spent in Italy, where he was a friend of the poet Lord Byron. He died at sea off the Italian coast. Apart from *The Mask of Anarchy* (1819), which was written in Rome, his best known works include *Prometheus Unbound* (1819), *The Cenci* (1819) and many shorter lyrics such as 'To the West Wind' and 'To a Skylark'.

Samuel Smiles (1812–1904) was a doctor and later a journalist and secretary to a railway company. As well as his most famous book, *Self-Help*, he published biographies of entrepreneurs and exhortations to moral self-improvement such as *Thrift* (1875) and *Duty* (1880).

Adam Smith (1723–90) was educated at Glasgow University, where he became Professor of Moral Philosophy in 1752. His *Theory of Moral Sentiments* was published in 1759. He left the university in 1763 and spent some time travelling in Europe, where he became acquainted with the work of French political economists. His best-known work, *An Enquiry into the Nature and Causes of the Wealth of Nations*, was published in 1776.

Sir Thomas Smith (1513–77) was a diplomat and statesman. In 1572 he was appointed Secretary of State by Elizabeth I.

Robert Southey (1774–1843) became friendly with Coleridge (see above), while studying at Oxford, and together they planned a 'Utopian Pantisocratic' society. After living in Spain and Portugal for a time in his twenties, he settled in Keswick, where he remained for the rest of his life as one of the 'Lake poets' (see also Wordsworth, below). As well as poetry, he published biographies and works of history. After youthful support of the French Revolution, he became more conservative with age.

The 'Spycatcher' Case. For three years, from 1985 to 1988, the British government fought an ultimately unsuccessful legal battle in Australia and Britain to prevent the publication of *Spycatcher*, a book by Peter Wright, a former agent for MI5 (the government secret service organization). Mr Wright's book alleged that the British secret service had been implicated in an attempt to assassinate President Nasser of Egypt, and that during the 1970s MI5 had been involved in burglary and bugging of political parties and trade unions, and had taken part in attempts to discredit and destabilize the Labour government of Harold Wilson. During the legal battle, the British government argued that Peter Wright was bound by the Official Secrets Act and that he had given undertakings that he would not divulge information acquired in the course of his duties unless authorized to do so.

Dugald Stewart (1753–1828) was Professor of Moral Philosophy at Edinburgh University from 1785 to 1810.

John Strachey (1901–63) entered Parliament in 1929 as a Labour MP and a supporter of Oswald Mosley, who in 1931 formed his own fascist New Party. Strachey broke away from Mosley and during the 1930s wrote books and pamphlets espousing the Communist cause. He was a Labour MP again from 1945 till his death. He moderated his Marxist position in the post-war period.

Jonathan Swift (1667–1745) was born in Dublin, ordained in 1694, and became Dean of St Patrick's, Dublin in 1713. His principal works include the *Journal to Stella* (1710), *Gulliver's Travels* (1726) and *A Modest Proposal* (1729).

Margaret Thatcher (1925–) now Lady Thatcher, was Conservative Prime Minister from 1979 to 1990.

R. S. Thomas (1913–) was born in Cardiff and ordained as a clergyman in the Church of Wales in 1936. His many collections of poetry include *Song at the Year's Turning* (1955) and *Laboratories of the Spirit* (1975).

E. P. Thompson (1924–93), historian and peace campaigner, was one of the leading figures of the post-war British Left. His books, mostly on eighteenth- and early nineteenth-century social history, include *The Making of the English Working Class* (1963), *Whigs and Hunters* (1975) and *Customs in Common* (1991). He also wrote a biography of William Morris, a science fiction novel (*The Sykaos Papers*, 1988) and many polemical essays on nuclear disarmament.

Anthony Trollope (1815–82), in addition to being one of the most prolific of English novelists, was by the end of his career an important civil servant in the Post Office. Perhaps his greatest contribution to British life was the invention of the pillar box. Best-known of his many novels are those in the 'Barsetshire' and the more political 'Palliser' series.

Sir Douglas Wass (1923–) was Permanent Secretary to the Treasury from 1974 to 1983 and Joint Head of the Home Civil Service from 1981 to 1983.

Sidney Webb, 1st Baron Passfield (1859–1947), was initially a civil servant and joined the Fabian Society in 1885. With his wife Beatrice Webb (1858–1943) he wrote numerous works on economic history and social reform, served on many royal commissions and helped to found both the London School of Economics and the *New Statesman*.

Rebecca West (1892–1983). Cicely Isabel Fairfield took the pen name Rebecca West from Ibsen's play, *Rosmersholm*. While still a teenager she was writing journalism in support of women's suffrage and social reform. In 1916 she published her first book, a study of the novelist Henry James. She went on to write many works of fiction, criticism and history, including the novels *The Return of the Soldier* (1918) and *The Fountain Overflows* (1958), a biography of St Augustine (1933) and a study of Yugoslavia, *Black Lamb and Grey Falcon* (1941).

Raymond Williams (1921–88) was born in the Welsh border village of Pandy, where his father was a railway signalman. From 1974 to 1983 he was Professor of Drama at Cambridge. His works include *Culture and Society 1780–1950* (1958), *The Long Revolution* (1961), *Drama from Ibsen to Brecht* (1968) and a number of novels.

Humbert Wolfe (1886–1940), born Umberto Wolff in Milan of Jewish parentage, was a civil servant as well as a poet, translator and critic.

Theobald Wolfe Tone (1763–98) was born in Dublin and published his first nationalist pamphlet in 1790. He spent his last three years in Paris and accompanied abortive French expeditions to Ireland in 1796 and 1798. He committed suicide following capture by the British authorities.

Mary Wollstonecraft (1759–97) was associated with a group that included Thomas Paine, the scientist Joseph Priestley and the philosopher and free-thinker William Godwin, by whom she had a daughter, Mary (future author of *Frankenstein* and wife of the poet Shelley (see above)). As well as the *Vindication of the Rights of Woman* (1792), her most famous work, Mary Wollstonecraft published *Thoughts on the Education of Daughters* (1787) and *A Vindication of the Rights of Men* (1790), written as a rejoinder to Burke.

William Wordsworth (1770–1850) was the most famous of the 'Lake poets' (see also Coleridge and Southey, above). Like Southey and Coleridge, he abandoned his youthful political radicalism, and in 1843 he succeeded Southey as Poet Laureate. His most celebrated works are the *Lyrical Ballads* (1798), the *Poems in Two Volumes* (1807, including the 'Intimations of Immortality from Recollections of Early Childhood') and *The Prelude* (1805–6, revised edition published 1850).

Copyright Acknowledgements

The editors and publishers gratefully acknowledge the following for permission to reproduce copyright material in this book:

Aurum Press: Margaret Thatcher, *The Revival of Britain*, London: Aurum Press, 1989. (III.24), (VIII.15)

Miss S. G. Bach: for use of Christabel Pankhurst, *Unshackled, the Story of How we Won the Vote*, London: Hutchinson, 1959. (III.22), (IV.19)

B. T. Batsford: Enoch Powell, *A Nation or No Nation?*, London: Batsford, 1978. (I.17)

BBC Enterprises: Lord Hailsham, *Elective Dictatorship*, London: BBC Richard Dimbleby Lecture, 1976. (I.5), (II.13)

Bellew Publishing: Shabbir Akhtar, *Be Careful with Muhammed! The Salman Rushdie Affair*, London: Bellew, 1989. (VI.13)

A. & C. Black: Sir David Lindsay Keir, *The Constitutional History of Modern Britain*, London: A. & C. Black, seventh edition 1964. (I.8)

The Blackstaff Press: *The Collected Poems of John Hewitt*, ed. Frank Ormsby, Belfast: Blackstaff, 1991. (VII.7)

Basil Blackwell Ltd: Vernon Bogdanor, *What is Proportional Representation?*, Oxford: Martin Robertson, 1984 (V.14); and for permission to quote from *The Prose Works of Jonathan Swift*, ed. Herbert Davis, Blackwell, 1941. (VII.3)

The British Library Board: *Magna Carta*, ed. Michael Borrie, London: British Museum Publications, 1976. (VI.4)

Sir Samuel Brittan: for permission to quote from 'Can Democracy Manage an Economy?' in *The End of the Keynesian Economy*, ed. Robert Skidelsky, London: Macmillan, 1977. (VIII.8)

Cambridge University Press: John Locke, *Two Treatises on Government*, ed. P. Laslett, Cambridge University Press, 1964, (III.10), (IV.2); 'Reply to the Nineteen Propositions of 1642' in *The Stuart Constitution: Documents and Commentary*, ed. J.P. Kenyon, Cambridge University Press, 1966 (II.5); and three extracts from *The Nineteenth Century Constitution*, ed. H. Hanham, Cambridge University Press, 1969. (III.17), (IV.9), (V.6)

Charter 88: for use of an extract from Charter 88 (I.18); and Lord Scarman

Samuel Selvon: for permission to quote from *The Lonely Londoners*, London: Longman, 1985. (VII.20)

Charles Strachey and family: for permission to quote from John Strachey, *The Theory and Practice of Socialism*, Gollancz, 1936. (V.7)

Sweet & Maxwell: Ponting/Official Secrets, from *Criminal Law Review*, 1985. (I.16)

R. S. Thomas: 'Reservoirs', from *Selected Poems 1946–68*, Newcastle: Bloodaxe, 1986. (VII.15)

Verso: Raymond Williams, *Resources of Hope*, London: Verso, 1989. (IX.13)

Virago Press: Harriet Taylor Mill, *On the Enfranchisement of Women*, Virago, 1983. (IV.17)

Every effort has been made to trace all copyright holders. In any outstanding instances, the publishers will be pleased to make the necessary arrangements at the earliest opportunity.

Index

Note: Page references in **bold** type indicate authors of extracts; references in *italics* indicate entries in the Biographical Notes.